Black Women in Latin America and the Caribbean

•••••••••••••••••••••••••••••••••••

Critical Research and Perspectives

EDITED BY MELANIE A. MEDEIROS AND
KEISHA-KHAN Y. PERRY

Rutgers University Press
New Brunswick, Camden, and Newark, New Jersey
London and Oxford

Rutgers University Press is a department of Rutgers, The State University of New Jersey, one of the leading public research universities in the nation. By publishing worldwide, it furthers the University's mission of dedication to excellence in teaching, scholarship, research, and clinical care.

Library of Congress Cataloging-in-Publication Data
Names: Medeiros, Melanie A., editor. | Perry, Keisha-Khan Y., editor.
Title: Black women in Latin America and the Caribbean : critical research and perspectives / edited by Melanie A. Medeiros and Keisha-Khan Y. Perry.
Description: New Brunswick, New Jersey : Rutgers University Press, [2023] | Includes bibliographical references and index.
Identifiers: LCCN 2022050898 | ISBN 9781978836303 (paperback ; alk. paper) | ISBN 9781978836310 (hardcover ; alk. paper) | ISBN 9781978836327 (epub) | ISBN 9781978836334 (pdf)
Subjects: LCSH: Women, Black—Latin America—History. | Women, Black—Caribbean Area—History. | Feminism—Latin America. | Feminism—Caribbean Area.
Classification: LCC F1419.B55 B53 2023 | DDC 305.48/89608—dc23/eng/20230223
LC record available at https://lccn.loc.gov/2022050898

A British Cataloging-in-Publication record for this book is available from the British Library.

This collection copyright © 2023 by Rutgers, The State University of New Jersey
Individual chapters copyright © 2023 in the names of their authors
All rights reserved

No part of this book may be reproduced or utilized in any form or by any means, electronic or mechanical, or by any information storage and retrieval system, without written permission from the publisher. Please contact Rutgers University Press, 106 Somerset Street, New Brunswick, NJ 08901. The only exception to this prohibition is "fair use" as defined by U.S. copyright law.

References to internet websites (URLs) were accurate at the time of writing. Neither the author nor Rutgers University Press is responsible for URLs that may have expired or changed since the manuscript was prepared.

rutgersuniversitypress.org

**Black Women in Latin America
and the Caribbean**

Dedicated to Black Brazilian feminist scholar-activist
Luiza Helena de Bairros (1953-2016).

Contents

Foreword
Reconfiguring the Politics of Knowledge: Writing
Transnational Black Feminism from the South   ix
CHRISTEN A. SMITH

Introduction   1
KEISHA-KHAN Y. PERRY AND MELANIE A. MEDEIROS

1   Reclaiming a Legacy: Black Women's Presence and
Perspectives in the Brazilian Social Sciences   18
EDILZA CORREIA SOTERO

2   Beyond Intercultural *Mestizaje*: Toward Black Women's
Studies on the Caribbean Coast of Nicaragua   37
MELANIE WHITE

3   The Significance of "Communists Wearing Panties"
in the Jamaican Left Movement (1974–1980)   56
MAZIKI THAME

4   Exercising Diversity: From Identity to Alliances
in Brazil's Contemporary Black Feminism   75
JULIA S. ABDALLA

5   "This Isn't to Get Rich": Double Morality and
Black Women Private Tutors in Cuba   95
ANGELA CRUMDY

6	A "Bundle of Silences": Untold Stories of Black Women Survivors of the War in Colombia CASTRIELA E. HERNÁNDEZ-REYES	113
7	The Burden of *Las Bravas*: Race and Violence against Afro-Peruvian Women ESHE L. LEWIS	131
8	A Creole Christmas: Sexual Panic and Reproductive Justice in Bluefields, Nicaragua ISHAN GORDON-UGARTE	148
9	Digital Black Feminist Activism in Brazil: Toward a Repoliticization of Aesthetics and Romantic Relationships BRUNA CRISTINA JAQUETTO PEREIRA AND CRISTIANO RODRIGUES	166

Notes on Contributors 187
Index 191

Foreword

Reconfiguring the Politics of Knowledge: Writing Transnational Black Feminism from the South

CHRISTEN A. SMITH

> Collective vision for liberation is necessarily transnational—our struggles are inherently connected. We are heartened that the world has been moved by Marielle's death. This show of international solidarity is a turning point. But we call on all of us to maintain this watchful eye for the months and years to come. Marielle's assassination was not the first, and unfortunately, it is most likely not the last bellicose act in this global struggle. The fight for black life requires us to remain vigilant at home and abroad. Justice for Marielle means justice for us all.
> —"On the Imperative of Transnational Solidarity: A U.S. Black Feminist Statement on the Assassination of Marielle Franco" (Caldwell et al. 2018)

On the evening of March 13, 2018, the shocking news of the death of Marielle Franco started to reverberate across Twitter and informal networks among Black feminists living in the Americas. When I first heard the news, I was simply overwhelmed. Pain, anger, fear, and disbelief hit me like a wave, and I immediately reached out to Keisha-Khan Y. Perry to process all of the emotions that were hitting us like a wave. As Black feminist anthropologists working in Brazil, we had been engaging with the Black feminist community in Brazil together since the early 2000s (Keisha-Khan Y. Perry has been doing the same work since the late 1990s). We were overtaken by the urgent need to say something in the face of such brazen and terrible misogynoir.[1]

I began a group chat on Twitter with Erica Williams, Wendi Muse, Tianna Paschal, and Kia Caldwell and called on the group to pen a collective statement. The group represented North American Black women who critically engage with the politics of gender, race, and violence in Brazil. For the next ten days and nights (while also balancing childcare and work responsibilities) we crafted a collective statement in response to the egregious tragedy and in the spirit of transnational Black feminist solidarity. At the heart of our charge was a simple acknowledgment: that at this moment more than ever it was our responsibility as U.S. Black women to stand up and speak out in solidarity with our sisters in Brazil who were under attack and who had suffered a great loss. We acknowledged the key role that U.S. imperialist politics and transnational, gendered anti-Blackness played in Marielle Franco and Anderson Gomes's deaths and also acknowledged the responsibility that we had (and have) as Black women living in the United States and carrying a U.S. passport: we must fight and refuse to be silent. On March 23, 2018 we published that statement, "On the Imperative of Transnational Solidarity: A U.S. Black Feminist Statement on the Assassination of Marielle Franco," on the online portal of *The Black Scholar*. The statement circulated widely—one additional voice in a global chorus of outrage. Transnational Black feminism is precisely this: an insistence on witnessing Black women's struggles in solidarity and sisterhood, and a refusal to be silent in the face of whatever injustice we encounter there. It is also the courage to speak up and speak out against the violence that faces Black women anywhere, recognizing that transnational solidarity is by definition an acknowledgment of the uneven power dynamics between "nations" that are a continued legacy of colonialism/slavery/Conquest and late capitalism/neoliberalism.[2] It is our responsibility as Black women living in the North to harness our (economic, national, imperialist) privilege in order to create *pequeñas brechas*/small openings in the veneer of patriarchal white supremacy and anti-Blackness.

Our lives as Black women are necessarily, globally intertwined, and there is no path toward our collective liberation that does not include dismantling hegemonic structures of imperialistic, patriarchal white supremacy. One critical aspect of this process is a radical Black feminist praxis of citational politics—engaging seriously with Black women's transnational intellectual contributions by centering our ideas about the world. This is especially the case in the plantation Americas, where imperialism, neoliberalism, heteropatriarchy, and white supremacy have defined Black women as disposable natural resources to be extracted, used, exploited, and discarded. This demarcation of violability includes our ideas and our innovations.

> What does it look like to dismantle the patriarchal, white supremacist, heterosexist, imperialist impetus of the neoliberal university (and its accomplices) by *centering* Black women's ideas and intellectual contributions? Embedded within this question we also find our response.
> —"Cite Black Women: A Critical Practice (A Statement)" (Smith et al. 2021)

In 2021, Erica Williams, Imani Wadud, Whitney Pirtle, and I published the "Cite Black Women Collective Statement on behalf of the Cite Black Women Collective" (Smith et al. 2021).[3] In it, we make the assertion that the project of dismantling the heteropatriarchal, white supremacist, heterosexist, imperialist impetus of the neoliberal university (and its accomplices) must necessarily center Black women's ideas and intellectual contributions. Fundamental to our assertion is the project of epistemic disruption: the necessary radical politics of citation. Citation in this sense is not merely mounting a bibliography. Rather, it is a Black feminist practice that reconfigures the politics of knowledge production by situating Black women's thought as the center of intellectual gravity. One of the very insidious dimensions of the legacy of colonialism/slavery/Conquest is the marking of Black women as violable. This violability is not only physical (characterized by the historical sexual and physical abuse of Black women's bodies) but also epistemic—the strip mining, appropriation, and colonization of Black women's ideas as part of the broader project of diminishment and erasure. This epistemic erasure has persisted through time and space. It is is one of the colonial legacies of our world and one of the markers of late racial capitalism. Imperialism compounds this process. Not only do Black women's ideas continue to be marginalized and obfuscated, but Black women writing, researching, thinking, and living in Portuguese and Spanish are almost invisible in the Northern academy. To cite and engage Black women's ideas with respect and care—especially ideas from Latin America and the Caribbean—is one antidote for this legacy of epistemic erasure, a gravity shift. *Black Women in Latin America and the Caribbean* is part of this gravity shift.

As Keisha-Khan Y. Perry and Melanie A. Medeiros note in the introduction to this book, "we see this volume, *Black Women in Latin America and the Caribbean: Critical Research and Perspectives,* as playing a key discursive role in challenging damaging misconceptions of Black womanhood." Indeed, it is.

Here we find Black women seriously engaging with Black women's experiences with politics and the fight for citizenship, rights, and representation across the Caribbean and Latin America. As Perry and Medeiros note, the recent election of Francia Márquez as vice president of Colombia is one such example of the kinds of radical change that Black women are forging in the region. It is important to note, as Perry and Medeiros also do, that these struggles for political representation are necessarily collective: they are the product of years of nonhierarchical, anti-individualist movement organizing. When Francia Márquez came to the University of Texas at Austin (UT Austin) in 2016 to participate on the "The Gendered Dimensions of Anti-Black State Violence" panel that I organized as part of the Black Matters Conference run by the Department of African and African Diaspora Studies, she directly challenged all of us to move away from the white supremacist, neoliberal tendency to reduce movements to one charismatic leader. Instead, she noted that her victories in the struggle for Black territorial rights and representation in Colombia and around the region have been the fruit of generations of collective struggle. I heard this assertion echoed repeatedly when I traveled to Colombia in May 2022 to serve as an international election observer with the Misión de Observación Electoral, a branch of the United Nations. I was part of a delegation of Black women, femmes, and nonbinary people from the United States organized by AfroResistance, a movement of Black women, femmes, and girls from Latin America who focus on promoting human rights, democracy, and racial justice throughout the Americas.[4] Our delegation's mission was to protect the democratic process by ensuring all Colombians were able to vote without hindrance. However, at the heart of our desire to protect democracy was a deeper sense of purpose as well. For the months leading up to the election, Francia Márquez suffered intense attacks on her campaign, including serious death threats. As we gathered, we were reminded of Marielle Franco's story and the dangerous stakes of Black women's political leadership in the region. To protect democracy as Black women signifies putting our bodies and our communities on the line. We are never safe. As a North American Black woman from the United States, I am well aware of the sacrifices that women like Fannie Lou Hamer, Ella Baker, and Shirley Chisholm made for the right to be considered for political leadership. For these women, like Francia Márquez and Marielle Franco, the fight for democracy and representation was about the very urgent need to protect Black life, not the neoliberal impetus to harness individual political power. Chronicling our collective and regional political struggles is also part of this broader fight for the preservation of Black life.

In her book *Escritos de Uma Vida*, Black Brazilian feminist scholar and organizer Sueli Carneiro writes of Brazil, "It is an ethical requirement, a presupposition for the consolidation of democracy and a condition for the country's reconciliation with its history, in the sense of building a more just and equitable future for all" (Carneiro and Evaristo 2018, 138).[5] Her words are applicable to Black women's national struggles across the region, however. The consolidation of democracy is a prerequisite for the elimination of inequality across the Americas. The contributions to this volume, in varying registers, demarcate the contours of this process of consolidation through Black women's experiences with community organizing, political struggles, and struggles for survival. As Perry and Medeiros note in the introduction to this book, "Writing from the crucial standpoint of Black women in Latin America and the Caribbean globalizes and engenders the political and social justice problems of Black people while also forging gendered diasporic politics." Diasporic politics build from our collective, transnational legacies of Black struggle toward a more just and inclusive world. And as the Combahee River Collective notes in its 1977 statement, "If Black women were free, it would mean that everyone else would have to be free since our freedom would necessitate the destruction of all the systems of oppression" (Combahee River Collective 1977).

What Melanie A. Medeiros and Keisha-Khan Y. Perry accomplish in this volume is nothing less than a radical intervention of tremendous importance. As they note in their introduction, this text adds to the growing literature being published in English on and by Black women from the Caribbean and Latin America that focuses on the Spanish- and Portuguese-speaking experiences (e.g., Caldwell 2007; Figueroa-Vásquez 2020; Perry 2013; Rivera-Rideu, Jones, and Paschel 2016; Smith and Leu forthcoming). It is a part of a quiet revolution that transnational Black feminists are engaging across the region: a movement that involves breaking down the barriers of language by engaging in radical, dialogic acts of translation (e.g., Alvarez, Caldwell, and Lao-Montes 2016; Machado and Perry 2021; Smith, Davies, and Gomes 2021; Smith and Leu 2023); refusing the frontiers of national borders in order to organize in solidarity with one another; creating the space for one another to speak; bonding together to denounce oppression in all of its forms; and reclaiming our intellectual histories one story at a time.

In February 2020, Lorraine Leu and I organized the Lozano Long Conference at the Lozano Long Institute for Latin American Studies at UT Austin. The conference, "Black Women's Intellectual Contributions: Perspectives from the Global South," gathered Black women scholar/activists/artists (nonhierarchically) in order to draw attention to the ways that Black women from Latin America have largely been excluded from contemporary debates in Black and Latin American studies. Race, gender/sexuality, and regional origin (which is inherently a classed categorization) compound to mute voices in unique ways. The duality of racism and sexism rampant in the Latin American academy erases Black women from Latin American studies. Black women are erased from Black studies because of its traditionally patriarchal structure. And Black women from Latin America have been overlooked in the canon of Black women's studies because of the tendency to overemphasize the experiences of English-speaking Black women within this global project. As a result, there is a need to radically diversify the discourses of each of these fields and to foreground Black women's contributions from Latin America to philosophical and political thought in the Americas.

The conference sought to address that need by engaging with Black women's intellectual contributions to the Americas from the perspective of the South: Latin America. We used the term "South" as a way to put Latin America in conversation with the Circum-Caribbean (a region conceptualized from coastal South America northward to the U.S. South). This conceptual zone has historically been marginalized in the public imagination as exotic, backward, out of the way, and specifically, Black. We also imagined the South to be a frame that allows us to push back against the coloniality of modern nation-state and regional formations that are both racialized and gendered. National borders and boundaries are not innocent configurations; rather, they are political land divisions steeped in the coloniality of power and designed to create arbitrary divisions on what is in fact Indigenous land. By centering Spanish-, Portuguese-, Indigenous-, and African-language speaking experiences from Latin America, we also sought to shift our interpretation of the South from an imperialistic North perspective to a decolonial non-anglophone perspective. This project was not an isolated one. What Melanie A. Medeiros and Keisha-Khan Y. Perry do here is part of that broader movement. We must acknowledge the significant theoretical and philosophical interventions that Black women have made and continue to make across the Caribbean and Latin America. Employing a multidisciplinary, transnational perspective, this movement rethinks the role that Black women's thought and praxis have played in defining the sociopolitical and cultural landscape of the Americas for the past 400 years, centering the experiences of Black women in Latin America and the movement of Black women throughout the Americas: movement, transit, and cultural flows. Part of the political struggle to redress Black women's erasure in the Caribbean and Latin American—especially in the Spanish- and Portuguese-speaking Americas—is to insist on reading and engaging with Black women's intellectual contributions from the southern Americas. We must critically engage with Black women's transnationalism, resonance, cosmopolitanism, and agency by locating Black women as agents of theory, movement, politics, and culture. This work recasts Black women as theorizers and transnational agents of change, and this is exactly what *Black Women in Latin America and the Caribbean* does here.

There is something refreshing about the project of gathering Black women's scholarship together into one volume—the way that the words feel on the page, the sense of community and belonging, the life of it all. I invite you to read and engage the contributions here with that open and refreshing spirit as your guide. We are writing our histories. We are chronicling our struggles. We are refusing to be silenced.

Notes

1. Moya Bailey and Trudy (2018) developed the term "misogynoir" to describe uniqueness of anti–Black women hatred.
2. M. Jacqui Alexander and Chandra Talpade Mohanty contend that that transnational examines the relationship between "the politics of knowledge, and the spaces, places and locations that we occupy." They also note, "The transnational is connected to neoliberal economics and theories of globalization—it is used to distinguish between the global as a universal system, and the cross-national, as a way to engage the interconnections between particular nations" (Nagar and Swarr 2010, 25).
3. Coeditor Keisha-Khan Perry is also part of the Cite Black Women Collective.
4. I would be remiss not to thank Janvieve Williams Comrie, Marcia Olivo, and Charo Mina-Rojas for inviting me to join this delegation and be part of this historic moment. For more information about the organization, see AfroResistance, www.afroresistance.org/.
5. Author's translation from the original Portuguese: "*É uma exigencia etica, um presupposto para a consolidaçao da democracia e condiçao de reconciliação do país com sua história, no sentido da construção de um futuro mais justo e igualidario para todos.*"

References

Alvarez, Sonia E., Kia Lilly Caldwell, and Agustín Lao-Montes. 2016. "Translations across Black Feminist Diasporas." *Meridians: Feminism, Race, Transnationalism* 14, no. 2: v–ix.

Bailey, Moya, and Trudy. 2018. "On Misogynoir: Citation, Erasure, and Plagiarism." *Feminist Media Studies* 18, no. 4: 762–768.

Caldwell, Kia L. 2007. *Negras in Brazil: Re-envisioning Black Women, Citizenship, and the Politics of Identity*. New Brunswick, NJ: Rutgers University Press.

Caldwell, Kia L., Wendi Muse, Tianna S. Paschel, Keisha-Khan Y. Perry, Christen A. Smith, and Erica L. Williams. 2018. "On the Imperative of Transnational Solidarity: A U.S. Black Feminist Statement on the Assassination of Marielle Franco." *The Black Scholar*, March 23. https://www.theblackscholar.org/on-the-imperative-of-transnational-solidarity-a-u-s-black-feminist-statement-on-the-assassination-of-marielle-franco

Carneiro, Sueli, and Conceição Evaristo. 2018. *Escritos de uma Vida*. Belo Horizonte, Brazil: Editora Letramento.

Combahee River Collective. 1977. *Combahee River Collective Statement*. www.blackpast.org/african-american-history/combahee-river-collective-statement-1977/.

Figueroa-Vásquez, Yomaira C. 2020. *Decolonizing Diasporas: Radical Mappings of Afro-Atlantic Literatures*. Evanston, IL: Northwestern University Press.

Machado, Taís Sant'Anna, and Keisha-Khan Y. Perry. 2021. Translation of "The Black Woman: A Portrait." *Feminist Anthropology* 2: 38–49.

Nagar, Richa, and Amanda Lock Swarr, eds. 2010. *Critical Transnational Feminist Praxis*. Albany: State University of New York Press.
Perry, Keisha-Khan Y. 2013. *Black Women against the Land Grab: The Fight for Racial Justice in Brazil*. Minneapolis: University of Minnesota Press.
Rivera-Rideau, Petra R., Jennifer A. Jones, and Tianna S. Paschel. 2016. *Afro-Latin@s in Movement: Critical Approaches to Blackness and Transnationalism in the Americas*. London: Palgrave Macmillan.
Smith, Christen A., Archie Davies, and Bethânia Gomes. 2021. "'In Front of the World': Translating Beatriz Nascimento." *Antipode* 53, no. 1: 279–316.
Smith, Christen A. and Lorraine Leu eds., 2023. *Black Feminist Constellations: Black Women in Translation and Dialogue*. The University of Texas Press: Austin.
Smith, Christen A., Erica L. Williams, Imani A. Wadud, and Whitney N. L. Pirtle. 2021. "Cite Black Women: A Critical Praxis (A Statement)." *Feminist Anthropology* 2, no. 1: 10–17.

**Black Women in Latin America
and the Caribbean**

Introduction

KEISHA-KHAN Y. PERRY AND
MELANIE A. MEDEIROS

On June 19, 2022, Francia Márquez, an environmental activist and the 2018 Goldman Environmental Prize winner, became the first Black woman elected to Colombia's executive branch as vice president. Despite her landmark win, critiques of Márquez's candidacy and appointment as well as violent verbal attacks and persistent death threats against her reflect a broader ideological problem with the devaluation of Black women's intellectual and political contributions across the Americas. We see this volume, *Black Women in Latin America and the Caribbean: Critical Research and Perspectives*, as playing a key discursive role in challenging damaging misconceptions of Black womanhood. This volume engages intellectual work by and about Black women while shedding light on the sociopolitical conditions that shape their participation and leadership in political struggles for citizenship rights and resources. A singular goal of this book is highlighting their contributions at this critical juncture in history, in which social movements such as *Vidas Negras Importam* (Black Lives Matter) and #NiUnaMenos (Not One Less) are increasing global awareness of the physical and structural violence that threatens Black women in the Americas, at the same time that the rise of authoritarianism threatens to dismantle their hard-won recognition and rights. Additionally, this volume explores the role of the social sciences in documenting anti-Black violence and forging hemispheric struggles against that violence.

A Transnational Black Feminist Legacy

Márquez represents a generation of activist-intellectuals in Latin America and the Caribbean who are leading the way for revolutionary change in political representation and whose influence extends beyond nation-state and even regional borders. Contributors to this volume, such as Colombian anthropologist Castriela Hernández Reyes, have benefited from Márquez's scholarship and activism. They have marched alongside her or have sat in audiences in which she spoke. Márquez has presented her work at North American universities (Brown, University of Texas at Austin, University of Massachusetts-Amherst [UMass-Amherst], etc.), at conferences, and in our classrooms. Christen Smith, author of this book's foreword and founder of the Cite Black Women campaign who encouraged people to "engage in a radical praxis of citation that acknowledges and honors Black women's transnational intellectual production" (CBW 2022; Smith et al. 2021), invited Márquez to speak at the University of Texas at Austin in 2016. Smith was also part of an African diasporic delegation that traveled to Colombia to witness the presidential electoral process. Reyes was part of a delegation of graduate students at UMass-Amherst that coordinated Márquez's visits to the Five Colleges on several occasions. In March 2010 and 2014, Angela Davis met with Márquez, and in September 2021, they participated in a conversation hosted by the University of California, Irvine and the International Coordinator of the Community Movement Builders' Pan African Solidarity Network. In a 2018 interview with Democracy Now, recorded in New York City, Márquez stated, "Afro-descendant communities have the lowest levels of basic rights and services. We don't have access to water, to health[care]." Essentially, Márquez has long been circulating in Latin American and Black studies spaces in the United States and has been key to building a vast Black diaspora solidarity network in support of radical Black politics in Latin America. We believe she has reshaped how U.S. academe understands gendered racial violence and social movements in Colombia and the broader region and that her exchanges with U.S. scholars and students have had a profound impact on her intellectual and political formation.

Another prominent contemporary example of a Black woman activist-intellectual with transnational significance is Brazilian sociologist-turned-councilwoman Marielle Franco (1979–2018). Franco was brutally assassinated because of her radical ideas and political praxis. Her master's thesis, the result of rigorous academic training at one of the nation's most renowned universities (Pontifical Catholic University of Rio de Janeiro, PUC-Rio), documents the human rights violations enacted by the Pacifying Police Units in Rio de Janeiro's poorest communities. It is a landmark account of systemic state violence and its genocidal impact on Black people in Brazilian cities. Franco is celebrated on a global scale. Solidarity groups continue to demand justice for her assassination (see Caldwell et al. 2018). In a recent interview for *NACLA: Report on the Americas*, Anielle Franco, who is now Minister of Racial Equality of Brazil, emphasized that her sister's murder is a reflection of the "institutional conditions of racial, gender, and homophobic violence that take the lives of many Black people, women, transgender people, and activists in Brazil," a "racist, misogynist society, a society that understands that our Black bodies are disposable" (2022). She highlights the role of education in her political formation, including her transformative studies at a historically Black college in the United States that prepared her for this political moment. One of Marielle Franco's most important legacies, as lived through her sister and other Black women, is the integration of intellectual work, global solidarity, and anti-racism.

In this vein, Marielle Franco's most significant legacy as a thought leader demands greater interest and critical inquiry. Dominican author Leuvis Manuel de Olivero published the book *Memória Viva* (Living Memory; 2020) about Franco's death and legacy. He was assassinated under similar circumstances in October 2021: shot to death in a moving vehicle after leaving a restaurant in Rio de Janeiro. Their overlapping work in life—the emphasis on how everyday people in urban communities resist violence despite devastation—and their similar deaths after denouncing violence in their scholarly work speaks to the radical implications of their work and the real material violence involved in eradicating insurgent knowledges. As Edwidge Danticat (2011) brilliantly reminds us, "Create dangerously, for people who read dangerously. This is what I've always thought it meant to be a writer. Writing, knowing in part that no matter how trivial your words may seem, someday, somewhere, someone may risk his or her life to read them" (10). Like Franco and Olivero, the authors in this volume bring us knowledge grounded in careful social science research attuned to the socioeconomic realities of Black women in Latin America and the Caribbean and the structural and everyday forms of violence that shape their political and intellectual work. As Mariana Mora (2019) writes, "*La memoria de Marielle se ha convertido en un campo de disputa entre distintos setores* [The memory of Marielle has been converted into a dispute of ideas among distinct parties]" (81). This book extends Mora's argument that Franco and numerous other Black women scholars continue to challenge and reshape the production of knowledge in the social sciences in Brazil and beyond.

The explosion of scholarship on Marielle's life and assassination necessarily discusses her inspiring global impact on a new generation of Black women and queer leftist politicians (Augusto 2020; Caldwell 2022). However, more studies must include how her ideas shaped public policy as well as the direction of the social sciences. On the night of Francia Márquez's electoral victory, she enthusiastically waved a flag demanding justice for the assassination of Marielle Franco. This provided the world with a vivid illustration of how these two

Black diasporic communities are deeply connected. Just as Márquez demanded justice for Franco, she has also invoked the name of Honduran Indigenous activist Berta Cáceres assassinated in 2016 and the nearly 150 Indigenous and Afro-Colombian activists murdered in environmental justice movements, rural advocacy groups, and trade unions in 2021. In the first half of 2022, fifty-two human rights activists and community leaders in Colombia were killed. The authors in this volume provide analyses of Black women's conditions in various countries across Latin America and the Caribbean. We hope that readers (experts and nonexperts alike) will see how the historical legacies of slavery and colonialism facilitate simultaneous processes of violence, exclusion, and political articulations of rights and resources.

Because of her feminist intellectual and political work, Franco has often been compared to the iconic Afro-Brazilian anthropologist and philosopher Lélia Gonzalez (1934–1994). Over the last two decades, interest in Gonzalez's vast collection of writings, speeches, and interviews has increased among scholars in Brazil and the broader African diaspora (Harrison 2022; Machado and Perry 2021; Lima and Rios 2020; Ratts and Rios 2010). While president of the Latin American Studies Association, Colombian anthropologist Mara Viveros-Vigoya organized the dossier *El Pensamiento de Lélia Gonzalez: Un Legado y Un Horizonte* (The Political Thought of Lélia Gonzalez: A Legacy and a Horizon). In their coauthored essay, Keisha-Khan Y. Perry and Edilza Sotero (2019) focus on Gonzalez's diasporic travels and affirm that Gonzalez is a "critical thinker in the Black radical and feminist traditions who should be known and taken more seriously in North America" (60). Luiza Bairros's (2000) classic essay "Lembrando (Remembering) Lélia Gonzalez" and Raquel de Andrade Barreto's comparative dissertation on Gonzalez and Angela Davis demonstrates Brazilian feminist scholars' ongoing commitment to examining her diasporic reach. In her chapter, sociologist Edilza Sotero outlines and honors the work of Lélia Gonzalez, Marielle Franco, and two other groundbreaking Black women social scientists: Luiza Bairros and Virgínia Bicudo. Sotero is one of the few scholars analyzing the historical continuities among Black women in the social sciences in Brazil, shedding light on an intellectual contribution that is often made invisible.

In North America, Sonia A. Alvarez and Kia Lilly Caldwell (2016) organized a two-part special issue of *Meridians: Feminism, Race, and Transnationalism*. This volume drew from Gonzalez's conceptualization of *Amefricanidade* (Amefricanity) to frame its focus on Black feminist cultures and politics across the Americas (see also Caldwell 2009). As Alvarez and Caldwell highlight, the basic premise of *Amefricanidade* regards forging diasporic solidarity based in common experiences of struggle with anti-Blackness across the Americas. This hemispheric view of anti-racism and feminist struggles is the focus of one of Gonzalez's few essays published originally in English, "For an Afro-Latin

Feminism" (1988), and much of her lectures in the United States in the 1980s that led to the book *Lugar de Negro* (1982) with Carlos Hasenbalg. What is most striking about Gonzalez's biography is that she moved extensively in Latin American studies and Black studies circles in the United States. While a Ford Foundation Scholar in 1984, she met Angela Davis for the first time (Perry and Sotero 2019). She also spoke French, Spanish, and English and traveled from Peru to Panama to Martinique to participate in Black liberation and feminist conferences to denounce racism and sexism in Brazil and the broader hemisphere. Gonzalez envisioned a diasporic response to a hemispheric system of gendered racial domination; hence, reading the chapters in this book together is about defining the "common experience of Black people in the Americas" (1988, 63) and articulating research agendas and political movements aimed at challenging the foundations of anti-Blackness on a global scale.

Furthermore, this book is critical to cultivating a general understanding of Black women's intellectual and political capacities in Latin American and Caribbean societies. Much of the existing scholarship involves interpretative essays on Black women's ideas and cultural and political work (Smith 2016b), as well as translations of critical writings by Black women from the region into English (Smith 2021; Smith, Davies, and Gomes 2021; Perry and Machado 2021; Williams 2021). There are plans to translate the entire collections of Gonzalez's writings to make her work more accessible in North America and Europe. As Bruna Barros, Feva, Jess Oliveira, and Luciana Reis's recent translation of Gonzalez's classic essay, "Racism and Sexism in Brazilian Society" (Gonzalez 2021), shows, the move to cite, translate, and engage Black women's writings is an important step is expanding what we know about the pervasiveness of gendered anti-Black violence in the region and how to cultivate critical dialogues about what to do with that knowledge. As Lélia Gonzalez's contemporary Benedita da Silva (who is still an activist politician in Brazil) has noted, "We must exchange experiences that can strengthen our struggles and search for new ways to unify Blacks in the Americas" (1997, 136).

As feminist anthropologists, we feel strongly that the campaigns for radical citational politics and English translations that subvert the continued overemphasis on the production of U.S. Black feminist works in Portuguese illustrate a step in the right direction. In the 2017 essay "bell hooks' 'The Oppositional Gaze' in Brazil: Translation and Black Diaspora Feminist Thought," Keisha-Khan Y. Perry discusses the prolific translation of hooks and other U.S. Black feminist scholars in Brazil. hooks has been one of the most translated and most cited Black feminist scholars in Brazil and arguably throughout Latin America. More recently, we have seen more Spanish and Portuguese translations of essays and complete works by Patricia Hill Collins, Angela Davis, and Assata Shakur. This dissemination of Black feminist knowledge has certainly led to rich diasporic conversations about Black feminist thought and praxis. However, one poignant critique of the *Meridians* 2016 journal special on Afro-Latin feminisms and scholarly works (theses, dissertations, articles, and books), which aimed to reverse the geographic flow of Black feminist ideas, has been the overreliance on North American feminist writings. In writing about Latin American feminisms, contributors to the journal issue still heavily cited North American feminists. As stated above, more translations of Black feminist scholars from Latin America into English can attempt to address this intellectual conundrum.

In putting together this volume, we aimed specifically to integrate the work of scholars based in North America, Latin America, and the Caribbean regarding the commonalities of Black women's experiences. While we understand that this approach does not decolonize English as the preferred language of knowledge exchange in the Americas, we do understand that putting these social scientists in conversation with one another challenges a hierarchy of knowledge and exchange. Scholars in Latin America are more familiar with social thought produced in North America and in English, and we are motivated by the need to reverse this trend. However, we are most inspired by their vivid illustrations of how the social sciences can be used in the process of eradicating all forms of subjugation.

Globalizing and Engendering Black Studies

Writing from the crucial standpoint of Black women in Latin America and the Caribbean globalizes and engenders the political and social justice problems of Black people while also forging gendered diasporic politics. In North America, we cannot ignore what is taking place in Latin America and the Caribbean, the region with the largest concentration of African-descendant peoples in the Western Hemisphere. South American and Caribbean colonies and nations received 95 percent of the enslaved Africans who survived the Middle Passage to the Americas (Slave Voyages 2022). In the 134 years since the last Latin American and Caribbean country abolished slavery (Brazil in 1888), racial ideologies and systemic racism have persisted, impacting the identities, perspectives, and experiences of African-descendant peoples across the region. How is it possible that Black people in Latin America and the Caribbean constitute the largest concentration of Africans in the diaspora, yet most Black studies programs still focus primarily on North America when discussing the Americas?

This book is primarily concerned with pushing the geographic and conceptual boundaries of Africana/Black studies, Feminist studies, and Latin American and Caribbean studies. The growth in Afro-Latin studies in the United States, with the support of major foundations such as the Mellon Foundation and the National Endowment for the Humanities, reflects an urgent recognition that there is a lacuna in our knowledge of Black populations in the Spanish- and Portuguese-speaking Americas. While there is some emphasis on Caribbean political thought, Afro-Latin history, culture, and politics are rarely taught and studied. Few universities in the United States, such as City University of New York, the University of Texas at Austin (UT-Austin), the University of Pittsburgh, Harvard, and the University of Pennsylvania, have significant concentrations of scholars doing this work on Afro-Latin America. Scholars such as Ruth Simms Hamilton at Michigan State University and Edmund T. Gordon at UT-Austin have shaped the field's current focus, but there is still little analytical attention given to women and gender distinctions in the production of knowledge, culture, and politics in countries such as Brazil, Colombia, Peru, and Cuba.

Just as Black studies needs engendering, women's and gender studies needs consideration of the ways in which systemic racism impacts the experiences and activism of Black women in the region. Although there is a large body of work centered on women and gender in Latin America and the Caribbean, this literature often lacks an intersectional approach that takes into consideration Black women's dynamic responses to injustice. Black feminist scholars have long advocated for an intersectional approach to examine the marginalization and oppression of Black women (Caldwell 2017; Crenshaw 1991), and Black feminist scholars have made substantial contributions to research on Black women's experiences and their activism in the region (e.g., Brazil, Caldwell 2007; 2017; Edu 2016; Falu 2020; Perry 2013, 2016, 2019; Smith 2016a, 2016b; Williams 2013, 2015). Since the publication of Ruth Landes's *The City of Women* in 1947, which focused on women's leading roles in Brazilian Afro-religious communities, Kia Lilly Caldwell's *Negras in Brazil: Re-Envisioning Black Women, Citizenship, and the Politics of Identity* (2006) has led the few books focused on Black women in Latin America. Additionally, coeditor Keisha-Khan Y. Perry's *Black Women against the Land Grab: The Fight for Racial Justice in Brazil* (2013) and coeditor Melanie Medeiros's *Marriage, Divorce and Distress in Northeast Brazil: Black Women's Perspectives on Love, Respect and Kinship* (2018) contribute to this canon. A key premise in these books is that Black women have knowledge and produce thought, and methodologically, they can be the focus of social scientific study. In her chapter, anthropologist Melanie White argues that rather than continue to center mestizx, institutional efforts at promoting intercultural education and research must prioritize the study of Black women's histories, lives, and experiences. While there is an explosion of master's theses and dissertations in Brazil focused on Black women, including contributor Julia Abdalla's (2020) award-winning dissertation on the Black feminist movement, other countries still lag behind.

We are deeply inspired by feminist anthropologist Faye V. Harrison's provocative essay "Refusing the God Trick: Engaging Black Women's Knowledge"

(2022). In this vein, we recognize that much of our interest in organizing this book stems from the "informal curriculum" with which we ourselves have had to contend. In graduate school and beyond, we have become accustomed to relying on this informal curriculum, which is, as Harrison reminds us, the bodies of knowledge (those produced by women, Black and Indigenous scholars, and nonacademic intellectuals) not typically included in our formal training. The "lessons from the informal curriculum," she adds, teaches "the ideologies, social relations, power dynamics, and practices shaping the producing, validating, reception, and circulation of anthropological knowledge" (182) in universities and broader societies. This book draws from Christen Smith's (2022) idea of "citational erasure" of Black women from formal sectors of knowledge production and learning. As she argues, our decision to foreground Black women's experiences and knowledges is not just as an intellectual act but also a recognition of the acute relationship between erasure/omission and the proliferation of intersectional violence in the academy and beyond (208–209), specifically the "historical patterns of race-gender exploitation that haunt the present" (211). Political scientist Maziki Thame's chapter on the rise of Black women in Jamaican politics shows an explicit correlation between grassroots movements and political formation, which can be read alongside Abdalla's chapter on the significance of Black women's grassroots organizing in Brazil.

For over two decades now, we have dedicated our research, writing, and teaching to amplifying the ideas and politics of Black women, and like our contributors, engaging them as intellectual interlocutors. Like Harrison and numerous others in the academy, we have built our careers on ideas that occupy the margins of knowledge production. Hence, this book is an effort to continue this feminist work, to make explicit the need to formalize the "informal curriculum," and to make Black women's ideas on Latin America and the Caribbean more accessible in U.S. academic spaces. Some contributors such as Thame have established academic careers albeit in spaces where Black women's thought still does not fully occupy the center of Black radical thought even when Black women scholars are prominent. Other contributors such as Angela Crumdy and Ishan Gordon are beginning their academic careers having benefited from Black feminist mentors such as Dána-Ain Davis who encouraged feminist theories, research methodologies, and citational practices as integral to their academic work. Black women anthropologists and sociologists such as Katherine Dunham, Lélia Gonzalez, Luiza Bairros, and Mara Viveros-Vigoya paved the intellectual road for this book's contributors to emerge. Our decision to edit this volume represents one piece of building on that intellectual legacy.

Putting together this volume forced us to remember our intellectual predecessors doing this work. African American feminist anthropologist Angela Gilliam wrote numerous essays that paved the way for our current studies on Black people in Latin America. Her essay "Black and White in Latin America"

(1974) provided some of the earliest rejections of Latin American racial exceptionalism and made a bold statement that remains relevant today: "We Blacks in the United States have much to offer the struggle in the African Diaspora, but let us humbly remember that we have a bit more to learn before we are truly internationally relevant and knowledgeable" (173). Perry's late Brown University colleague Anani Dzidzienyo was one of the first to introduce the term "Afro-Latin" in his classic 1978 essay, "Activity and Inactivity in the Politics of Afro-Latin America," and in turn became a foundational figure in the field of Afro-Latin studies. At Brown University, he was critical in building Portuguese and Brazilian studies and encouraged hundreds of students to study Portuguese. It is also necessary to remember that it was choreographer and anthropologist Katherine Dunham who in 1952 sued a hotel in São Paulo after she was refused entry—a lawsuit that led the Brazilian legislature to pass a bill outlawing all forms of discrimination in public spaces. Ruth Simms Hamilton at Michigan State University also established the Afro-Latin Project (Dzidzienyo was on its board) and recruited numerous Afro-Latin students and noteworthy Black Brazilian scholars such as Vera Benedito, who wrote a master's thesis on Caribbean immigrants to South America and a dissertation on affirmative action in the workplace. Luiza Bairros was one of Hamilton's most renowned students, and she went on to become the minister of Brazil's Secretariat for the Promotion of Racial Equality (2011–2014). More recently, a fellowship in Hamilton's memory supported the doctoral research and writing of Sônia Beatriz dos Santos and Luciane Rocha, two former activists of the Criola Black women's organization who completed their PhDs at the University of Texas at Austin. This participation of Afro-Latin students in U.S. academe certainly impacted Black studies circles and shaped how scholars like us would enter our research fields in Latin American and Brazilian studies. Much of the research on gendered racism that the authors explore in this volume stem from this long history of researching gendered race, racialization, and class-based inequality in the field that now constitutes Afro-Latin studies in the United States. More importantly, the increase in the numbers of Black students in Latin American and Caribbean universities in recent decades also has meant an expansion of the body of work in the social sciences that explores the cultural and political realities of the Black communities from which these students have emerged.

A Note on Race/Racism and Its Particularities

This book places great emphasis on hemispheric Blackness and diasporic solidarities in a global gendered anti-racism guided by transformational scholarship produced in the social sciences across the Americas. Although this is our explicit intellectual and political aim, we are still attuned to the particularities of Black women's experiences and the vastness of the historical processes that produces systems of subjugation in disparate geographic locations. We recognize that as a technology of power fabricated by Europeans, the construction of race as a social identity category occurs within specific historical, social, cultural, and political economic contexts. While the construction of race as identity and processes of racialization vary across nation-state contexts within Latin America and the Caribbean, racial ideology throughout the region differs substantially from that of countries such as the United States. Until the 1970s, pseudoscientists in the United States argued that there was substantial genetic differentiation between people with different phenotypic traits and that differentiation corresponded with characteristics such as intellect and skills and used the ideology of hypodescent to categorize people as "Black." In Latin America and the Caribbean, the construction of racial categories and identities is grounded in more than the myth of significant genetic difference. In Latin America, contemporary racial categories are largely the product of historical ideas about miscegenation (*mestizaje* in Spanish; *mestiçagem* in Portuguese), and the racialization of people incorporates characteristics such as class, communication style, education, occupation, clothing and hair style, and geographic location. Racial categories and identities in the region are also continually in flux and relational (Hordge-Freeman 2015), with perceptions about someone's racial identity and an individual's own identity transforming across time and space depending on the context. Yet, as Smith (2016a) notes, Blackness is "an incontestable 'fact' born out of history, social experience, and violent encounter" (13), and anti-Blackness undergirds much of the gender and class subjugation that people experience in societies. Centering Black women's ideas and practices reveals how race, gender, sexuality, and class interact to produce systemic violence and marginalization. This volume encourages us to examine the interconnectedness of historical processes of domination and exclusion. More importantly, as gendered racial discourses about Blackness and indigeneity have circulated over time and space and shaped socioeconomic relations, insurgent radical ideas have also traveled, and political communities have formed in a common struggle.

Today, we continue to write against the backdrop of proliferated scholarship that would argue that "racial democracies" and racial fluidity have indexed a level of racial tolerance in Latin America and the Caribbean that has not existed in the United States, where overt forms of racism and segregation were institutionalized. As Brodwin Fischer, Keila Grinberg, and Hebe Mattos show in their essay, "Law, Silence, and Racialized Inequality in the History of Brazil" (2018), and Paulina L. Alberto shows in her book *Black Legend: The Many Lives of Raúl Grigera and the Power of Racial Storytelling* (2022), anti-Black discourses and racial inequality persisted throughout Latin American history even in contexts where racial laws or codes did not exist. Efforts to "whiten" (and thus make more "modern") the populations of South American nations through encouraging immigration from Europe, and the persistent and pervasive discrimination of people of African descent who are racialized as Black, belie the ideology of a racial democracy across the region. And in countries where Afro-descendant people are in the vast majority, people who are racialized as Black (e.g., Haitians and Haitian-descendants in the Dominican Republic) also face oppression and marginalization. While this is not her primary focus, Thame's chapter illustrates the nuances of anti-Black gendered racism in a predominantly Black context such as Jamaica. Similarly, Crumdy's chapter explores how even countries such as Cuba, which attempted to eliminate race-based inequality through a more inclusive social safety net after the Cuban revolution, have failed to eliminate a social hierarchy that corresponds to racial categories. In short, the widespread preference for whiteness in Latin America and the Caribbean affords privilege to members of a society who exhibit characteristics associated with whiteness, challenging myths surrounding racial equality in the region. Black people in Latin America and the Caribbean face inequities along the lines of education, labor, income, housing, political representation, health, and violence (e.g., in Brazil, IBGE 2019).

For Black women in Latin America, gender inequality intersects with other forms of oppression such as systemic racism and class inequality. For many Black (and Indigenous) women, the benefits of greater gender equality are not guaranteed (Lebon 2010). As Sotero points out in her chapter, the study of labor, undertaken by Brazilian sociologist Luiza Bairros, is central to understanding the ways in which gender and racial ideologies perpetuate class inequality to the detriment of Black women. For example, Black and Brown Brazilian women are more likely than white women to work in the informal labor force (47.8 percent work in the informal labor force versus 34.7 percent of white women; IBGE 2019) and Black and Brown Brazilian women earn 44.4 percent of what white men earn and 58.6 percent of what white women earn (IBGE 2019). In her chapter, Thame examines the ways in which Black women involved in leftist politics in 1970s Jamaica recognized workers' rights as a women's rights issue, particularly for Black women challenging the historical legacy of slavery on Black women's labor conditions. And in her chapter, anthropologist Crumdy explores how retired Black Cuban women rely on clandestine informal sector labor as English tutors to supplement their state pension. Yet, despite the complexity of gendered racial inequalities in postrevolutionary Cuba, Crumdy's chapter shows a nuanced understanding of how leftist politics can simultaneously aim to dismantle systemic racism and sexism while upholding historical legacies of slavery and colonialism.

Part of the historical legacies of slavery and colonialism, racialized and gender violence disproportionately affect Black women in Latin America and the Caribbean. In Brazil, where Black women make up 26 percent of the Brazilian population (CFEMEA 2016), women identifying as Black or Brown are twice as likely to be victims of violence than white women (IBGE 2019). In her chapter, anthropologist Eshe Lewis explores the ways that stereotypes about Black Peruvian women's aggression and sexuality are a product of the "social and political exclusion of Afro-descendant women in Peru," and mask the lived realities of the interpersonal violence (IPV) that many Black women experience. Presenting findings from ethnographic research with users of IPV support services, Lewis centers Black women's perspectives to examine the myriad ways IPV, as a form of gendered and racial violence, manifests to impact women's lives. And Reyes discusses the ways in which the armed conflict in Colombia transformed Black territories in devastating ways as part of a "colonial/modern racial project of war," of which Black women are carriers of embodied memories of violence. Through their powerful stories, Reyes counters hegemonic portrayals of the armed conflict that erase Black women's experiences. Furthermore, in her discussion of the importance of Black women's studies, White uses violence against Black women as a prime example as to why and how intercultural universities must commit to change-making scholarship and resources that recognize the specificities of Black women's experiences.

Another enduring legacy of colonialism, across the Americas, is that Black women grapple with racist tropes that hypersexualize them, while experiencing structural inequities that jeopardize their reproductive health and access to health care (Caldwell 2017). In her chapter, Gordon, an anthropologist, outlines the impact respectability politics have on the reproductive health of young Black women in Nicaragua. Additionally, taking us beyond representations and expectations of Black womanhood, Thame similarly shows how activism around reproductive justice on a societal scale shapes Black women's political participation.

As the chapters in this book demonstrate, examining the life experiences of African-descendant women at the intersection of race, gender, and class is integral to understanding how the historical legacies of slavery and colonialism and social and structural inequities affect their daily lives and subjectivities (Caldwell 2017; Hill Collins 2000). Intersectional approaches demonstrate that Black women face racialized gender inequality in both public and private spheres; such inequality mutually reinforces systemic racism that minotitizes Black women. Black women's experiences and perspectives merit critical study and analysis to understand how historical, social, and political economic factors that impact their lives, "sanction and perpetuate their social and political invisibility" (Caldwell 2007, 1), and confine them to a marginal position in their societies' "matri(ces) of domination" (Hill Collins 2000; Hordge-Freeman 2015). Yet, as the rest of this introductory essay has demonstrated, Black women have made powerful intellectual and political contributions in the pursuit of a more equitable and just society. Thame's chapter on Black women in leftist politics in 1970s Jamaica explores the significant contribution that Black women made both to the broader leftist political agenda and to efforts to secure women's rights to consumer and labor protections and paid maternity leave, issues that were and are particularly salient for Black women in postcolonial Jamaican society. In her chapter, Abdalla, a sociologist, examines the growing plurality within the Black feminist movement in Brazil and its transition from an organized movement confined to activist and political domains to a large-scale, decentralized, and multifaceted movement that has greatly impacted political culture. And in their chapter, sociologists Bruna Pereira and Cristiano Rodrigues argue that online activism is forging new narratives and turning subjectivity and intimacy into political concerns, broadening the scope of Black feminist activism in Brazil.

Volume Overview

In short, this book presents the results of valuable, critical social science research that centers Black women as knowledge producers and bearers and emphasizes Black women's innovative, theoretical, and methodological approaches to gendered racism, activism, and Black politics in Latin America and the Caribbean. This volume situates these social and political analyses as interrelated and dialogic, and it contributes a transnational perspective to contemporary conversations surrounding the continued relevance of Black women as a category of social science inquiry. While this volume is loosely organized around four thematic foci, the chapters explore topics and issues that intersect and overlap in ways that transcend thematic boundaries. Chapters 1 ("Reclaiming a Legacy: Black Women's Presence and Perspectives in the Brazilian Social Sciences") and 2 ("Beyond Intercultural Mestizaje: Toward Black Women's Studies on the Caribbean Coast of Nicaragua") explore the role of Black women scholars in the social sciences and the importance of Black women's studies, often overlooked or deprioritized amid regional academic initiatives focused on multiculturalism, for understanding and addressing the enduring challenges facing Black women in Latin America and the Caribbean.

Building off of Sotero's discussion in chapter 1 on Black women's intellectual contributions to movements for racial justice, chapters 3 to 5 examine Black women's activism and their agency. Chapters 3 ("The Significance of 'Communists Wearing Panties' in the Jamaican Left Movement (1974–1980)" and 4 ("Exercising Diversity: From Identity to Alliances in Brazil's Contemporary Black Feminism") examine Black women's dynamic participation in political movements. In chapter 3, Thame highlights Black women's activism surrounding labor in the 1970s, and in chapter 5 ("'This Isn't to Get Rich': Double Morality and Black Women Private Tutors in Cuba") Crumdy examines the ways in which Black Cuban women circumvent Cuban labor policies as a means of survival.

The volume's third thematic emphasis centers on the critical issue of Black women's experiences of racial and gendered violence. Chapters 6 ("A 'Bundle of Silences': Untold Stories of Black Women Survivors of the War in Colombia") and 7 ("The Burden of *Las Bravas*: Race and Violence against Afro-Peruvian Women") interrogate Black women's experiences of violent conflict and intimate gender-based violence to challenge the erasure and invisibility of those experiences. In chapters 2 and 7, White and Lewis introduce the ways in which racist tropes about Black women's sexuality are weaponized to justify the oppression of and violence against Black women, and the remaining two chapters in the volume further investigate the structures that hinder and support Black women's intimate lives. Chapters 8 ("A Creole Christmas: Sexual Panic and Reproductive Justice in Bluefields, Nicaragua") and 9 ("Digital Black Feminist Activism in Brazil: Toward a Repoliticization of Aesthetics and Romantic Relationships") highlight the discourses and politics surrounding Black women's sexual and romantic entanglements. Additionally, with chapter 9, Pereira and Rodrigues further contribute to Abdalla's discussion, in chapter 4, of the multifaceted Brazilian Black feminist movement. When read together, the chapters in this volume offer a hemispheric framework for understanding the lasting legacies of colonialism, transatlantic slavery, plantation life, and persistent socioeconomic and cultural violence.

References

Abdalla, Julia S. 2020. *Alianças, encontros e margens: Feminismos negros e interseccionalidade na Frente de Mulheres Negras de Campinas e Região*. PhD diss., University of Campinas, Brazil.

Alberto, Paulina L. 2022. *Black Legend: The Many Lives of Raúl Grigera and the Power of Racial Storytelling*. Cambridge: Cambridge University Press.

Alvarez, Sonia A., and Kia Lilly Caldwell, editors. 2016. "African Descendant Feminisms in Latin America." *Meridians: Feminism, Race, and Transnationalism* 14, no. 1, and 14, no. 2.

Augusto, Geri. 2020. "For Marielle: Mulhere(s) da Maré—Danger, Seeds and Tides." *Transition* 14, no. 129: 246–264.

Bairros, Luiza. 2000. "Lembrando Lélia Gonzalez." *Afro-Ásia* 23. https://periodicos.ufba.br/index.php/afroasia/article/view/20990.

Caldwell, Kia. 2006. *Negras in Brazil: Re-envisioning Black Women, Citizenship, and the Politics of Identity*. New Brunswick, NJ: Rutgers University Press.

———. 2009. "Transnational Black Feminism in the 21st Century: Perspectives from Brazil." In *New Social Movements in the African Diaspora: Challenging Global Apartheid*, edited by Manning Marable and Leith Mullings, 105–120. New York: Palgrave Macmillan.

———. 2017. *Health Equity in Brazil: Intersections of Gender, Race, and Policy*. Champaign: University of Illinois Press.

———. 2022. "#MariellePresente: Black Feminism, Political Power, and Violence in Brazil." *Souls*, 22, no. 2–4: 213–238.
Caldwell, Kia L., Wendi Muse, Tianna S. Paschel, Keisha-Khan Y. Perry, Christen A. Smith, and Erica L. Williams. 2018. "On the Imperative of Transnational Solidarity: A U.S. Black Feminist Statement on the Assassination of Marielle Franco." *The Black Scholar*, March 23. https://www.theblackscholar.org/on-the-imperative-of-transnational-solidarity-a-u-s-black-feminist-statement-on-the-assassination-of-marielle-franco/.
CBW (Cite Black Women). 2022. Homepage. Accessed June 28, 2022. www.citeblackwomencollective.org/.
CFEMEA (Centro Feminista de Estudos e Assessoria). 2016. "Mulheres negras são grupo social com menor representatividade no legislativo municipal." Brasília: CFEMEA. www.cfemea.org.br/index.php/alerta-feminista/4610-mulheres-negras-sao-grupo-social-com-menor-representatividade-no-legislativo-municipal.
Crenshaw, Kimberlé. 1991. "Mapping the Margins: Intersectionality, Identity Politics, and Violence against Women of Color." *Stanford Law Review* 43, no. 6: 1241–1299.
Danticat, Edwidge. 2011. *Create Dangerously: The Immigrant Artist at Work*. Princeton: Princeton University Press.
Dzidzienyo, Anani. 1978. "Activity and Inactivity in the Politics of Afro-Latin America. *SECOLAS Annals* 9 (March): 48–61.
Edu, Ugo. 2016. "Untangling Discursive Sexualities: Afro-Brazilian Women, Sterilization and Identity Movements in Salvador, Bahia, Brazil." In *Human Rights, Race, and Resistance in Africa and the African Diaspora*, edited by Toyin Falola and Cacee Hoyer. New York: Routledge, 47–63.
Falu, Nessette. 2020. "Ain't I Too a Mulher? Implications of Black Lesbians' Wellbeing, Self-care, and Gynecology in Brazil." *Journal of Latin American and Caribbean Anthropology* 25, no. 1: 48–66.
Fischer, Brodwin, Keila Grinberg, and Hebe Mattos. 2018. "Law, Silence, and Racialized Inequality in the History of Brazil." In *Afro-Latin American Studies: An Introduction*, edited by Alejandro de la Fuente and George Reid Andrews, 130–176. Cambridge: Cambridge University Press.
Gilliam, Angela. 1974. "Black and White in Latin America." *Présence Africaine* 92, no. 4: 161–173.
Gonzalez, Lélia. 1988. "For an Afro-Latin Feminism." In *Confronting the Crisis in Latin America: Women Organizing for Change*. Santiago, Chile: Isis International. https://feministarchives.isiswomen.org/47-books/confronting-the-crisis-in-latin-america-women-organizing-for-change/828-for-an-afro-latin-american-feminism.
———. 2021. "Racism and Sexism in Brazilian Culture." Translated by Bruna Barros, Feva, Jess Oliveira, and Luciana Reis. *Women's Studies Quarterly* 49 (2021): 371–394.
Gonzalez, Lélia, and Carlos Hasenbalg. 1982. *Lugar de Negro*. São Paulo: Editora Marco Zero.
Harrison, Faye V. 2022. "Refusing the God Trick: Engaging Black Women's Knowledge." *Cultural Anthropology* 37, no. 2: 182–190.
Hill Collins, Patricia. 2000. *Black Feminist Thought: Knowledge, Consciousness, and the Politics of Empowerment*. 2nd ed. New York: Routledge.
Hordge-Freeman, Elizabeth. 2015. *The Color of Love: Racial Features, Stigma, and Socialization in Black Brazilian Families*. Austin: University of Texas Press.

IBGE (Instituto Brasileiro de Geografia e Estatística). 2019. *Desigualdades sociais por cor ou raça no Brasil.* Rio de Janeiro: IBGE. https://biblioteca.ibge.gov.br/visualizacao/livros/liv101681_informativo.pdf.

Landes, Ruth. 1947. *The City of Women.* Albuquerque: University of New Mexico Press.

Lebon, Nathalie. 2010. "Introduction: Women Building Plural Democracy in Latin America and the Caribbean." In *Women's Activism in Latin America and the Caribbean: Engendering Social Justice, Democratizing Citizenship,* edited by Elizabeth Maier and Nathalie Lebon, 3–25. New Brunswick, NJ: Rutgers University Press.

Machado, Taís de Sant'Anna and Keisha-Khan Y. Perry. 2021. "Translation of 'The Black Woman: A Portrait.'" *Feminist Anthropology* 2. no. 1: 38–49.

Medeiros, Melanie A. 2018. *Marriage, Divorce and Distress in Northeast Brazil: Black Women's Perspectives on Love, Respect and Kinship.* New Brunswick, NJ: Rutgers University Press.

Mora, Mariana. 2019. "Marielle Franco, una huella inspiratadora." *LASA FORUM* 50, no. 3: 80–81.

Olivero, Leuvis Manuel de. 2020. *Memória Viva.* São Paulo: Câmara Brasileira do Livro.

Perry, Keisha-Khan Y. 2013. *Black Women against the Land Grab: The Fight for Racial Injustice in Brazil.* Minneapolis: University of Minnesota Press.

———. 2016. "Geographies of Power: Black Women Mobilizing Intersectionality in Brazil." *Meridians: Feminism, Race, Transnationalism* 14, no. 1: 94–120.

———. 2017. "O olhar oposicional de bell hooks no Brasil: tradução e pensamento feminista negro diaspórico." In *Brazil: Translation and Black Diasporic Feminist Thought (1970–2010),* edited by Izabel Brandão, Ildney Cavalcanti, Claudia de Lima Costa, and Ana Cecília Acioli Lima, 510–518. Floriánopolis, Brazil: EDUFAL, Editora da UFSC.

———. 2019. "The Resurgent Far Right and the Black Feminist Struggle for Social Democracy in Brazil." *American Anthropologist* 122, no. 1: 157–162.

Perry, Keisha-Khan Y. and Edilza Sotero. 2019. "Amefricanidade: The Black Diaspora Feminism of Lélia Gonzalez." *LASA FORUM* 50, no. 3: 60–64.

Ratts, Alex and Flavia Ríos. 2010. *Lélia Gonzalez.* São Paulo: Selo Negro.

Ríos, Flavia and Marcia Lima. 2020. *Lélia Gonzalez: Por um feminismo Afro-latino-americano: ensaios, intervenções e diálogos.* Rio de Janeiro: Zahar.

Silva, Benedita da and Medea Benjamin. 1997. *Benedita da Silva: An Afro-Brazilian Woman Story of Politics and Love.* Pasadena, CA: Food First Books.

Slave Voyages. 2022. The Trans-Atlantic Slave Trade Database. Accessed May 20. www.slavevoyages.org/.

Smith, Christen A. 2016a. *Afro-Paradise: Blackness, Violence, and Performance in Brazil.* Champaign: University of Illinois Press.

———. 2016b. "Towards a Black Feminist Model of Black Atlantic Liberation: Remembering Beatriz Nascimento." *Meridians* 2016: 71–87.

———. 2021. "An Introduction to Cite Black Women." *Feminist Anthropology* 2, no. 1: 6–9.

———. 2022. "Citation, Erasure, and Violence: A Memoir." *Cultural Anthropology* 37, no. 2: 206–213.

Smith, Christen A., Archie Davies and Bethânia Gomes. 2021. "'In Front of the World': Translating Beatriz Nascimento." *Antipode: A Radical Journal of Geography* 53, no. 1: 279–316.

Smith, Christen A., Erica L. Williams, Imani Wadud, and Whitney N. L. Pirtle. 2021. "Cite Black Women: A Critical Praxis (A Statement)." *Feminist Anthropology* 2, no. 1: 10–17.

Williams, Erica Lorraine. 2013. *Sex Tourism in Bahia: Ambiguous Entanglements.* Champaign: University of Illinois Press.

———. 2015. "Mucamas and Mulatas: Black Brazilian Feminisms, Representations, and Ethnography." In *Transatlantic Feminisms: Women and Gender Studies in Africa and the Diaspora*, edited by Cheryl Rodriguez, Dzodzi Tsikata, and Akosua Adomako Ampofo, 103–122. Lanham, MD: Lexington Books.

———. 2021. "A Tale of Two Women: Genealogies of Black Feminist Anthropology in Brazil." In *Genealogies of the Feminist Present: Lineages and Connections in Feminist Anthropology*, edited by Lynn Bolles and Mary H. Moran, *American Ethnologist* (AES) website, May 24. https://americanethnologist.org/features/collections/legacies-and-genealogies-in-feminist-anthropology/a-tale-of-two-women-genealogies-of-black-feminist-anthropology-in-brazil.

1
Reclaiming a Legacy

∙∙∙∙∙∙∙∙∙∙∙∙∙∙∙∙∙∙∙∙

Black Women's Presence and Perspectives in the Brazilian Social Sciences

EDILZA CORREIA SOTERO

> Our objective is that we, Black women, set off to create our own references, not looking at the world from the perspective of men, both Black and White, or White women. The meaning of the expression "creating our own references" is that we want to be side by side with our partners in the struggle for social change, we want to become spokespersons of our own ideas and needs. In short, we want a position of equality in this struggle.
> —First National Meeting of Black Women Newsletter, 1988

In all phases of Brazil's history, during moments of resistance and struggle for liberation, Black Brazilian women's political actions are identifiable. Oriented by a critical praxis and commitment to social change, Black women have produced knowledge that has made significant contributions to Brazilian intellectual traditions. However, records of their intellectual production—research, books, academic articles, theses, newspapers, and media—have often been forgotten in history or ignored. As part of an effort to rectify this erasure, in this chapter, I focus on four Black Brazilian women scholars whose work in the social sciences centers race, frequently interconnected with gendered analyses. Even though they had distinct research foci and perspectives, I argue that their work promotes social change and is a critical contribution to the social sciences in Brazil.

Throughout this chapter, I employ an inscription-erasure-reinscription framework. I use *inscription* to demonstrate how these women's life experiences are reflected in their writing and other work. I explore how the *erasure* of their intellectual contributions has been a systematic social process connected to how race- and gender-based discrimination creates barriers to Black women's representation in the social sciences. To analyze their erasure as a social process, I discuss their scholarly and political contributions and efforts to silence or rebuke those contributions. Lastly, to overcome erasure, *reinscription* is a method of retrieving and presenting academic and life trajectories concurrently to contemporary audiences. Therefore, this chapter takes a historical and biographical approach to the lives and work of Black scholars Virginia Bicudo, Lélia Gonzalez, Luiza Bairros, and Marielle Franco, highlighting their contributions to the social sciences. All four women had academic training in the social sciences and used their professional training to work as professors, public administrators, or political representatives. Another distinctive characteristic they share is their activism, which centered the rights of Black women specifically and the Black population in general.

The institutionalization of the social sciences in Brazil began circa 1930 with the emergence of the first undergraduate classes in São Paulo and then in Rio de Janeiro.[1] In Brazil, the social sciences are an area of distinction and legitimacy for scholars of race relations, and in this chapter, I explore how each of these four women are connected with traditions of racial studies in the social sciences. Virgínia Bicudo's studies on racial attitudes developed frontier analyses between sociology and psychology. Later, Lélia Gonzalez devoted her analytical efforts to understanding Brazilian culture, centering the categories of race, gender, and class to explain the effects of colonial exploitation, racism, and sexism on the formation of Brazilian society and the Americas. In turn, Luiza Bairros focused her scholarship on labor, the effects of contemporary capitalist exploitation, and the ways in which racism is perpetuated. A critique of capitalism is also at the center of the analysis proposed by Marielle Franco, highlighting the problem of state violence against Black populations in Brazilian favelas. The life and intellectual trajectories analyzed in this chapter reflect the substantive contributions Black women have made to the field of social science in Brazil, from its constitution in the early 1930s to the present day.

Virgínia Bicudo: A Pioneer in the Social Sciences

Virgínia Leone Bicudo was born on November 21, 1910, in the city of São Paulo. She was the second of six children. Her parents were Giovanna Leone, an Italian immigrant who arrived in Brazil in 1897, and Teophilo Julio, the son of enslaved parents.[2] She was born just twenty-two years after the end of slavery in Brazil, and her lived experiences share a striking resemblance with those of other Black and poor people at that time, including the experience of her family's migration from rural areas to urban centers in hopes of social ascension (Butler 1998). Migration was common among Black men and women intellectuals and activists in Brazil, especially those born in the first decades of the twentieth century, such as Carolina Maria de Jesus, Abdias Nascimento, Alberto Guerreiro Ramos, and others.

In 1930, at the age of twenty, Virgínia Bicudo received a teaching degree from the Escola Normal Caetano de Campos (ELSP), a public school in São Paulo, and began to build a career in the field of education. Starting as a health educator, she worked at the São Paulo State Department of Education's School of Mental Hygiene Service, focusing on the treatment of psychological problems in children (Maio 2010). Anthropologist Janaína Damasceno Gomes (2013) dedicated her doctoral dissertation to the study of Virgínia Bicudo's trajectory and explains the many ways in which Bicudo was a pioneer throughout her life: "Bicudo's trajectory reveals processes such as the professionalization of women through teaching and training as a health educator, the entrance of women into higher education, trajectories of social ascension of Black and mixed families . . . the emergence of sociology as a discipline for analyzing and understanding Brazil and its institutionalization at the graduate level. Through it [her life] we can still see the introduction of psychoanalysis in Brazil. (25) In 1938, Bicudo was one of the first students to graduate from the Political and Social Sciences program at the *Escola Livre de Sociologia e Política* (ELSP), the only woman in her class of ten students."[3]

Unlike other intellectuals of her generation, Bicudo became recognized in the field of psychoanalysis during her lifetime rather than after her death. Therefore, interviews that she gave to newspapers recalling her childhood and early professional life exist within the historical archives. In one of those interviews, she explains how her decision to study the social sciences was related to the racism she suffered since her childhood: "As a child, I suffered color prejudice. I wanted a degree in sociology because, if prejudice was the problem, I should study sociology to protect myself from it, because it is formed at the sociocultural level" (Bicudo 1994). For Bicudo, the social sciences could help her to better understand the ways in which racism affects the lives of Black people as well as their subjectivities. Despite the Brazilian elite's discourse touting racial harmony, as a child living in São Paulo during the first decades of the twentieth century, Bicudo experienced tense race relations in the city. As scholars like Kim Butler (1998) and George Andrews (1991) have argued, racial discrimination and segregation in Brazil tended to be more intense in urban centers like São Paulo. Employing the study of racial discrimination to understand problems she experienced in her own life, Bicudo merged social and psychological studies, which would become a distinctive element of her research and scholarship.

During her training in the social sciences, Bicudo studied psychology, especially Freud's ideas, and psychoanalysis. While still an undergraduate student at ELSP, Bicudo became the first woman in South America to be psychoanalyzed as a patient of psychoanalyst Adelheid Koch (from 1937 onward). Despite her growing interest in psychoanalysis, Bicudo continued her studies in sociology, a more well-established discipline in Brazil at the time. She became one of the first three researchers to graduate from ELSP's master's program in social sciences, the first of its kind. Under the guidance of her adviser, sociologist Donald Pierson, she finalized her master's thesis in 1945.[4] The thesis, titled *Estudos sobre Atitudes Raciais de Pretos e Mulatos em São Paulo* (*Study of Racial Attitudes of Blacks and Mulattos in São Paulo*), offers an analysis of Black Brazilians' perspectives on and ideas about racial relations in São Paulo between 1941 and 1944; it was not published until 2010.

The academic path taken by Bicudo reflects her interests and influences. Her analysis of racial attitudes helped to shape the understanding of prejudice as a social phenomenon. Her approach combined psychological and social elements to explain, among other issues, how socioeconomic barriers reduced Black people's opportunities in society. In her research, in addition to affirming the prevalence of racial prejudice and not just class prejudice in Brazilian society, Bicudo also concluded that Black people tended to internalize a negative image about themselves and that this process has a significant impact on individuals during childhood (Bicudo 2010). This groundbreaking analysis contributed to the scholarship on race in Brazil, elevating the understanding of racism at both the societal level and the individual level.

Later, as a researcher on a UNESCO project, she coordinated a study on racial attitudes, this time among poor and middle-class children and adolescents from different racial groups.[5] The project, titled *Attitudes of Students from School Groups in Relation to the Color of Their Peers*, investigated students' stereotypes about, attitudes toward, and perceptions of other children and included interviews carried out with more than 4,000 children and adolescents in the city of São Paulo. Through this study, Bicudo identified the influence of family on children's attitudes. She argued that children's behavior, including racial prejudice and discrimination, could be understood by examining the interactions and relationships they had with other children and with their families (Bicudo 1955). Bicudo's study of children in their social interactions proposed to challenge the notion that racism is an innate personality trait rather than a social phenomenon.

The results of Bicudo's study, as well as scholarship from the lead researchers on the UNESCO study, were published as a book (Bastide and Fernandes 1955). However, a few years later, Bicudo's chapter was suppressed in a reprint of the publication (Bastide and Fernandes 1959), preventing her work from becoming known to a larger academic audience until recently.[6] Although in 2010 her master's thesis was printed, her chapter from the UNESCO project research has not reemerged. This lack of access to Bicudo's scholarship has contributed to her absence from publications celebrating the pioneers of the social sciences in Brazil.

Even today, Bicudo and her groundbreaking intellectual work are virtually unknown in the Brazilian social sciences. Some may suggest this happened because she moved almost completely away from the field of social sciences to dedicate herself to psychoanalysis after her participation in the UNESCO research project and until her death in 2003. However, this would be an inaccurate argument, as it cannot explain the erasure of her many contributions to an interdisciplinary field, including sociology, psychology, race studies, and children's studies. The absence of her name and the lack of citations acknowledging her original ideas surrounding race relations in Brazil are part of the systematic erasure of Black scholars, and in particular Black women's contributions to the social sciences.

Analyzing Virgínia Bicudo's trajectory, it is evident that inscription and erasure took place almost concomitantly. As she was a Black woman scholar of race relations interested in connecting the social sciences and psychology, her stance as a sociologist was constantly questioned by others in the field. At the start of her career, Bicudo sought to secure her place in the Brazilian field of sociology. Yet her contributions were forgotten until works such as Janaína Gomes's *Os Segredos de Virgínia* (2013) sought to rescue her memory and contribution to sociology from its erasure. The reinscription of Virgínia Bicudo also helps to redefine the field of social sciences in Brazil as intricately connected with the development of the field of psychology and its emphasis on the individual dimension.

Bicudo's academic work requires continued analyses to reveal her legacy, which includes perspectives on racism and how individuals reflect and react within broader social and cultural contexts. Additionally, among Black intellectuals, Bicudo's scholarship on race relations has influenced scholars such as Neusa Santos Sousa. Sousa's (1983) *Tornar-se Negro* (*Becoming Black*) highlights how racism affects the mind and the body through a psychoanalytical approach that was inspired by Bicudo. Another intellectual whose scholarship connecting psychoanalysis, racial relations, and the social sciences has been reinscribed into the Brazilian social sciences is the scholar activist Lélia Gonzalez.

Lélia Gonzalez: A Scholar of Brazilian Culture

A prominent leader in Brazil and transnationally, Lélia Gonzalez was born in 1935. She grew up in Rio de Janeiro, where she later studied and built her professional career. With academic training in history, geography, communications, and anthropology, Gonzalez published studies that, like Bicudo, also combined her training in psychoanalysis. Her intellectual work centered on understanding the effects of racism and sexism in Brazilian society and culture and its impacts on the lives of Black women.

In recent years, Lélia Gonzalez's life as an intellectual, politician, teacher, and activist has received attention in academic work, especially among Black scholars, dedicated to the study of different aspects of her scholarship. Recently there have been collections of her writing (Gonzalez 2018, 2020), biographies (Ratts and Rios 2010), analyses regarding several aspects of her scholarship (Viana 2006; Barreto 2005; Cardoso 2014), and her place as an intellectual and activist in the African diaspora (Perry and Sotero 2019). Considering the recent and prolific work about Lélia Gonzalez, this chapter focuses on her life and intellectual trajectory and scholarship as a social scientist, specifically the reinscription of her innovative approach to interpreting Brazilian society and the broader Americas.

Gonzalez's experiences as an activist started in the early 1970s during the time that she obtained a master's degree in communication at the Federal University of Rio de Janeiro (UFRJ) and took part in different initiatives of the Black movement, such as the Sociedade de Intercâmbio Brasil África (Brazil Africa Exchange Society, SINBA) and later the Instituto de Pesquisa das Culturas Negras (Research Institute of Black Cultures, IPCN). While dedicating herself to completing her master's degree, Lélia offered a course in Black Culture at the Escola de Artes Visuais do Parque Laje (Parque Laje School of the Visual Arts). The course discussed Black culture and African heritage and dealt with areas such as literature, visual arts, and popular culture as well as issues such as language, religion, identity, racism, and exclusion. An innovative proposal in the Brazilian social sciences, the course addressed several topics with the proposition of attracting a diverse audience of not only traditional academics but also young Black students, artists, intellectuals, and activists: "As a teacher in *Parque Laje*, Lélia sought to develop a work of critical reflection that enables the designation of the place of Black people in Brazilian culture. And, in trying to point to such a place, she also intend[ed] to bring its contribution towards the need of Black people to place themselves and their ancestors as a striking presence in our cultural reality" (Gonzalez 1977, 7). As a researcher, Gonzalez saw herself as a person of knowledge on a path to rescue a collective memory, which she defined as "a place of inscriptions to restore a history not written" (Gonzalez 1984, 226). Gonzalez established herself as a professor at the Pontifical Catholic University of Rio de Janeiro (PUC-RJ), teaching courses such as Anthropology and Brazilian Popular Culture, remaining a professor at the institution for eighteen years.

Throughout the 1980s, Gonzalez made a series of trips to Africa and within the Americas and Europe, participating in seminars and congresses and doing research on African women. Those events marked an intense period in her life for her emergence as a relevant intellectual at an international level. She also became a spokesperson on Brazil at conferences and other spaces, working to disseminate the ideas of Black women movement leaders (Perry and Sotero 2019).

During this period, she also authored several articles and books. In these publications, she offered her interpretation of Brazilian society, sharing her perspectives with both national and international audiences. Gonzalez's international presence also contributed to the inclusion of Afro–Latin American issues into Africana studies and diaspora studies in the United States. Anani Dzidzienyo (2007) notes that as a Black woman from Brazil in the early 1980s, Lélia was an uncommon presence in international seminars and conferences. In the United States, her presence initiated an ongoing intellectual project, an epistemological commitment of Black studies scholars to engage perspectives focusing on transnational issues.

From the 1970s onward, Gonzalez's scholarship defended the need for intellectual thought that escapes the cunning of Western reason and that denounces cultural racism in Brazilian society. Previous race-related Brazilian scholarship produced "distortion, folklorization and commercialization of Brazilian Black culture," with perverse effects for Black women in the labor force (Gonzalez 1979). Class exploitation and sexual exploitation placed Black women into two social roles: "domestic" and "mulattos" (Gonzalez 1979). When addressing the super-exploitation of Black women, Gonzalez argued that the Left and the feminist movement failed to recognize the centrality of the problem. Nevertheless, her criticism did not prevent her from recognizing herself as a feminist and leftist. When it comes to the super-exploitation of Black women, Gonzalez's approach was similar to that of intellectual activists such as Claudia Jones, who did not shy away from criticizing the neglect of Black women's socioeconomic problems by the Left (Jones 1949).[7]

Lélia Gonzalez conceived racism as both a material (based on capitalistic exploitation) and a symbolic phenomenon. In the symbolic field, she considered the cultural, psychological, ideological dimensions of racism. To her, the manipulation of the social representation of Black people resulted in a self-image of naturalized subordination. In this perspective, she resembled authors such as sociologist Patricia Hill Collins (2002) who uses the concept of *controlling images*—images used to naturalize and justify racism and sexism, poverty, and other forms of social injustice. Building on the foundation of Bicudo, Gonzalez used a psychoanalysis framework combined with analytical tools in the social sciences to analyze the effects of racism and sexism. Throughout her work, one can find concepts such as alienation, repression, denial, and neurosis to describe the effects of racism.

Throughout the 1980s, Gonzalez expanded her gaze to the Americas, focusing her scholarship on the African diaspora and on Indigenous peoples. Gonzalez proposed a historical and cultural perspective using the notion of *Améfrica Ladina*, in opposition to the idea of Latin America.[8] According to Gonzalez, racism must be understood in relation to colonialism and imperialism. From this understanding, she formulated the political-cultural concept of *Amefricanidade* (Amefricanity), referring to the historic and dynamic process of adaptation, resistance, reinterpretation, and creation of new life forms. The concept prioritizes the common experience of Black and Indigenous women and men on the continent. Gonzalez understood Amefricanity as a phenomenon of everyday life, present in speech, gestures, movements, and ways of being. The term *pretuguês* is an *amefricana* example of reinterpretation and adaptive transformation, revealing the heritage of the languages of African peoples in the Portuguese spoken in Brazil.

Gonzalez's political-cultural analyses also concern movements for social change. She argues that Black women's participation and leading role in social transformation processes occurred especially in the dimension of popular mobilization, even though they were present in the partisan political and feminist movements as well.[9] However, because of grassroots political-cultural forms of resistance in their communities, Black women faced challenges in addressing all dimensions (popular, political, and feminist) of their political practice at once. Referring to their experience in the 1980s, Gonzalez argues that the Black movement gave the basis for the participation and organization of Black women. A primordial place to organize and exercise a critical posture, Black movement organizations have been foundational to Black men and women's struggle against class exploitation and racial discrimination. Even so, the presence and performance of women in the Black movement produced tensions and struggle against sexism, as Luiza Bairros explains in her recollection of Gonzalez:

> I met Lélia Gonzalez when I joined the Movimento Negro Unificado—Unified Black Movement—(MNU) in 1979. She was a member of the National Executive Committee.... At the time there was no one with her ability to pulverize racist arguments in the debates we participated in, to defend the

legitimacy and necessity of the Black movement when all self-styled progressive sectors accused us of being divisive in the popular struggle. When most of the MNU militants still did not have a deeper elaboration on Black women, Lélia served as our spokesperson against the sexism that threatened to subordinate the participation of women within the MNU, and the racism that prevented our full insertion in the women's movement (Bairros 2000, 342).

Bairros, as well as many Black women of her generation, developed their political approach and practice in the Black women's movement by learning from leaders such as Gonzalez and others who became reference points in the struggle for social justice. Throughout the years, Gonzalez's relevance among Black organizers, activists, and intellectuals has increased, and yet the recognition of her work in the social sciences has still been limited.

Challenging decades of erasure, Black women in the social sciences are leading efforts to reinstate Gonzalez as a central figure in the field. Rios and Lima's recent book *Por um Feminismo Afro-Latino-Americano* (2020) anthologizes some of Lélia's writings from the 1980s and '90s, much of which had been forgotten or scattered in low-circulation or out-of-print publications, and has quickly become a national bestseller. Other recent efforts to organize her ideas include books, academic articles, translations (Machado and Perry 2021), documentaries (Costa, n.d.; Vieira 2017), and other forms (Motta 2019).

Gonzalez provides a critical case for understanding the significance of inscription-erasure-reinscription as a necessary process of documenting Black women's intellectual trajectory and influence on the Brazilian social sciences. In her case, the inscription of her perspectives is visible in the circulation of her scholarly ideas, her participation in academic congresses, and her position as a professor at an important university in Brazil. Her ascendence in Brazilian academe provides strong evidence that Gonzalez's scholarship was not ignored by her peers. Despite this, after her death, for the vast majority of social scientists in the 1990s and 2000s her scholarship fell into oblivion. Gonzalez's reinscription in the social sciences reflects the increased interest in her writings by younger generations of social scientists, especially over the last five years. Yet her work is underutilized in social science courses, demonstrating the limitations of this reinscription at the level of institutional change in the teaching of intellectual traditions.

The Sociological Legacy of Luiza Bairros

Luiza Bairros became a leader within the Black women's movement throughout the 1990s and 2000s, inspiring generations of Black women to pursue an intellectual activism committed to social transformation and emancipation.

Her trajectory both in academia and social movements reveals her efforts to expand the participation of Black women and men in Brazilian society. Despite the tremendous impact she had on racial transformation in Brazilian society, the same process of inscription-erasure-reinscription can be observed in Bairros's academic trajectory. She developed groundbreaking research on the labor market, a relevant area to understand Brazilian society; however, her intellectual contribution to these discussions in the social sciences remains scarce. Born in Rio Grande do Sul in 1953, she graduated with a degree in Business Public Administration from the Federal University of Rio Grande do Sul (UFRGS) and began her political activism in the student movement. Following the path of activism, she left Rio Grande do Sul and helped found the Movimento Negro Unificado (MNU) in 1978, where she served as the first national coordinator (between 1991 and 1994) and founded the MNU Women's Group in 1991. Choosing to live in Salvador, Bahia, she built an academic and professional career as a sociologist.[10]

Bairros held several positions in public management, serving as a public policy developer in areas such as labor and institutional racism.[11] Bairros also worked as secretary for the promotion of racial equality in the government of the State of Bahia, a position she held between 2008 and 2010. She was later appointed minister of the Department of Policies for the Promotion of Racial Equality by President Dilma Rousseff between 2011 and 2014. The executive positions she occupied helped her promote actions against the absence of policies for the Black population in the governmental sphere and in organizations.

As a scholar, Bairros dedicated herself to investigating racial discrimination in the labor market, focusing on the ways racism affected the creation of a working class in Bahia. She also dedicated herself to studying the connections between gender relations and labor, especially regarding Black women.[12] In 1987, she defended her master's thesis "Pecados no 'Paraíso Racial': O Negro na Força de Trabalho da Bahia, 1950–1980" (Sins in the 'Racial Paradise': The Black Person in Bahia's Workforce, 1950–1980). In her research, she argued that racism could be perceived in everyday life with multiple consequences, including the reproduction of social classes in Bahia (Pinho 2020). Among the significant contributions of her research to the social sciences was her demonstration of how racism impacted employment access and types of positions Black people occupied. In her research, she demonstrates how capitalism and racism intertwine, creating disadvantages for Black people in the labor market. Bairros has made groundbreaking contributions to the field of labor studies in Brazil, incorporating a racial perspective to the analysis of the world of work (e.g., Bairros, Castro, and Barreto 1992). This was unusual at the time, as most approaches maintained a Marxist perspective and completely ignored race as a relevant element in their analyses. Other scholars subordinated racial dynamics in their analyses of social class.

In addition to her research on the labor market, during the 1990s, Bairros also worked as a sociology professor at the Catholic University of Salvador and a researcher at the Federal University of Bahia (UFBA) Human Resources Center. At the latter, she coordinated the project "Race and Democracy in the Americas," in partnership with the National Conference of Black Political Scientists (NCOBPS).[13] Developed between 1998 and 2002, the project aimed to promote an exchange between Black Brazilian and U.S. scholars and students. The project was born from the partnership established by Bairros with a group of scholars based in the United States doing research on Latin American and Caribbean studies in political science. The work of those scholars was groundbreaking at the NCOBPS, especially because the organization contained a large group of scholars who focused mainly on the United States and continental Africa. At the time, Bairros was a graduate student at Michigan State University, under the supervision of the pioneer diaspora scholar and organizer of the Afro-Latin Project Ruth Simms Hamilton.[14] Remembering their first contact with Bairros, during NCOBPS meetings, K. C. Morrison wrote, "Bairros added quality of information and a set of interpretations that facilitated the panels and the discussions about a collaborative project" (2003, 27). Bairros's interactions with Black political scientists in the United States and the collaborative project she built with them reveals how she conducted an academic activism, promoting a network of researchers, students, activists, representatives, and public office holders interested in building an agenda for comparative analysis between Brazil and the United States.

In her personal and collective politics, Bairros sought to break the invisibility of Black men and women, both in academia and in public policy. A permanent feature in her work points to the way she critically examines the systematic erasure of Black intellectual traditions, as she explained in an interview: "There are Black intellectuals who play a key role, in their universities or their political organizations, trying to promote new ideas, new ways of interpreting racial politics in Brazil and the processes that determine it. But there is also enormous resistance to facing racism, which comes from within the academia itself, generally from white academics. And such resistance does not depend on whether they have studied the racial issue or not" (Pompeu and Bairros 2016). Bairros's professional trajectory in public administration and her legacy in the social sciences are important to the fight against the invisibility of Black intellectuals. The struggle today is embraced by a greater number of intellectuals in universities largely due to affirmative action and other policies in higher education geared toward combating racism in Brazil. Slowly, some recognition of the aforementioned scholars comes at the hands of this generation of Black scholars in the social sciences. An example is the Luiza Bairros Award for papers presented at the Annual Meeting of the National Association for Graduate Studies and Research in Social Sciences (ANPOCS). The award, proposed by the Ethnic and Racial Relations Committee, intends to give visibility to Brazilian scientific production on Ethnic and Racial Relations, racism, racial inequalities, and intersectionality.

However, the invisibility dilemma, inside and outside academia, is still prevalent for Black women. In some cases, even when a Black woman is elevated to a prominent position, she is often reduced to a symbol or token that people dispense instead of having a deep knowledge of her ideas and intellectual contributions. Such is the case with Marielle Franco, whom I discuss next. While in recent years Franco has become a symbol and inspiration in the fight for citizenship rights and in the struggle against racial violence in Brazil and worldwide, her work in the social sciences remains relatively unexamined.[15] The visibility of Marielle Franco has not prevented erasure of her significant scholarly contributions, providing another case of the inscription-erasure-reinscription process in Brazilian academe.[16] To contribute to the effort to reinscribe her work and deepen perspectives on her scholarship, the next section provides an overview of her academic career as a sociologist working on public policy.

Marielle Franco: Heiress and Inspiration

Marielle Franco's life and intellectual trajectory were marked by multiple places of belonging. Heir to the activist and intellectual legacy of other Black women in the social sciences such as Virgínia Bicudo, Lélia Gonzalez, and Luiza Bairros, she defined herself as a Black woman, mother, *favelada* (favela resident), lesbian, parliamentarian, and scholar. Born in 1979, in the city of Rio de Janeiro, Franco grew up in the Complexo de Favelas da Maré. At the age of eleven, she started working as a street vendor alongside her parents. Like many Black girls and women in Brazil, she also worked as a domestic worker. At the age of nineteen, she became the mother of Luyara Franco. Since childhood, Franco's life has been marked by the articulation of gender, race, and class oppression. However, she revolted against oppression to walk her own path. In her youth, she became part of the collective struggle and organization of her community residents. Building on her connections with social movements in the favelas, carnival groups, the university student movement, and the funk movement, Franco represented urban and peripheral Black youth in Rio de Janeiro and connected her experiences to those of others in Brazil and in the African diaspora.

Franco's admission to university was made possible, in part, by a preparatory course organized by the community of Maré, for which she also worked as secretary.[17] She matriculated as a student in the social sciences at the Pontifical Catholic University of Rio de Janeiro (PUC-RJ) and received a scholarship targeting low-income students. After completing her training in the social sciences, Marielle devoted her attention to the field of public administration, studying public security policy in the state of Rio de Janeiro. In her 2014 Universidade Federal Fluminense master's thesis, she analyzes the use of Unidades de Polícia Pacificadora (Pacifying Police Units, UPPs), which she classifies as a fragile, unfinished, and inconsistent security policy (Franco 2014).[18] Her master's thesis remains one of the most important social science studies on pacifying police forces and anti-Black state violence.

In her academic work, Marielle documented how the occupation of favelas by the UPP began with a military intervention by specialized police groups and later the occupation of favela territories by the government. According to Franco, when the UPPs were implemented, the state promised they would replace armed troops with the practice of community policing, a promise that was never fulfilled. Without that transition, the UPPs became yet another instrument of the penal state, specialized in the repression and social control of the working-class population. When analyzing the UPPs, Marielle examines their impact on the daily lives of favela residents and public perception of favelas. Her work points to forms of resistance and initiatives that could help to produce a public security policy attentive to the experience of citizenship rights in a broader way. For her, the demilitarization of the police and the need for greater dialogue with civil society, especially favela residents, were pivotal points. In her analysis, Franco also criticizes neoliberalism, describing the "neoliberal-penal" Brazilian state, of which young Black men are the greatest victims. As she writes, "It is not the armed, violent and warlike power of the State that assures the bases for strengthening security, on the contrary, it only serves to expand repression and class domination" (Franco 2014, 121). In her view, public security should be based on the guarantee of social, political, and economic rights and human rights in a broad way. In her analysis of public safety, Marielle developed a critical interpretation of contemporary forms of racial capitalism. Her work can be placed in the Black radical tradition, as put by Cedric Robinson: "It is not the province of one people to be the solution or the problem. A Black radical tradition formed in opposition to that civilization and conscious of itself is one part of the solution" (Robinson 2000, 318).

Franco's criticism of the role of the police force and public security policy reflects her experience as a favela resident as well as her political activism. She started working in politics in 2006, while studying social sciences, as a staff member to Marcelo Freixo who was elected state deputy in Rio de Janeiro. Among the functions she performed, she served on the Commission on Human Rights.[19] After ten years working as a staff member, she ran for a council position in the city of Rio de Janeiro in 2016. With a campaign inspired by the South African concept of *Ubuntu*, her slogan said, "I am because we are." In her political discourse, she defended not only the desire to occupy space in politics but also a change in the way of doing politics in Rio de Janeiro. By stating her position as a Black woman, mother, *favelada*, and activist for human rights and LGBTQIA+ rights, she managed to attract a broad range of support within favelas' residents, people in the Black movement, women, and youth. Elected as a PSOL (Socialism and Freedom Party) representative, Marielle became one of six women elected that year. In a total of fifty council members, she was the only Black woman in the city council and one of only two Black people on the council. As council member, she presided over the Commission for the Defense of Women and took part in the monitoring committee of the Federal Military Intervention in Rio de Janeiro. Her term as a council member followed President Michel Temer's February 2018 decree institutionalizing the military occupation already underway in the city, which resulted in escalated tensions between the police and community members.

Increased political tension and police corruption are the probable causes of the political assassination of Franco and her driver Anderson Gomes on March 14, 2018. Although the Brazilian police conducted some arrests in 2019, the crime remains unsolved. However, this attempt to silence Franco did not stop the struggle. In one of her last speeches at the Rio de Janeiro city council, Franco rebelled against attempts at silencing her, stating, "I will not be interrupted." A social movement erupted at the transnational level as a result of her example, fighting against attempts at derailing social movements.

Using the inscription-erasure-reinscription framework to analyze well-known figures such as Marielle Franco reveals that erasure as a process may not equally affect all areas of a Black woman's life. The erasure of her scholarship in the social sciences illustrates how racism and sexism work to obscure Black women's agency in specific areas, even if they achieve visibility in others. In cases where a legacy could be reduced to a singular memory, reinscription can help to reestablish multidimensionality, broadening knowledge of an inspiring body of scholarship such as that of Marielle Franco.

Creating Paths to See the Horizon: Black Women Reinventing the World

Throughout this chapter, I have discussed some aspects of the lives and work of Virgínia Bicudo, Lélia Gonzalez, Luiza Bairros, and Marielle Franco as a brief overview of Black women's perspectives and contributions to the Brazilian social sciences. In presenting their histories, I demonstrate how their life trajectories were marked not only by their engagement in social movements, especially Black women organizations, but also by their academic career in social sciences. Even though they are not representatives of the entire diversity of thought and perspectives of Black Brazilian women in the social sciences, their experiences reveal the ways in which different forms of oppression (such as gender, race, class, and sexuality) impacted them and their work.

The analyses of their lives allow us to understand that, in the same way their trajectories reveal the challenges facing Black women scholars, their work is critical in movements toward social change. Yet the erasure of Black women's scholarly contributions throughout Brazilian history have prevented generations from exploring the innovative and significant knowledge scholars such as Bicudo, Gonzalez, Bairros, Franco, and others have produced in the social sciences. Recently, however, the visibility of these scholars outside of academia has propelled (mostly) Black women scholars to reinscribe their ideas, translating their writings into other languages and discussing their contributions in contemporary scholarship.

To close, the contributions of these Black women must be seen within a broader diasporic framework. It is necessary to relate their scholarship to that of other Black, Brown, and Indigenous social scientists in the Americas and in the diaspora as an intellectual project that maps and systematizes their contributions. An analysis of their scholarly production and research methods can help us to understand how they used the theoretical tools of the social sciences to inform their feminist and anti-racist analyses. The paths taken by these Black women and countless others have marked the ground that paves the history of the Brazilian social sciences. Recognizing this fertile soil allows a generation of social scientists today to get a foothold and look to the horizon, not only to think about the future but also to retrieve stories from the past that are waiting to be told.

Notes

1 The Escola Livre de Sociologia e Política de São Paulo had the first bachelor's degree program in sociology, founded in 1933. In 1934, the University of São Paulo opened its first social sciences class. In 1939, the Federal University of Rio de Janeiro also started offering classes in the social sciences.
2 The only name on Theophilo Julio's birth certificate was that of his mother, Virginia Julio. Common during this period, he adopted the surname of his godfather and boss, Bento Augusto de Almeida Bicudo (a plantation owner). This relationship guaranteed Theophilo access to schooling, which was still very limited at the time. To learn more about this practice and the complicated network of relationships during slavery in Brazil, see Mattoso (1982).
3 The first Political and Social Sciences class took place at the Escola Livre de Sociologia e Política de São Paulo in 1933.
4 Donald Pierson (1900–1995), a U.S. sociologist trained at the University of Chicago, worked as a university professor and conducted research on race in Brazil during the 1930s and 1940s.
5 The United Nations Educational, Scientific and Cultural Organization (UNESCO) project represented an effort to develop research to help explain racism after the end of World War II. Brazil was one of the countries chosen for conducting research (Maio 2000).

6 In addition to Virgínia Bicudo's chapter, the reprint also suppressed papers by Oracy Nogueira and Aniela Ginsberg.
7 See also Thame, in this volume.
8 Magno coined the concept *Améfrica Ladina* in the 1981 book *Améfrica Ladina: Introdução a uma Abertura*. Magno points out the prominence of Amerindian and African elements in the region's social configuration, in contrast to the historical narrative that emphasizes the influence of Spain and Portugal.
9 The three modes of participation, popular, political, and feminist, is a proposal by the Peruvian feminist sociologist and theorist Virginia Vargas (2019).
10 Luiza Bairros completed her master's in social sciences in 1997 at the Federal University of Bahia (UFBA). In 1997 she completed her PhD at Michigan State University.
11 Luiza Bairros coordinated the Employment and Unemployment Survey (PED) at the Department of Labor and Social Action of the State of Bahia. She worked as a consultant to the United Nations Development Program (UNDP) from 2001 to 2003, in preparation for the Third World Conference against Racism. She also worked as a consultant to the Program to Combat Institutional Racism, helping to implement the Program to Combat Institutional Racism in the cities of Recife-PE and Salvador-BA, and in the Public Prosecutor's Office of Pernambuco, from 2003 to 2007.
12 See also Thame, in this volume.
13 Among the activities promoted by the project were two international seminars: one in Salvador (2000), another in Sacramento, California (2001), and the publication of a special issue of the CRH journal, edited by Luiza Bairros with contributors from Brazil and the United States (Bairros 2006).
14 Ruth Simms Hamilton was a professor at Michigan State University, where she founded the African Diaspora Research Project (ADRP) in 1986. Through the ADRP, Brazilian students and scholars were invited to assist in research and pursue graduate degrees. In addition to Luiza Bairros, Vera Lucia Benedito was also a graduate student at the university under the supervision of Dr. Hamilton.
15 Scholars have been working to understand the discourses and images associated with the image of Marielle (Aragão and Dutra 2020), but there is a lack of analysis on key aspects of her life, such as her scholarship.
16 To exemplify, a search done in December 2021 at the SciELO portal (https://scielo.org/), a virtual library that brings together scientific journals produced in Brazil, resulted in only four articles with citations for Marielle Franco, and none of the articles engaged with Marielle's research as a sociologist.
17 The preparatory courses for university admission are initiatives that emerged in Brazil in the late 1970s. During the 1990s, groups created courses as social projects to support students and Black and poor communities. Both the Pré-vestibular-Vestibular para Negros e Carentes (PVNC) in Rio de Janeiro and the Instituto Cultural Steve Biko in Salvador are organizations created to support Black and poor people in the admission process to universities in Brazil. Since the 1990s, these courses have become popular spaces for educational training and for critical formation about social reality, racism, and discrimination.
18 A public policy implemented by the government of Rio de Janeiro, the first UPP started in 2008. The UPP had as its model the installation of police command posts in the communities and a discourse of "Community Police." The project

argued that it was combating drug trafficking in the state's favelas and was motivated by large events being hosted by Rio de Janeiro in 2014 and in 2016 (the FIFA World Cup and the Olympics). In practice, the UPPs continued a policy of military occupation of the favelas of Rio de Janeiro under a banner of "pacification," which concealed the perpetuation of the violence suffered by favela residents (Fleury 2012).

19 On the commission, Franco monitored cases of police violence and provided legal advice to victims' families, including families of police officers killed on duty.

References

Andrews, George Reid. 1991. *Blacks and Whites in São Paulo-Brazil (1888–1988)*. Madison: University of Wisconsin Press.

Aragão, V., and C. Dutra. 2020. "Quem é Marielle Franco? Uma Proposta de Investigação das Imagens Construídas Pelos Discursos Midiáticos." *Colineares* 7, no. 2: 46–66.

Bairros, Luiza. 1987. "Pecados no 'Paraíso Racial': O Negro na Força de Trabalho da Bahia, 1950–1980." PhD diss., Universidade Federal da Bahia, Brazil.

———. 2000. "Lembrando Lélia Gonzalez 1935–1994." *Afro-Ásia* 23 (January): 347–368.

———. 2006. "Raça e Democracia Nas Américas." *Caderno CRH* 15, no. 36. https://periodicos.ufba.br/index.php/crh/article/view/18741.

Bairros, Luiza, Nadya Araújo Castro, and Vanda Sá Barreto. 1992. "Negros e Brancos num Mercado de Trabalho em Mudança." *Ciências Sociais Hoje* 1992: 32–54. Rio de Janeiro: Anpocs.

Barreto, Raquel de Andrade. 2005. *Enegrecendo o Feminismo ou Feminizando a Raça: Narrativas de Libertação em Angela Davis e Lélia Gonzáles*. PhD diss., Pontifícia Universidade Católica do Rio de Janeiro.

Bastide, Roger, and Florestan Fernandes, eds. 1955. *Relações Raciais Entre Negros e Brancos em São Paulo: Ensaio Sociológico as Origens, as Manifestações e os Efeitos do Preconceito de Côr no Município de São Paulo*. São Paulo: Anhembi.

———. 1959. *Brancos e Negros em São Paulo*. São Paulo: Companhia Editora Nacional.

Bicudo, Virgínia Leone. 1955. "Atitudes dos Alunos dos Grupos Escolares em relação com Cor dos seus Colegas." In *Relações Raciais entre Negros e Brancos em São Paulo*, edited by Roger Bastide and Florestan Fernandes. São Paulo: Anhembi, 227–310.

———. 1994. "Já Fui Chamada de Charlatã: Depoimento a Cláudio João Tognolli." *Folha de São Paulo*. São Paulo: Caderno Mais, June 5. http://acervo.folha.com.br/fsp/1994/06/05/72.

———. 2010. *Atitudes Raciais de Pretos e Mulatos em São Paulo*. São Paulo: Sociologia e Política.

Butler, Kim D. 1998. *Freedoms Given, Freedoms Won: Afro-Brazilians in Post-abolition São Paulo and Salvador*. New Brunswick, NJ: Rutgers University Press.

Cardoso, Cláudia Pons. 2014. "Amefricanizando o feminismo: o pensamento de Lélia Gonzalez". *Revista Estudos Feministas* [online] 22, no. 3: 965–986. https://doi.org/10.1590/S0104-026X2014000300015.

Costa, Elisio, dir. n.d. *Lélia Gonzalez: Feminismo Negro no Palco da História*. https://cultne.tv/en/movimentos-sociais/mulher-negra/192/lelia-gonzalez/video/2083/lelia-gonzalez-black-feminism-on-the-stage-of-history.

Dzidzienyo, A. 2007. "Africana Studies: The International Context and Boundaries." In *A Companion to African-American Studies*, edited by Lewis R. Gordon and Jane Anna Gordon, 568–589. Oxford: Blackwell.

Fleury, Sonia. 2012. "Militarização do Social como Estratégia de Integração: O Caso da UPP do Santa Marta." *Sociologias* 14, no. 30: 194–222.

Franco, Marielle. 2014. *UPP—A Redução da Favela a Três Letras: Uma Análise da Política de Segurança Pública do Estado do Rio de Janeiro*. PhD diss., Universidade Federal Fluminense, Brazil.

Gomes, Janaína Damasceno. 2013. *Os Segredos de Virgínia: Estudo de Atitudes Raciais em São Paulo (1945–1955)*. PhD diss., Universidade de São Paulo. https://doi.org/10.11606/T.8.2013.tde-14032014-103244.

Gonzalez, Lélia. 1977. "A Presença Negra na Cultura Brasileira." *Jornal Mensal de Artes* 37 (March).

———. 1979. "Cultura, Etnicidade e Trabalho: Efeitos Linguísticos e Políticos da Exploração da Mulher." Eighth Meeting of the Latin American Studies Association, Pittsburgh, PA.

———. 1984. "Racismo e sexismo na cultura brasileira." *Revista Ciências Sociais Hoje*, Anpocs, 223–244

———. 2018. *Primavera para as Rosas Negras: Lélia Gonzalez em Primeira Pessoa*. São Paulo: Diáspora Africana.

———. 2020. *Por um Feminismo Afro-latino-americano: Ensaios, Intervenções e Diálogos*. Rio de Janeiro: Jorge Zahar Editor.

Hill Collins, Patricia. 2002. *Black Feminist Thought: Knowledge, Consciousness, and the Politics of Empowerment*. New York: Routledge.

Jones, Claudia. 1949. "An end to the neglect of the problems of the Negro woman!." *PRISM: Political & Rights Issues & Social Movements* 467: 3–19.

Machado, Juliana, Rubia Luiza Silva, Tanja Baudoin, Ulisses Carrilho, and Zezé. 1988. *First National Meeting of Black Women Newsletter*. Rio de Janeiro.

Machado, Taís Sant'Anna, and Keisha-Khan Perry. 2021. Translation of "The Black Woman: A Portrait." *Feminist Anthropology* 2: 38–49.

Magno, M. D. 1981. *Améfrica Ladina: Introdução a uma Abertura*. Rio de Janeiro: NovaMente Editora.

Maio, Marcos Chor. 2000. "The UNESCO Project: Social Sciences and Race Studies in Brazil in the 1950s." *Portuguese Literary & Cultural Studies* 4, no.5: 51–64.

———. 2010. "Educação Sanitária, Estudos de Atitudes Raciais e Psicanálise na Trajetória de Virgínia Leone Bicudo. *Cadernos Pagu* [online] 35: 309–355. https://doi.org/10.1590/S0104-83332010000200011.

Mattoso, K. M. 1982. *Ser Escravo in Brazil*. São Paulo: Brasiliense.

Morrison, Minion K. C. 2003. "Race and Democracy in Brazil and the United States: The Evolution of a Program." *National Political Science Review* 9: 6–30.

Motta. 2019. Hospedando Lélia Gonzalez (1935–1994): Projeto de Pesquisa da Biblioteca/Centro de Documentação e Pesquisa da EAV Parque Lage.

Perry, Keisha-Khan.Y., and Sotero, Edilza. 2019. "Amefricanidade: The Black Diaspora Feminism of Lélia Gonzalez". *LASA Forum* 50, no. 3: 60–64

PINHO, Osmundo. 2020. Luiza Bairros: Um legado sociológico e uma inspiração intelectual. *LASA Forum* 51, no. 2: 99–102.

Pompeu, Fernanda, and Luiza Bairros. 2016. "Assim Falou Luiza Bairros." *GELEDÉS*, October 1, 2016. www.geledes.org.br/assim-falou-luiza-bairros/.

Ratts, Alex, and Flavia Rios. 2010. *Lélia Gonzalez*. São Paulo: Selo Negro.

Rios, Flavia, and Márcia Lima, eds. 2020. *Por um Feminismo Afro-Latino-Americano: Lélia Gonzalez*. Rio de Janeiro: Zahara.

Robinson, Cedric J. 2000. *Black Marxism: The Making of the Black Radical Tradition*. Chapel Hill: University of North Carolina Press.

Sousa, Neusa Santos. 1983. *Tornar-se Negro: As Vicissitudes do Negro em Ascensão Social*. Rio de Janeiro: Graal.

Vargas, Virginia. 2019. "Latin American Feminisms and Their Transition to the New Millennium." In *Key Text for Latin American Sociology*, edited by Fernanda Beigel, 319–337. London: SAGE Publications Ltd.

Viana, Elizabeth do Espírito Santo. 2006. *Relações Raciais, Gênero e Movimentos Sociais: O Pensamento de Lélia Gonzalez (1970–1990)*. PhD diss., Universidade Federal do Rio de Janeiro.

Vieirah, Beatriz Santos, dir. 2017. *Em Busca de Lélia*. https://embaubaplay.com/catalogo/em-busca-de-lelia/

2

Beyond Intercultural *Mestizaje*

Toward Black Women's Studies on the Caribbean Coast of Nicaragua

MELANIE WHITE

For the last forty years, the rise of Black feminisms and Black women's studies in U.S. institutions of higher education has led to the proliferation of U.S.-based Black feminist scholarship on Black women across the Americas. By contrast, and despite the organizing efforts of Black feminists in Latin America, the institutionalization of Black women's studies continues to face significant challenges in most areas of the region. On the one hand, long-standing myths of *mestizaje* and racial democracy, which uphold narratives of a racially and culturally uniform population forged through racial mixture, have historically silenced discourse on gendered racial difference in educational settings. On the other hand, the shift from this brand of "monocultural mestizaje" to "mestizo multiculturalism" in the late 1980s and 1990s paradoxically led to the fortification of gendered racial hierarchies when Latin American states began to recognize racial, ethnic, and cultural diversity in mostly nominal ways.[1]

In the educational context under multiculturalism, the mere acknowledgment of difference has often translated into a relinquishing of the responsibility to center gendered, structural anti-Blackness and social and epistemic transformation. In many instances, however, faculty and curriculums in Latin American institutions of higher education continue to ignore the experiences of Black populations, let alone Black women, altogether. If the emergence of multiculturalism in late twentieth-century Latin America has proven to be an extension of preexisting barriers in the study of Black women's experiences and in research by and about Afro-Latin American women, what have efforts toward the systematization of race- and gender-based research and inquiry looked like in regional institutions committed to decolonizing approaches to education, such as intercultural community universities? In other words, how have Latin American community-based educational institutions grappled with multiculturalism's silencing of structural power relations?

In the 1970s and 1980s, in response to decades of cultural domination, forced assimilation, and social neglect, Indigenous and Afro-descendant communities throughout Latin America mobilized for collective autonomous rights, including the right to community-based, intercultural education. This political organizing is precisely what gave way to the noteworthy yet deeply flawed Latin American "multicultural turn" and the attendant development of several intercultural community universities, beginning in the early 1990s.[2] Latin American intercultural community universities are necessarily multiethnic given the demographics of their regions and are intended to incorporate the experiences, knowledges, languages, and cultures of local Black and Indigenous groups into their structure, administration, approach to research, and pedagogy.

This chapter considers the relationship between intercultural higher education and the production of scholarship on Black women on the Caribbean Coast of Nicaragua. Specifically, I identify key advances and challenges in the study of Black women's histories, lives, and experiences at the University of the Autonomous Regions of the Nicaraguan Caribbean Coast (URACCAN). In addition to my intermittent experiences as a student, teacher, researcher, and volunteer at the university's Bluefields campus between 2014 and 2020, I employ URACCAN as a case study for two primary reasons: (1) it is the oldest and most established intercultural community university in Latin America, with three decades of experience in defining its purpose as a multiethnic, intercultural, and community-based university, and (2) it is one of the very first Latin American intercultural institutions of higher education to integrate a gendered perspective of interculturality into its core mission. As such, it is uniquely capable of instituting a critical race- and gender-based approach to the study of Black women in Caribbean Nicaragua. Moreover, more so than any other intercultural community university in the region, URACCAN's origins and pedagogical model are rooted in the leadership and activism of Afro-descendants and particularly Afro-descendant women.

For all of this critical work around race, ethnicity, and gender, however, it is puzzling that Black women's studies has yet to emerge as its own independent field and discipline at URACCAN. Like Kia Lilly Caldwell (2016), who has written about the importance and challenges of producing scholarship on Black women in the Brazilian academy, I believe in the value of developing a systematic field that is committed to the study of Black women's experiences and intellectual contributions in Caribbean Nicaragua. Indeed, the field of Black Latin American women's studies is severely needed throughout all corners of the Black diaspora given the persistent and structural erasure of Black Latin American women's thought and political organizing (Perry 2009; Smith 2016). In Nicaragua, a settler colonial state that is literally and figuratively divided in roughly two halves, Black women on the country's Caribbean Coast have been imagined and represented as little more than tropical and exotic sensual beings by the country's Pacific mestizx elite for more than a century (Morris 2012). Courtney Morris succinctly captures this spatial, racial, and gendered dynamic when she writes that "Black women have become the symbolic representation of the excessive, animalistic sexuality of the region" (Morris 2012, 100). This perception of Black Caribbean women in Nicaragua structures their position both at a national scale and in their local communities (see Gordon-Ugarte, this volume).

For example, Socorro Woods Downs highlights that structural race- and gender-based discrimination leads to a local situation in which Black women from the region strive to be "good mothers and wives, rather than people with their own life inspirations" (Woods Downs 2005, 11). Demonstrating a striking resemblance to the "culture of dissemblance" (Clark Hine 1989) as practiced by Black women in the Reconstruction-era U.S. Midwest, Black women in Caribbean Nicaragua often feel that their only recourse in counteracting "controlling images" (Hill Collins 1990) about themselves is to resign to silence. For Woods Downs (2005), "creating space for [Black] women to speak and be heard is an important means for self-recovery" (13). It is in this spirit that she wrote the first book on Black women in Caribbean Nicaragua and in which I write now to advocate for Black women's studies in the region.

The chapter consists of the four following sections: First, I provide an overview of the historical, sociopolitical, and educational context in Caribbean Nicaragua that led to Black (and Indigenous) organizing for autonomous institutions of higher education in the region. Next, I discuss how this goal was achieved via Nicaraguan constitutional multiculturalism, the communal and pedagogical mission of URACCAN, and the advances the university has made toward the development of Black women's studies in the region. I then discuss some of the institutional challenges to and offer suggestions that might help in establishing Black women's studies at the university. Finally, I conclude with a reflection on the critical importance of centering Black women's studies in the contemporary Nicaraguan political moment.

Coloniality and Education in Caribbean Nicaragua

The Caribbean Coast of Nicaragua is a region rich in racial, cultural, linguistic, and biological diversity whose geographies have historically been home to both Indigenous and Afro-descendant populations. Among the Indigenous groups are the Miskitu, Mayangna, and Rama, while the two Afro-descendant groups are the Creole and Garifuna (who are also Indigenous). Since the early twentieth century, the region has also been increasingly populated by mestizxs from Pacific Nicaragua. "Mestizx," the gender-neutral version of "mestizo," is a Latin American racial category—albeit a highly fraught one—used to denote people who are of European and Indigenous descent. In Caribbean Nicaragua, a distinction is made between "mestizxs costeñxs" (mestizx Caribbean Coast residents), who are those mestizxs who have lived in the region for more than forty years, and "mestizxs colonos," who are those who migrated to the region beginning in the 1990s and are seen as settlers with vast cultural differences from the region's native populations. Although the Caribbean Coast only makes up approximately 15 percent of the national population, it represents most of Nicaragua's racial, cultural, and linguistic diversity. Additionally, even though the region comprises more than half of the national Nicaraguan territory, it has long been treated as an internal colony of predominantly mestizx Pacific Nicaragua. This relation is a historically rooted reality, as it was a British protectorate during the colonial period and has faced centuries of colonial intervention by both the Spanish empire and the postcolonial Nicaraguan state.

Indeed, throughout the region's British colonial history, the Spanish Crown maintained a nominal claim to the area. Though ultimately unsuccessful at securing a presence in the region, when Nicaragua gained independence in 1821, it continued the Spanish legacy of attempting to assert sovereignty over the Caribbean Coast. In 1894, the Nicaraguan state—undeniably influenced by the major U.S. presence and enclave economy on the Caribbean Coast—succeeded at its mission and militarily annexed the region to Nicaragua. This late-nineteenth-century occupation marked the start of a long trajectory of forced cultural assimilation and racist policies toward the Black and Indigenous racialized region (Gordon 1998).

One of the foremost effects of annexation was the devaluation of Black and Indigenous histories, languages, cultures, and forms of social and political organization. With it came the exploitation of the region's natural resources by mestizx Nicaraguans and North American interests; the placement of mestizxs in regional government and administrative positions; the mandate that all public education in the region be conducted in Spanish; and the declaration of Spanish as the region's official language (Cunningham 2006). The effects of these mestizx nationalist policies impacted the educational development of

Black and Indigenous costeñxs. The requirement of Spanish language instruction in all coastal schools, for example, led to the immediate closure of Moravian Church–affiliated schools in the region for a period of eleven years at the turn of the century (Holland 1990).

The violent impact of the Spanish language mandate cannot be overstated. As Woods Downs (2005) notes, "Creole students became insecure at an early age, due to the fact that they were forced to speak an unknown language" (62). Even when Black and Indigenous students from the Caribbean Coast began to be taught by native teachers in the mid-twentieth century, the confusion, anxiety, and harm caused by a Spanish-based education had detrimental and long-lasting effects. Despite these assimilationist policies, the Nicaraguan state was unable to nationalize the Caribbean Coast for the larger part of the twentieth century. This failure was in part due to the U.S. occupation of Nicaragua in the early twentieth century, as well as to the rise of the U.S.- and capital-friendly Somoza family dynasty from 1936 to 1979. Under Somoza rule, the United States comfortably maintained its capitalist enterprise in the region, while the Nicaraguan state adopted a policy of neglect toward it (Baracco 2016). It was not until the departure of U.S. companies from the region in the 1960s that renewed attempts at national integration would be made by the Somozas, mostly in the form of "modernizing" agrarian reform programs that expanded the agricultural frontier and incentivized mestizx occupation of Caribbean coastal lands (Baracco 2016).

Caribbean Coast education reform was not a part of the Somoza state's developmental measures. Instead, for much of the twentieth century, education on the Caribbean Coast remained primarily in the hands of colonial religious institutions such as the Moravian Church.[3] While Moravian primary schools were developed in the latter half of the nineteenth century, it was not until 1923 that a Moravian secondary school was established in the region. In 1960, Moravians administered twenty-three primary schools and two secondary schools on the Coast (Holland 1990). In terms of higher education, the few students who had the resources to do so were forced to travel far away to Pacific Nicaraguan cities like León and Managua to attend university. This experience was often violently exclusionary, as Black and Indigenous costeñxs faced racism from mestizx students and professors and anti-Black and anti-Indigenous university curriculums. It is within this context that Black and Indigenous costeñxs began to organize around the need for higher education in their communities in the 1970s.

Autonomy and Intercultural Higher Education at URACCAN

The first time that the idea of instituting higher education in Caribbean Nicaragua was raised in a systematic fashion was during a meeting of university-educated Caribbean Coast leaders that took place in 1978, just one year before the revolutionary FSLN (Sandinista National Liberation Front) successfully toppled the Somoza dictatorship in 1979 (Dennis and Hobson Herlihy 2003). Following the nationalist revolution, a civil war ensued as a result of not only U.S. anticommunism and the Reagan administration's funding of a counterrevolutionary ("Contra") war movement on the Caribbean Coast but also the very real and endogenous resistance of Black and Indigenous costeñxs (many of whom fought as Contra combatants) to Sandinista ethnonationalism. While the Contra war and the revolutionary government's military response to it led to massive destruction, death, and community displacement on the Caribbean Coast, the civil conflict also led to a peace negotiation process and an autonomy regime through which Black and Indigenous costeñxs were able to put forth their demands for higher education. It is precisely this activism around autonomy, of which higher education was an integral part, that ushered in the era of multicultural rights recognition in Nicaragua.

In 1987, the Nicaraguan National Assembly ratified an autonomy statute (Law 28) in the nation's new constitution that recognized the multicultural nature of Nicaragua and granted specific political, cultural, economic, educational, and property rights to Black and Indigenous communities on the Caribbean Coast. With regard to education, Law 28 included a specific provision on the right to culturally sensitive, bilingual education in the region. Thus, with the support of the new autonomy law and the recognition of the importance of autonomous higher education institutions for sovereign knowledge production in the face of ongoing material and epistemic colonization, Black and Indigenous leaders established two universities on the Caribbean Coast in the early 1990s: URACCAN and the Bluefields Indian and Caribbean University (BICU). BICU has eight campuses in the region, including in Bluefields, Bilwi, El Rama, Corn Island, Paiwas, Bonanza, Waspam, and Pearl Lagoon. URACCAN has four campuses in Bilwi, Bluefields, Las Minas/Siuna, and Nueva Guinea, as well as four extensions, or university branches, in Bonanza, Rosita, Waslala, and Waspam.

Afro-descendants, and especially Afro-descendant women, were central to this educational development and to the administration and philosophical outlook of URACCAN, in particular. For instance, instrumental to the development of URACCAN's Intercultural Bilingual Education Program (PEBI) was Angela Brown, a Creole woman and bilingual teacher who served as the director of the Southern Autonomous Region's program until 1993 (Sanmiguel 2012). From 1994 to 2002, Miskita-Creole feminist and Indigenous rights activist Myrna Cunningham Kain served as the founding rector of URACCAN and was replaced in 2002 by a Creole woman, Alta Hooker Blandford. It is precisely as a result of the racialized and gendered contours of the university's founding administrators that a gender perspective has been integrated into the university's pedagogical model and vision for intercultural community-based education, most notably through the creation of a research center for gender-based research, special diplomas focused on gender, and a new master's degree program in Gender, Ethnicity, and Intercultural Citizenship (as of 2018). Additionally, URACCAN's demographics reflect a commitment to gender parity. Approximately 50 percent of administrators, professors, and students at URACCAN are women (Hobson Herlihy 2011). In 2018, 63 percent of URACCAN's graduates were women and 6 percent were Creole and Garifuna (URACCAN 2018). Though university reports do not provide statistical breakdowns by race and gender, given the percentage of women graduates, it is likely that at least half of Black graduates in 2018 were women.

Interculturality from a Gender Perspective

Since its inception as the first intercultural university in Latin America, URACCAN was designed with the vision of strengthening the autonomy process in Caribbean Nicaragua through the deployment of an intercultural community-based framework. Critical of facile multiculturalisms that stop at the mere recognition of racial, ethnic, and linguistic diversity, the Regional Autonomous Educational System (SEAR) on the Caribbean Coast understands interculturalism as "the practice of dialogue between people of different cultures as a means of communicating and exchanging knowledge within a context of mutual respect, empathy, and solidarity" (Cunningham, 2017, 81). Though closely related to multiculturalism, interculturalism was conceived with the intention of adopting a more critical lens. This is due, in part, to its conceptual grounding in Latin American decolonial thought and regional struggles against epistemic colonization (Cupples and Glynn 2014). While Indigenous intercultural universities throughout Latin America are committed to decolonial intercultural frameworks, what sets URACCAN apart is that it integrated a gendered perspective of interculturality into its institutional vision and structure early on in its history. This development was in large part due to the work of the university's Center for Studies and Information of the Multiethnic Woman (CEIMM) established in 2002 but with origins in the late 1990s.

Indeed, in addition to URACCAN's demographics and establishment of a new master's degree in Gender, Ethnicity, and Intercultural Citizenship, CEIMM is a key emblem of the institution's commitment to advancing a critical perspective of gender and patriarchy and to promoting women's studies and gender-based research. CEIMM was founded with the mission of promoting interculturality through a gendered perspective within the university, of heightening the visibility and demands of Indigenous and Afro-descendant women, and fomenting a critical gender consciousness that takes racial and ethnic differences into account. There is a CEIMM branch at each of URACCAN's four main campuses in the region, all of which conduct research, publish, present, and lead workshops on issues related to gender such as self-esteem, women's rights, and gender-based violence. CEIMM often partners with local feminist activists to do this consciousness-raising educational work.

In 2019 and 2020, I volunteered at the Bluefields branch of CEIMM and was able to witness its crucial gender-based and woman-centered work via conferences, symposiums, workshops, research studies, and a book publication. Much of my own work at CEIMM revolved around its 2018–2019 research study titled "Gender, Violence, and Spirituality" that was published as a four-part research publication of the same name in late 2019. I participated in post-fieldwork follow-up workshops in Bluefields and Corn Island and cowrote a report with CEIMM researcher Socorro Woods Downs analyzing the study's data. The study sought to identify the various forms of both interpersonal and structural gender-based violence experienced by women of various ages, occupations, class positions, and racial and ethnic backgrounds in the region, as well as to address the causes and consequences of—as well as the methods used by study participants to cope with—these violences.[4]

During my time at CEIMM and through my participation in their organized events, the critical role that the center occupies on the Caribbean Coast became increasingly clear. One of the most striking aspects of CEIMM's work in the region is that it adopts the role of a community resource and support program. While CEIMM staff are primarily tasked with leading research investigations, their approach to research and knowledge production is an activist one. The very fact that their research designs entail educational workshops and follow-ups with participants, as opposed to moving forward with their collected data without consulting their interlocutors, demonstrates a great deal of care for the members of their communities. This is especially significant in a regional context in which many Black and Indigenous women, particularly those in rural communities, have limited access to educational opportunities and critical resources to address their experiences with gender-based violence.

In the Bluefields workshop I participated in during November 2019, CEIMM staff lectured on human rights, citizenship, the Nicaraguan law criminalizing violence against women (Law 779), and sexual and reproductive rights and health. During a discussion on citizenship and ethnic hierarchy in Nicaragua and the Caribbean Coast, an Afro-Indigenous Mayangna and Creole participant and URACCAN alumna felt safe enough to share her experience of being discriminated against by a mestiza professor while she was a student at the university. A speaker of the Miskitu language, she was once told by a professor that all languages other than Spanish were prohibited in her classroom. When a classmate corrected the professor by pointing out that costeñx students have the right to a bilingual education under autonomy, the professor doubled down and responded that they would never learn Spanish if they spoke other languages in class. The other members of the workshop, as well as the staff, affirmed her experience, anger, and frustration.

In the Corn Island workshop that also took place in late November, some of the topics that were lectured on include gender inequality, sexual and gender-based violence, racial discrimination, feminism, and LGBT discrimination. In light of this material, participants were encouraged by staff to discuss methods of self-care as well as coping strategies, especially to manage living in a society in which the rates of gender-based violence are exceptionally high. Workshop participants, all of whom were women, reflected on the harmful reality that there are no therapists or psychologists present on the island and that one cannot always trust their family or friends as, in many instances, they are the perpetrators of the gender-based violence they experience. In discussing the presence of patriarchal masculinity and violence in their lives, many participants opened up and shared anecdotes from their own experiences and those of women they know to meditate on its pervasiveness in the lives of Corn Island women. The workshop resembled a support group in this moment as the women were prompted to respond to each other with collective care and advice. CEIMM staff facilitated a workshop not only in which Black and Indigenous women could be vulnerable with and feel supported in their experiences but also that encouraged participants to facilitate an environment of collective care themselves. This process helped ensure that participants would be both familiar with and comfortable enough to employ the tools of trauma-informed facilitation and communal support long after the staff departed from the island.

Upon returning to Bluefields, I began to study the data from CEIMM's research investigation to cowrite a report on its findings. What stood out the most to me was the severity of the situation of sexual and gender-based violence in the region. In the words of a Corn Island research participant, "On this island, there are no exceptions. Every woman has experienced domestic violence" (URACCAN-CEIMM 2018, 111). Also striking was the extent to which the available regional resources to receive support in cases of gender-based violence were inadequate. Many interviewees reported that when they decide to seek the little institutional support available, they experience further violence. For example, police station workers, most of whom are mestizo men, often question survivors as to what they might have done to "instigate" the violence they experience. Interviewees also stated that reporting cases of gender violence at *Comisarías de la Mujer* (women's police stations), before they were ordered shut by the Nicaraguan state in early 2016, was equally as violent.[5] Even female representatives, who are often mestizas, asked probing, victim-blaming questions.

For Black women and girls in Caribbean Nicaragua, these forms of sexism and patriarchy are compounded by anti-Black racism. Courtney Morris notes, "As members of a community whose claims to citizenship and national belonging are perceived by the Mestizo nation as being at best tenuous, and at worst, fictitious, there is little empathy for [Black women's] experiences of violence and sexual exploitation" (Morris 2012, 286). A central part of the reason that Black women are not perceived to be legitimate victims of gender-based violence has to do with the particular history of anti-Black misogyny in Nicaragua: "Black women's personal stories of violence and abuse must also compete with larger historical discourses of Afro-Nicaraguan women's tropical hypersexuality and libidinal nature that position them as being "un-rapeable" (Morris 2012, 288). As elsewhere in the Black diaspora, Black women and girls in Caribbean Nicaragua are criminalized even when victimized and in search of help. On the Coast, there is the added element that Black women and girls must report in Spanish rather than in their native Creole. This not only deters them from reporting but provides yet another basis for discriminatory treatment by Spanish-speaking and anti-Black mestizxs. Between structural barriers and communal silencing, Black women and girls in Caribbean Nicaragua have few places of institutional support where their experiences with racialized and gendered violence will be taken seriously.

Alongside regional women-centered activist organizations, CEIMM is one of the few spaces that is dedicated to challenging the social conditions that continue to impact and shape the life chances of costeña women. Importantly, CEIMM is well attuned to questions of difference and centers a localized and place-specific version of intersectionality theory that accounts for the region's multiethnic context. The center's official statement on gendered interculturality, for example, emphasizes that the oppressions that women of diverse racial and ethnic backgrounds experience are not uniform but are instead experienced in multiple, "hierarchically distinct" ways according to their differences (Gómez Barrio and Dixon Carlos 2018, 8). Recognizing differential experiences among Caribbean Coast women is conceived of by CEIMM as critical to the regional autonomy process: "One cannot speak of building autonomy if one does not work to eliminate the barriers that impede the development of women in general, and of Indigenous and Afro-descendant women, in particular" (Gómez Barrio and Dixon Carlos 2018, 9).

Yet, for all of CEIMM's critical work, there have nevertheless been significant obstacles to highlighting the unique and particular experiences of marginalized women at the center, including Black women. Some of these obstacles include but are not limited to an uncritical larger institutional approach to interculturality; the overburdening of the center as the go-to place for all matters concerning gender; URACCAN's incorporation into the Nicaraguan state's university system, which requires the institution to comply with national standards and expectations; and a national and regional context of heightened political polarization, surveillance, and anti-race and anti-gender discourse sentiments that in some instances has led to armed demonstrations at URACCAN campuses. Out of all these challenges, the most significant roadblock to the growth of Black women's studies at CEIMM and URACCAN has by far been the university's approach to interculturality. The following section provides an in-depth discussion of some of the key limitations of the intercultural university model. It also provides insight into the steps that would help facilitate the systematization of Black women's studies at CEIMM and URACCAN more broadly.

Challenges to Establishing Black Women's Studies in a Mestizx Intercultural Context

Closely tied to Black feminisms in the region, Black women's studies on the Caribbean Coast of Nicaragua exists mostly as a dispersed and nonsystematized body of multigenre work, including activist reports, local university theses, international dissertations, workshop resources, oral histories, and a select few traditionally published books—including those published abroad. Much of this work has been conducted from the 1990s to the present. Notable among these are *"I've Never Shared This with Anybody": Creole Women's Experience of Racial and Sexual Discrimination and Their Need for Self-Recovery* (2005) by Creole feminist scholar Socorro Woods Downs, *Black Autonomy: Race, Gender, and Afro-Nicaraguan Activism* (2016) by U.S.-based anthropologist Jennifer Goett, and *To Defend This Sunrise: Black Women's Activism and the Authoritarian Turn in Nicaragua* (2023) by U.S.-based Black feminist scholar Courtney Morris. While works such as these are present in URACCAN and CEIMM libraries, they have not been systematized along with other works by and about Black women for use in potential courses, workshops, and outreach programs in Black women's studies. The structured compilation and instruction of literature by and about Black Coast women would be a significant contribution to regional knowledge production for generations to come. While intercultural universities and centers like URACCAN and CEIMM are especially poised to undertake this kind of intellectual and pedagogical project, there are some key structural and institutional barriers that would need to be addressed to ensure its feasibility. Perhaps the biggest challenge to instituting Black women's studies at URACCAN and CEIMM in the current conjuncture is their intercultural educational framework adopted in the era of multicultural mestizaje.

Interculturality in the context of autonomous higher education in Caribbean Nicaragua has the potential to function as a critical framework of multiethnic solidarity given its origins in decolonial philosophy. However, its application in the context of late twentieth and early twenty-first-century

Nicaraguan multiculturalism has often blunted its radical potential. Juliet Hooker has argued that the multicultural reforms that took place in Nicaragua in the 1980s did not entail a decisive break from earlier mestizx nationalist discourses that erased Black and Indigenous populations by holding that all Nicaraguans were biologically and culturally mixed; instead, the era marked a turn to "mestizo multiculturalism," which emphasizes the mixed-ness, or mestizx-ness, of the nation as a whole (Hooker 2005, 16). In other words, mestizx elites in Nicaragua reconciled their adoption of multiculturalism by infusing it with mestizx nationalist discourse (Hooker 2009). State officials wielded the multicultural narrative of ethnic diversity to reinforce Nicaragua's identity as a quintessentially mestizx nation. In doing so, they made symbolic progressive strides and alleviated their responsibility to combat white/mestizx supremacy and anti-Black and anti-Indigenous racism. Woods Downs (2005) captures the predicament in a nutshell: "With the autonomy law a complete shift came about from not talking about race at all, to using the term multi-ethnicity. The point is that racism, racial discrimination, and power differences between the ethnic groups are still masked, but now in a new way" (60).

As an approach to education that grew out of Nicaraguan mestizx multiculturalism, interculturality has the potential to—and has often wound up—reinforcing mestizx supremacy. Indeed, even though the intercultural discourse of Caribbean Coast educational institutions purports to center and encourage difference and the intercultural sharing of diverse experiences in a multiethnic and gendered context, it tends to folklorize and celebrate group differences without critically attending to race, class, gender, and other social hierarchies and fault lines. An apt yet ironic illustration of this dynamic is presented in a reflection by an URACCAN student who was part of a study on why Black students drop out of the university's Bluefields campus. Noting interculturality as one of the campus's strengths, she shared, "We were taught about identity and interculturality. This prevented us from having culture shock, especially when we went to the Pacific. We learned to appreciate and respect each other as brothers and sisters beyond any differences among us.... I thank URACCAN for that knowledge. It helped me a lot to accept myself and feel proud of who I am. Most of all, it helped in overcoming differences with Spanish speaking people. I will forever be grateful" (Garth Sambola, Hodgson Lewis, and Baez 2017, 34).

This former student's comments reveal an institutional approach that characterizes interculturality as an anthropological curiosity and a question of interpersonal relation rather than a framework to critically analyze structural positioning and potential paths toward social transformation. While the sense of racial and ethnic pride she developed represents an important by-product of interculturality, the fact that it helped instruct her on how to overlook historically and structurally rooted tensions with "Spanish speaking people," or mestizxs, reveals a privileging of and catering toward the individual positions of mestizxs that fails to decenter and interrogate structural white/mestizx supremacy. This anecdote is a prime example of intercultural mestizaje, a process by which superficial diversity is extolled while mestizxs are centered and white/mestizx supremacy is reinforced. In practice, it appears as though the intent behind intercultural education is not to learn about critical histories of struggle, colonialism, and the oppression of Black and Indigenous costeñxs, but rather to teach Black and Indigenous students how to interact with and assimilate into the culture of the national majority.

In order for Black women's studies to be established as a discipline at URACCAN, then, there would need to be a radical reformulation of how interculturality is applied on campus. Rather than a cover for the false pretexts of equality, horizontal relations, and facile, unearned solidarity, interculturality would need to be reoriented around critically dissecting the racialized and gendered structures of power that differentially position each racial and ethnic group in the region. This would also entail the necessary process of interrogating mestizaje and mestizx identity and positioning on the Caribbean Coast. It is only in this context of a truly critical "interculturalism" that Black women's studies can be established as a discipline. Otherwise, the endeavor of attending to Black women's unique experiences of oppression will be flattened as mere ethnic and cultural difference.

The issue of patriarchal anti-Black discrimination within the intercultural classroom is also a major deterrent to the potential development of Black women's studies at URACCAN. On a fundamental level, it means that Black women students at the university are not learning in safe environments or settings receptive to their experiential knowledges, intellectual interests, and investigative curiosities as university documents purport. In many cases, and as the following example from URACCAN's Bluefields campus demonstrates, the discrimination Black women experience at the university is a driving force behind their decisions to "drop out," or exit the violence they experience at the institution: "When classes started, I had my hair long with dry curls, but after a while I decided to cut my hair. I guess this was the worst thing I could have done. After that, my teacher didn't accept me as part of the class. She claimed that she had never seen me before and that I was not part of that group. This was a reason why I decided to leave. I tried my best to show what I could do, but it was useless. At some point, I felt invisible and discriminated against" (Garth Sambola, Hodgson Lewis, and Baez 2017, 35). Considering this student's racist and sexist experience as a former undergraduate at URACCAN, it is worth reflecting on how the university's "intercultural gender perspective" model has deeply failed Black women students. What is the significance of an intersectional approach to education that is not only unattuned to the intersections of Black costeñas' experiences and oppression but that actively marginalizes and causes harm to them for merely existing?

On a similar note, what is the point of a bilingual intercultural education if the language of the dominant culture is the default requirement in the classroom and the use of Black and Indigenous languages renders students invisible? Another Black student who dropped out of the Bluefields campus of URACCAN shared that racial and linguistic discrimination was a major factor in their decision: "On several occasions I was not allowed to present my work in my language since the professor told me that he didn't speak Creole. Because of this I didn't present several works" (Garth Sambola, Hodgson Lewis, and Baez 2017, 35). Even though Law 162 (Law on the Official Use of the Languages of the Communities of the Atlantic Coast of Nicaragua) and the regional autonomous education system prohibit discrimination based on language, the reality in the intercultural university classroom is far different. In order for a Black women's studies program to be able to flourish at URACCAN, Black students would need to fully and truly have the right to speak, write, and present in their native language. More than that, the overarching barrier that is the gendered anti-Black racism of professors, staff, and other students would need to be addressed in a deep and meaningful way.

Yet another key issue is that much of the knowledge produced about Black women's experiences in the context of intercultural education on the Caribbean Coast tends to be inserted into broader, more general analyses encompassing the experiences of all women in the region. This was certainly the case with CEIMM's 2018–2019 study given that only a select amount of participants were asked about how they identify. This creates a situation where post-study analyses, reports, and publications are written in pan-racial and pan-ethnic terms. While such totalizing analyses can certainly be helpful in gauging trends on the Caribbean Coast as a whole, it makes it difficult to account for the differences in gendered and racialized experiences among costeñas. This tendency has its roots in the fact that interculturality, when rooted in mestizx multiculturalism and expressed as intercultural mestizaje, glosses over important differences to represent the nation—or in this case region—as a whole, as multiethnic and thus mestizx in essence. This is not to mention the challenge wrought by the tendency of mestizxs to weaponize interculturality discourse and argue that a specific focus on Black or Indigenous rights not only goes against the principles of mutual, nonhierarchical interaction and relation but is ethnonationalist and "racist" against mestizxs (Goett 2006, 37–38). As elsewhere in the diaspora, most notably in Brazil and the United States, calls of "reverse racism" and efforts to ban critical race pedagogies and upend affirmative action reflect a culture of white supremacy that is also endemic to Nicaragua and its Caribbean Coast.

In order for Black women's studies to be possible at URACCAN, the anti-Black and rote allegiance to the idea of the Caribbean Coast as a multiethnic space that must always be represented and written about as such would need to be completely abandoned. Rather than advance the university's intercultural gender perspective, this approach drowns out specificity and important differences among diverse women whose experiences require deep study and individualized attention. This attention must be more than a cursory review of the different cultural traditions of women of various ethnic groups in the region, which is often the approach taken in the classroom. A promising route that might be taken in this direction is the establishment of various branches within CEIMM dedicated to women from each ethnic group in the region. As a center for the study of and information on the "multiethnic woman," CEIMM is indeed uniquely positioned to take on such a project and kickstart the development of Black women's studies at URACCAN.

Black Women's Studies Now

In the thirty-one years that have elapsed since URACCAN's founding in 1992, the university has played a critical role in Caribbean Nicaragua. Tens of thousands of Black and Indigenous students have graduated from the intercultural community-based university, at least half of whom have been women. Additionally, URACCAN has had a significant role in the development both of regional autonomy and of a critical consciousness around ethnicity and gender in the region. Its unique intercultural gender perspective has certainly made it one of the most committed Latin American intercultural universities with regard to the pursuit of ethnic and gender-based justice. A large part of its pathbreaking work in this area is due to the efforts of CEIMM, which has diligently worked to advance critical gender consciousness in the region's multiethnic communities. Through CEIMM, URACCAN has engaged not only in important research studies that center questions pertinent to women's lives in the region but also in community outreach and support in the form of workshops, informational lectures, and symposiums. While there have been significant challenges along the way, it is difficult to overemphasize the importance of their work. Since 2002, CEIMM has been one of the very few spaces throughout the entire Caribbean Coast that has been specifically dedicated to issues of gender and especially gender-based violence in the lives of the region's women. This has been no easy feat in a national and regional context that, as Black feminist scholars of the region such as Socorro Woods Downs and Courtney Morris note, have historically worked to silence racial and gender-based discrimination. Yet, precisely because of the critical role that CEIMM occupies in various communities on the Caribbean Coast, it is crucial to consider how the center might continue to prioritize women's studies in a way that is inclusive of some of the region's most marginalized women, of which Black and Indigenous women certainly form part.

This chapter has explored the particular need to center and contribute to the growth of Black women's studies in the region. Given the long trajectory of gendered anti-Black racism in Nicaragua toward the Caribbean Coast and the Black women who live there, it is critically important that a center like CEIMM and a community-based intercultural university like URACCAN highlight the full extent of marginalization that the women they serve have historically experienced. While some of this history has been captured in various interspersed research studies as well as institutional discourse on the importance of highlighting the region's diversity at URACCAN and CEIMM, the legacies of mestizaje and white/mestizx supremacy in the form of mestizx multiculturalism and intercultural mestizaje continue to occlude the degree to which racialized patriarchy has been fundamental to Nicaraguan national formation and the history of the Caribbean Coast. This erasure creates a situation where Black women live the effects of gendered anti-Blackness while their experiences are silenced or not fully explored in public life, including in the university setting. The consolidation of an intercultural framework in virtually all aspects of life on the Caribbean Coast in the wake of Nicaragua's multicultural turn has dominated most discussions of race and gender-based activism in the region and foreclosed targeted political organizing against gendered anti-Black racism.

However, intercultural mestizaje need not run its course in Caribbean Nicaragua. It is a framework and practice that can and ought to be challenged and dismantled via the formation of a field devoted specifically to the study, research, and teaching of Black women's history, experiences, theory, and organizing in the region. Centering Black women and the conditions that shape their lives will not only counteract their silencing but will also be a critical step toward the eradication of all forms of racialized patriarchal violence in Caribbean Nicaragua given the foundational nature of anti-Black misogyny to the marginalization of the region. Thus, developing the field of Black women's studies would be a major contribution toward the fight against all gendered racisms in Caribbean Nicaragua. CEIMM and URACCAN are exceptionally well positioned to pursue the discipline of Black women's studies given their ethical and political commitments to multiethnic gender equity.

Finally, I would be remiss not to mention the significance of Black women's studies in the contemporary political moment. Across the Americas, Black (and Indigenous) populations are experiencing what some scholars have identified as a period of post-multiculturalism and racist retrenchment that includes the stripping away of the rights and gains achieved during the multicultural era (Hooker 2020). Given these hemispheric developments, it is of urgent importance not only to assess what the transition means for Black (and Indigenous) people in the Americas but also to reignite critical conversations and analyses around the gendered anti-Black (and anti-Indigenous) racisms fueling this shift. Indeed, in Nicaragua, the sobering reality of racist resentment for the limited set of rights Black and Indigenous people and women have gained over the years and the current government's increasingly austere methods of repression (in the context of the contemporary Nicaraguan political and authoritarian crisis) point to the need to abandon flawed multicultural discourses that emphasize the facile recognition of difference. In its stead, may a sharpened analysis of the foundational nature of gendered anti-Blackness (and anti-Indigeneity) emerge. Such an analysis will be crucial to the formation of Black women's studies in Caribbean Nicaragua.

Notes

1 From the late 1980s until the second decade of the twenty-first century, a series of cultural, political, educational, and territorial rights for Indigenous and Afro-descendants were constitutionally recognized throughout Latin America. Juliet Hooker (2005) coined the concept of "mestizo multiculturalism" to identify how multicultural rights recognition in Nicaragua has reified mestizx nationalist narratives.
2 See Rahier (2019).
3 The Protestant Moravian Church, which arrived on the Caribbean Coast in 1849, offered the region's population spiritual and moral guidance, health services, and an Anglicized, English education.
4 For more on gender-based violence, see the chapters by Lewis and by Hernández Reyes in this volume.
5 Comisarías across Nicaragua have since been reopened.

References

Baracco, Luciano. 2016. "The Historical Roots of Autonomy in Nicaragua's Caribbean Coast: From British Colonialism to Indigenous Autonomy." *Bulletin of Latin American Research* 35, no. 3: 291–305.
Caldwell, Kia Lilly. 2016. "Black Women's Studies in the United States and Brazil: The Transnational Politics of Knowledge Production." In *Race and the Politics of Knowledge Production: Diaspora and Black Transnational Scholarship in the United States and Brazil*, edited by Gladys L. Mitchell-Walthour and Elizabeth Hordge-Freeman, 15–25. New York: Palgrave Macmillan.
Clark Hine, Darlene. 1989. "Rape and the Inner Lives of Black Women in the Middle West: Preliminary Thoughts on the Culture of Dissemblance." *Signs: Journal of Women in Culture and Society* 14, no. 4: 912–920.
Cunningham Kain, Myrna. 2006. *Racism and Ethnic Discrimination in Nicaragua*. Bilwi, Puerto Cabezas: Centro para la Autonomía y Desarrollo de los Pueblos Indígenas.
———. 2017. "Indigenous Peoples' Conflicts and the Negotiation Process for Autonomy in Nicaragua." In *Indigenous Peoples' Rights and Unreported Struggles: Conflict and Peace*, edited by Elsa Stamatopoulou, 28–54. New York: Institute for the Study of Human Rights.

Cupples, Julie, and Kevin Glynn. 2014. "Indigenizing and Decolonizing Higher Education on Nicaragua's Atlantic Coast." *Singapore Journal of Tropical Geography* 35, no. 1: 56–71.
Dennis, Philip A., and Laura Hobson Herlihy. 2003. "Higher Education on Nicaragua's Multicultural Atlantic Coast." *Cultural Survival Quarterly* 27, no. 4: 42. www.culturalsurvival.org/publications/cultural-survival-quarterly/higher-education-nicaraguas-multicultural-atlantic-coast.
Garth Sambola, Ivania, Yelicet Hogdson Lewis, and Courtney Baez. 2017. "Exploring the Situations of Afro-descendant Students Who Drop Out from URACCAN Bluefields: Causes, Consequences and Retention Strategies." Diploma thesis, University of the Autonomous Regions of the Nicaraguan Caribbean Coast.
Goett, Jennifer. 2006. "Diasporic Identities, Autochthonous Rights: Race, Gender, and the Cultural Politics of Creole Land Rights in Nicaragua." PhD diss., University of Texas at Austin.
———. 2016. *Black Autonomy: Race, Gender, and Afro-Nicaraguan Activism*. Stanford: Stanford University Press.
Gómez Barrio, Nuria, and Bernadine Dixon Carlos. 2018. *La Perspectiva Intercultural de Género desde la Mirada de URACCAN*. Bluefields, Nicaragua: URACCAN-CEIMM.
Gordon, Edmund T. 1998. *Disparate Diasporas: Identity and Politics in an African Nicaraguan Community*. Austin: University of Texas Press.
Hill Collins, Patricia. 1990. *Black Feminist Thought: Knowledge, Consciousness, and the Politics of Empowerment*. New York: Routledge.
Hobson Herlihy, Laura. 2011. "Rising Up? Indigenous and Afro-descendant Women's Political Leadership in the RAAN." In *National Integration and Contested Autonomy: The Caribbean Coast of Nicaragua*, edited by Luciano Baracco, 221–242. New York: Algora Publishing.
Holland, Clifton. 1990. *Expanded Status of Christianity–Country Profile: Nicaragua*. San José, Costa Rica: PROLADES.
Hooker, Juliet. 2005. "'Beloved Enemies': Race and Official Mestizo Nationalism in Nicaragua." *Latin American Research Review* 40, no. 3: 14–39.
———. 2009. *Race and the Politics of Solidarity*. Oxford: Oxford University Press.
———, ed. 2020. *Black and Indigenous Resistance in the Americas: From Multiculturalism to Racist Backlash*. Lanham, MD: Lexington Books.
Morris, Courtney. 2012. "To Defend this Sunrise: Race, Place, and Creole Women's Political Subjectivity on the Caribbean Coast of Nicaragua." PhD diss., University of Texas at Austin.
———. 2023. *To Defend This Sunrise: Black Women's Activism and the Authoritarian Turn in Nicaragua*. New Brunswick: Rutgers University Press.
Perry, Keisha-Khan. 2009. "The Groundings with My Sisters: Toward a Black Diasporic Feminist Agenda in the Americas." *The Scholar and Feminist Online* 7, no. 2. https://sfonline.barnard.edu/africana/print_perry.htm.
Rahier, Jean Muteba. 2019. "The Multicultural Turn, the New Latin American Constitutionalism, and Black Social Movements in the Andean Sub-Region." In *The Andean World*, edited by Linda J. Seligmann and Kathleen S. Fine-Dare. New York: Routledge.
Sanmiguel, Raquel. 2012. "A Postcolonial Comparative Study of Secondary Education and Its Ideological Implications for West Indian Communities in Puerto Limón,

Costa Rica; Bluefields, Nicaragua; and Old Providence Island, Colombia." PhD diss., University at Albany, State University of New York.

Smith, Christen. 2016. "Towards a Black Feminist Model of Black Atlantic Liberation: Remembering Beatriz Nascimento." *Meridians: Feminism, Race, Transnationalism* 14, no. 2: 71–87.

URACCAN (Universidad de las Regiones Autónomas de la Costa Caribe Nicaragüense). 2018. "Perfil Institucional," 34. www.uraccan.edu.ni/sites/default/files/2020–05/Perfil%20Institucional%20URACCAN%202018%20actualizado.pdf.

URACCAN-CEIMM (Universidad de las Regiones Autónomas de la Costa Caribe Nicaragüense-CEIMM). 2018. "Primer borrador de transcripciones para investigación Acción-Participativa desde una perspectiva intercultural de género." Bluefields, Nicaragua: URACCAN-CEIMM.

Woods Downs, Socorro. 2005. *"I've Never Shared This with Anybody": Creole Women's Experience of Racial and Sexual Discrimination and Their Need for Self-Recovery*. Managua, Nicaragua: CEIMM.

3

The Significance of "Communists Wearing Panties" in the Jamaican Left Movement

••••••••••••••••••••

(1974–1980)

MAZIKI THAME

In *Comrade Sister: Caribbean Feminist Revisions of the Grenada Revolution*, Laurie Lambert asks, "What would it mean to reimagine the Grenada Revolution with women at its center? How do they shape the ideology of revolution, and how do they make themselves the beneficiaries of political power?" (2020, 1). My study of the Committee of Women for Progress (CWP), an affiliate of the Workers Liberation League (WLL, which became the Workers Party of Jamaica [WPJ] in 1978), seeks to follow the path of Lambert in "foregrounding the roles played by women" in our reading of Caribbean struggles for social transformation and revolution (9). It examines the praxis of the CWP (disparagingly called "communists wearing panties") in terms of their struggles for social change. Those struggles both shaped and were shaped by the women's national movement and left politics.

In the period between 1972 and 1980, there were radical changes in Jamaican society under the leadership of the People's National Party (PNP) led by Michael Manley, including the inclusion of socialist ideals. Popular and scholarly analysis of the period often attributes those changes to the efforts and leadership of Manley himself. But this chapter points to the ways in which women of the CWP shaped and directed the politics and policies of the period and took power for themselves as power brokers and beneficiaries of initiatives. Although the CWP continued its work after the defeat of the PNP in 1980, this chapter focuses mainly on its work during the 1970s. The 1970s were marked by mass upheaval in Jamaica and was a period in which social justice was thought of through the lens of left politics. The CWP believed that at the root of revolution was the rise of the proletariat. Further, its analysis of society was anchored in the everyday lives and struggles of Black women, especially in their lives as mothers caring for families. My use of the term "communists wearing panties" is part of the foregrounding of women in left politics during a period of strong anticommunist and sexist sentiment within both the Left and the wider society. I have also appropriated the phrase to indicate how these women's politics were tied to their inner and private lives.

In this chapter, I first establish my intent to reframe leader-centric understandings of the politics of the 1970s and to think instead about the period from the perspective of political movement and more specifically through the women's movement, of which the CWP was central. Centering the women's movement, I focus on the notion that Black women on the left deployed embodied politics. I highlight this through considering the figures of Linnette Vassell, who led the CWP, and Beverly Manley-Duncan, who led the PNP Women's Movement (PNPWM). I discuss the CWP in relation to the political left broadly by examining its relationship to the WPJ, the PNP, and the PNPWM and also by exploring the nature of CWP politics and the CWP's ideological view of liberation. I examine the CWP's politics and contributions to national and women's liberation within the frames of two specific struggles: the struggle for consumer rights and for paid maternity leave. I conclude my chapter with a return to Lambert's questions and the implications of the CWP's struggle for the present.

Reframing the Politics of the 1970s: Black Women on the Left and Embodied Politics

Little attention has been paid to the national movement that propelled Manley's left turn and successes of the 1970s, in which the WPJ and its affiliates participated (T. Munroe 1988; Gray 2012; Lewis 2019). Manley's 1972 electoral victory was part of popular mobilization against the Jamaica Labor Party (JLP), rooted in a need to address the deleterious conditions faced by Black Jamaicans. Though independence had come in 1962, with the JLP forming the first government, racial frustration around the conditions, mobility, power, and status of the Black majority in Jamaica led to the flowering of Black Power, which culminated in the Walter Rodney riots in 1968. Black Power activists viewed the JLP as anti-Black (see Campbell 1985 Lewis 1998; Quinn 2015). Though Michael Manley was a Brown Jamaican, son of Norman and Edna Manley, important PNP figures of the decolonization generation and beneficiaries of racial, class, and political privilege in Jamaica, he came to be associated with the struggles of the dispossessed. He projected pro-poor politics locally and anti-racism and Third Worldism internationally. His charisma was important to his power and popular mobilization, but the self-motivated actions of the marginalized themselves, their social and political movement, was also important to social change in the period.[1] In that regard, Rupert Lewis argues that though the Left needed Manley and that political analysis in Jamaica was Manley-centric (Scott 2001, 157), Manley was radicalized by the period and was not a lone orchestrator. Manley, Lewis argues, was changed and challenged by the wider national movement (135–136).

Under Manley and the PNP's governance, the agendas pursued by the CWP as part of the women's movement had the potential to change the world of women, their children, and the class dynamics that impacted the most disadvantaged in Jamaica. But the CWP's agendas, actions, and responses to social problems were also telling signals of how women wore their struggle on and through their (Black) bodies. This is visible in the experiences of the leaders of the women's movement: Linnette Vassell and Beverly Manley. Vassell and Manley represented the mass of the Black population, though their class locations shifted by virtue of their education and relationship to the top of local politics. Linnette Vassell was from the rural peasantry and working class, in a mother-headed household, while Beverly Manley was from the capital city, Kingston, and lower-middle class. Their politics were rooted in their beginnings and the struggles of ordinary Jamaican people, and they faced discrimination as Black women with proximity to those at the bottom of the social hierarchy. Because they chose left politics and alongside other women of the Left were in a struggle for power within politics itself, they became targets of sexist, classist, racist, and pro-capitalist attacks. As women and as Black women their radicalism compounded their location on the fringes of power. Carole Boyce Davies (2008) points to such marginalization of Black communist women as "the most neglected among contemporary examinations of Black women" (16). We see such marginality in the case of the CWP, with public hostility toward the group and its causes, even within the PNP which they supported and defended.

Class and racial conflict played out within the organizations of the Left and shaped the responses of the public regarding the struggles of women and the women themselves. For instance, Beverly Manley-Duncan recalls that Vassell was rebuffed as a rural Black girl leading a middle-class organization

(Interview with Author 2016). The space Vassell was given in the WLL/WPJ is of significance because it troubled the symbolic representations of power in the nation and opened space for Black women. The appearance of the body of Vassell as a leader on the platform implicitly called for the need to deconstruct racial and class norms. The racial question is an important one which was not overtly tackled in the politics of the CWP. Race was significant to how the women were read and whether they were deemed to have legitimacy in power. Personal attacks on Vassell were racial in nature—she was routinely ridiculed on public radio, called out as black and ugly, and summarily hated.[2] Vassell's courage in standing firm as the leader of the CWP and as a Voluntary Price Inspector (VPI), which I discuss later in this chapter, put her in physical battle with capitalist interests and was thus itself a marker of change.

Although the PNP and the PNPWM as organizations were not Left as a whole, they had leftist tendencies within them, with Beverly Manley being an important member on the left. Beverly Manley's class background and race were important to her place in the PNP and the struggle of the day. Michael Manley's marriage to her (given their class and race positionalities) was seen as positive and in step with the social changes of the day by progressive forces. It was thus a politically significant marriage, a joining of Brown and Black, privileged, and dispossessed individuals. But Manley-Duncan recalls that members of the PNP along with sections of the public contributed to her awareness that she "wasn't supposed to marry aristocracy" (Interview with Author 2016). In that context, Michael Manley's defense of her in the face of opposition within the party was the avenue through which she had political space that she deployed in the interest of the communities from where she came.

Linnette Vassell and Beverly Manley's personal experiences are emblematic of those of Black women in everyday life and in the movement on the left, which is important to conceiving their politics as embodied and as personally and socially transformative. The presence of the bodies of Vassell and Manley on the front lines of the movement and their specific politics transformed the racial/color, gender, and class dimensions of power. Since independence, power had been male, based in wealth and class privilege, and held by ethnic minorities including white and Brown people. Through Vassell and Manley, who acted alongside others like them, we see how Black women deployed embodied politics and how their private lives influenced their politics. Fixmer and Wood explain that embodied politics is personal and physical action seeking change through everyday acts of resistance in local sites where injustices occur (2005, 237–238). Additionally, I find it useful to think in terms of Honor Ford-Smith's concern that the body "is understood as a site for integrating thought and action," "a field for the inscription of power, and a "floating signifier" that can both inhabit and subvert the dominant representations that justify hierarchies of race or gender" (2019, 154–155). This is also why I have appropriated the term "communists wearing panties," insofar as gender and the inner worlds of women were important to their political practices.

The 1970s Left Alliance and the CWP

Perry Mars argues that the Caribbean Left, like other left movements outside the region, had "middle class, intellectual-type leadership, and an ideological orientation anchored in a critique of capitalism and imperialism, and advocacy of some form of socialism" but also tended toward Black consciousness and nonviolent democratic struggles (1998, 40). Their priority issues were anti-imperialism, democracy, race and class, socialism, and Left Unity (63). These concerns were central to the work of the Workers Liberation League (WLL) formed in 1974 and to the creation of the Workers Party of Jamaica as a Marxist-Leninist party in 1978. Michael Manley's victory and left turn as leader of the PNP was a marker of what the larger grouping of the Left saw as a democratic opening in Jamaica. A core element of the political strategy of the WPJ was to give "critical support" to the PNP and to push it further left of where it stood. Within the PNP in the 1972–1980 period, there was struggle for ascendancy between left and right groupings, yet notably the PNP Left was not generally aligned with the WPJ.[3] On the other hand, the women of the Left seemed to display a higher level of solidarity expressed in alliances between the Beverly Manley–led PNPWM and the Vassell-led CWP on women's issues. The CWP's goal was movement building (CWP 1978b, 5).

Beverly Manley-Duncan argues that WPJ women (including the CWP) pushed the struggle when others were ready to give up and PNP women learned from them how to mobilize support and insistence on discipline. She recalls that where the mainly grassroots women of the PNP were doubtful of the possibilities, the professional women of the WPJ pushed forward and were "a serious group of women" (Interview with Author 2016).

The CWP was founded by women of the Workers Liberation League (WLL) in 1976. Its leadership and core membership came from the WLL and WPJ for social outreach of the party, and they recruited members into the WPJ. The Organizing Bureau of the WPJ, which "dealt with membership, allocation of party tasks, finances, and party security," was "also responsible for the Committee of Women for Progress" (Lewis 2019, 104). CWP members would report to the WPJ Central Committee on their CWP work as part of their WPJ activities. The CWP, however, did not publicly declare itself as communist and claimed to be primarily agitating for women as a constituency. It was part of the WPJ strategy for its various affiliates, like the CWP, to hold the line that they were not associated with the WPJ for various reasons, including the secrecy of democratic centralism within the party, the wider anticommunist political context, and the role affiliates played in reaching audiences beyond the Left and

Table 3.1
The CWP and the Left Alliance in the 1970s

Committee of Women for Progress (CWP): An affiliate of the WLL/WPJ that collaborated closely with the PNPWM on women's issues	
The Workers Liberation League (WLL), which became the Workers Party of Jamaica (WPJ) in 1978, influenced the PNP on the left.	The PNP Women's Movement (PNPWM), led by Beverly Manley, supported and was supported by the PNP.
People's National Party (PNP), led by Michael Manley, prime minister of Jamaica (1972–1980)	

within the Left that may have been anti-WPJ.[4] (See table 3.1 for a brief explanation of the relationships between the CWP, WPJ, PNP and PNPWM).

The agendas of the CWP mirrored the WPJ's application of Marxism/Leninism to the Jamaican social situation whereby the working class (often seeming to include all oppressed groups) was to be mobilized as the engine of revolution. Rupert Lewis argues of the WLL/WPJ, "We thought of the nation largely in relationship to the class structure, the way in which the social forces were aligned, issues of oppression, issues largely relating to the failure to realize the aspirations of the '38 generation, and building a politics that identified the working class as against the bourgeoisie, as against the middle strata, as being the force that could correct the political and social situation as we saw it in the 1970s" (cited in Scott, 2001, 146). To achieve their ends, alliance with and influence of the PNP and anti-imperial activism were seen to go hand in hand. Internal documents defined the CWP's role as pulling the "embryonic progressive movement of women into a consistently democratic path, [sic] win them to Marxism-Leninism and widen their influence" (CWP, n.d.b, 4–5). Since the CWP publicly claimed independence from the WPJ, the public reference to the group as "communists wearing panties" was meant to "out" the members' attachment to the WLL/WPJ.[5] It would also serve to marginalize them in the context of anticommunist sentiment within the nation and the Left. Beverly Manley-Duncan pointed to such sentiment within the PNP, which demanded that she explain her relationship with the CWP. She says tensions were evident at the National Executive Council (NEC) of the party but that Michael Manley was open to shifting the balance of power within the party, since he was "a compromiser, a balancer" who was unwilling to repeat the anticommunist breach that occurred in the PNP in the 1950s (Interview with Author 2016). At the same time, as Beverly Manley-Duncan became more leftist, she began to be in increasing ideological disagreement with Michael Manley (2008, 165). By the time Michael Manley committed to an agreement with the International Monetary Fund (IMF), their politics had diverged such that she could no longer give him the support he needed as a wife. The intersection of her radical gender and class politics made it clear to her that "the first group to feel the negative impact of any [IMF] agreement would be the women" (Manley 2008, 190–192).[6] In critiquing the Left within the PNP, Manley-Duncan says the party was not strong on gender and did not always support its women. She recalls an instance where a minister of government in an executive meeting insisted that Manley control his wife—that as first lady, she should be home cutting ribbons (Interview with Author 2016). Manley says she was laughed at inside and outside of the party, facing ridicule at party meetings where she would be met with objections when she rose to speak: "that woman thing again" (148–149).

Mars argues that women's equality in left parties was assumed and was not "viewed as a special problem for debate" (1998, 82), but WPJ women recognized women's unequal power, even if there was limited official debate and mobilization around it, at least not until close to the time of the party's dissolution in the late 1980s. Though women faced sexism in the party, they were swayed by the single-minded vision of the struggle as defined by the WPJ, expressed in the WPJ's demand that members should not derail their efforts by prioritizing lenses other than the working-class struggle, including matters of race and gender. When party women did assert their rights or were critical of "anti-woman behavior and tendencies," they were called names and isolated.[7]

Yet there was room for women within the WLL and WPJ party structure. Joan French, then active in the National Union for Democratic Teachers (NUDT), an affiliate of the WLL/WPJ seeking to democratize the Jamaica Teachers Association (JTA) and a member of the Sistren Theatre Collective, contrasts the incorporation of women into the struggle of the WPJ with the experience of women in the PNP. French concludes that on one hand, women were integral to the WPJ struggle (Interview with Author 2015). On the other hand, the women's movement was not integral to the PNP and depended on the leadership of Beverly Manley to argue its merits. Under Beverly Manley's leadership, Kaufman argues, the PNPWM became one of the most effective voices of the party's Left (1985, 143). Manley-Duncan points out, however, that it was Michael Manley who "asked the party if they could revive the women's movement," and she did "everything under his umbrella." She says she could "take on the PNP" given the protection of her husband, and would literally intervene: "Comrade Chair, can I have your protection to speak?" Even though she had "to fight" to get reforms, she concludes that without his protection, she could not have played the role she did (Interview with Author 2016). Beverly Manley also argues that it never occurred to the PNPWM that it could become independent under the PNP; it was a "follow-the-leader" movement (cited in Kaufman 1985, 174). On the other hand, the CWP had its own leadership and led its own struggle for women of Jamaica as independent of, as well as interlocked with, the WPJ.

CWP members' intimate relationships with WPJ men is also of importance in terms of their intertwining politics and ideology. For instance, Ingrid Munroe, who was a member and at one point leader of the Organization of Women for Progress (a rebranded CWP), was eventually married to the general secretary of the WPJ, Trevor Munroe. She credits him with motivating the women in their protest action for paid maternity leave after Michael Manley outlawed protesting in front of Jamaica House.[8] These relationships were part of the intimate and political lives of the men and women of the movement. This dynamic is also visible in Beverly Manley's role as wife of the prime minister. Her marriage gave her and the CWP access to the highest leadership of the nation, and she describes educating Manley in their private conversations about the realities of those at the bottom of the social hierarchy (Interview with Author 2016).

Women's Liberation as Centering the "Working Class"

Perry Mars argues that though left parties in the Caribbean had "strong women's chapters," they emphasized party women's role in electoral mobilization rather than women's rights (1998, 82). I argue that the CWP's anti-capitalist activism sought to address the lived reality of women and expand their rights.[9] The CWP's national engagement took shape through a concern for the conditions of women as a constituency negatively impacted by capitalism (not women as victims of gender oppression). The work of the CWP made women into political actors as well as beneficiaries of social transformation. The targets of their mobilization were the state, the opposition JLP, the private sector, and international agents of capitalist expansion—the United States and the IMF. The Left deemed that the leader of the JLP, Edward Seaga, was a puppet of the United States and global capitalism. The CWP identified these forces as "downpressors" and urged women to side with the PNP or WPJ (CWP 1984). This meant they played an electioneering role in addition to other activities. In the 1976 election, they called on women to "vote for progress" and the party that would best allow them to "fight the enemy—imperialism and [aid] the struggle for women's rights" (CWP, n.d.f). In 1980, they encouraged voters and specifically women not to be deterred by escalating violence: "Sisters when October 30 comes, if it rain, if sun hot, if they fire shots at you, if hurricane come, whatever happen, if it is the last thing you do, we must go out and vote" (CWP 1980b, 2). They called on women to vote for the party that allows women to make "more progress, get more laws like Maternity Leave Law, more Voluntary Price Inspectors, the progressive movement for the third term" (CWP 1980a). Essentially, the CWP's election activities were geared toward creating the conditions that would expand women's rights. To that end, they propagandized that the 1980 election was a fight between continued progress or reversals for women—what they referred to as "setting back the clock" (Vassell 1980). The proverbial clock had been set forward by progressive legislation and public policies through the PNP. A JLP victory would mean a turn to the right politically, and this was not seen as being in the interest of the Black majority and Black women especially, who suffered from the inherited anti-Black colonial social structure. The 1970s were the beginning of substantive change that came through the support of a left-leaning government in power, and thus the stakes for the 1980 election were extremely high, which was visible in increasing violence between the two sides of the political spectrum by the end of the 1970s.

In addition to the defense of rights, the CWP's electioneering activities were important to building its confidence and women's agency overall. In assessing the impact of the 1976 election mobilization process on CWP women themselves, the group found participation was impacted by "inexperience and shyness of a number of our women in pamphleteering" but that as their effort progressed, women showed increased willingness and enthusiasm. While members could not assess their impact on the elections, they noted that the women's issues emerged as a focal point in that election and that women turned out in record numbers (CWP, n.d.c). In 1980, the CWP encouraged specific actions for women—discuss ideas, register to vote, demand time from work to vote, and share childcare responsibilities to facilitate voting (CWG, n.d.h). The CWP consistently promoted women's participation in their own struggles and with a view of the kind of sacrifices required of them, such as the need to find childcare while promoting voter participation. They also encouraged women to "join CWP" or in other words, their own struggle (CWP 1978b, 5).

Judith Soares contends that the issues taken on by the CWP reflected the acceptance by women that the struggle for the working class should take priority over the struggle for women's liberation. Soares points to their mobilization of women against the high cost of living (high rentals and unemployment) in campaigns for consumer rights in the 1980s. Women also fought for low prices for basic goods and discussed consumer problems faced by women of the lower classes (Soares 1991, 163). Alternately, I would argue that the struggles of women for the transformation of the conditions of working-class women was the route through which the CWP sought women's liberation. Their agendas were also consistent with Marxist analysis of women's role as low-paid laborers and caregivers in capitalism as key to their oppression and liberation.[10] The provision of childcare and paid maternity leave were consequently seen as integral to facilitating women's beneficial involvement in the public sphere and the economy. For Black women in the Caribbean, their liberation could not be separated from their place in global capitalism as descendants of nonwaged enslaved people. The legacy of racial slavery kept them at the bottom of racial and class hierarchies in the region and globally—they had inherited poverty and dispossession. The CWP's anti-imperial, anti-capitalist struggle and its demand for food and shelter rights to have the means to care for its offspring were critical to the struggle for Black women's liberation, which also held a radical vision of emancipation. The CWP saw the conditions of working-class women as determined by their location in local capitalism and the global problem of imperialism, not their relations with men, and, as such, mobilized against gendered manifestations of imperial domination for women. Their role would be to expose women's conditions, seek to change them, educate women on the relationship between change in their conditions and change in the entire economic and social system, and give a global view of women's conditions, their oppression, and advances (CWP, n.d.d). The CWP's global vision occurred within the frame that the "entire thrust of the organization is anti-imperialist, anti-colonial, anti-racist, anti-apartheid, against foreign domination and oppression" (CWP 1985).

The CWP's official position was that it was not fighting against men since "some suffer the same conditions as us. We see men according to their class. These men and women react to issues according to their interests of their class. We in the CWP cannot fight apart from men who suffer the same conditions as us and whose struggle is the same as ours. Although we face special problems as women, our lot will never be better until our country has true economic independence, equality and justice (CWP, n.d.d)." The CWP defined the main enemy as imperialism, the national struggle as women's struggle and women's issues, the ground on which to seek national liberation. They concluded that the people needed to control their resources for women's positions to be improved (CWP, n.d.a). Women's liberation as such would be an outgrowth of their struggle for national liberation. In that vein, the CWP would cite Michael Manley in explaining their goals: "One wants to relate this whole concept of women's liberation to national liberation. We don't believe that liberation of women in the Jamaican context is an end in itself, but rather it is the process by which a half of the population achieves its freedom and exercises it in a new creative and naturally enriching partnership" (CWP 1978b).

Descendants of enslaved Africans had inherited a nation whose independence would be imperiled by global white supremacy and capitalism's global racial division of labor. Working-class Jamaican men also experienced "downpression," and there was a need to tie women's struggle to the national struggle against imperialism. But there is an extent to which the CWP's particular emphasis on working-class women did not grapple with the fact that women, regardless of class, experienced sexism and oppression as a function of patriarchal relations of power. Amy Thame, then member of the WPJ and CWP, recalls how women in 1970s Jamaica had to complete their housework and the care of men and children before going out to protest (Interview with Author 2017). Men did not face those difficulties of the sexual division of labor, and they had power over women in general. The struggle against patriarchy at home and within the nation was, in that context, underdeveloped within the CWP.

The Right to Eat and Women's Embodied Politics

Jamaica faced an economic crisis in the latter half of the 1970s as a result of an economic downturn driven by the flight of capital in response to Manley's turn to the left, U.S. interference in the economy and local politics as part of its cold war in the Caribbean, and the PNP's economic management. After its 1976 electoral victory, the PNP entered into a contentious agreement with the IMF, worsening the hardships facing ordinary people, which were compounded by the actions of the private sector, resulting in food scarcity. The CWP responded with an assault on the distribution sector, agitation for the extension and maintenance of price controls, and through acting as Voluntary Price Inspectors (VPI), which the CWP advocated should have prosecutorial powers. The VPI program was set up to deal with the problem of food distribution, which was characterized by hoarding, "marrying of goods," overcharging, and unfair distribution through a system of "brown paper bags" in which scarce food was hidden and distributed to favored customers in stores.[11]

Volunteers investigated shortages and price gouging in food distribution stores. They were, at times, in physical confrontations with store personnel when they faced objections to them carrying out their duties. In terms of their successes in addressing the food crises, the VPI reported convincing supermarket managers to stock reputedly scarce goods on shelves when they were present and to sell goods in smaller amounts for affordability. In the period of PNP government, the CWP also pushed the PNP to expand its "progressive credentials" by resisting the IMF and forces that could push the party to the political right. To that end, they tasked themselves to "expose the role of the private sector, especially in food distribution problems (through for instance, journalism); unite with organizations to pass consumer protection laws—outlaw double stamping, stamp of manufacture date to prevent hoarding, increase penalties for breach of trade law; demand that the Jamaica Manufacturers Association (JMA) publish prices at which they sell to distributors; call on government to strengthen [the] Prices Commission including through giving Voluntary Price Inspectors (VPI) powers of prosecution; shop in groups to strengthen protection against brown paper bag; act as VPI; protest; Act now" (CWP 1980c). The consumer struggle was especially revealing of the character of the CWP's struggle as attached to the intimate lives of women and the ways in which they were required to embody political struggle. Barbara Gordon, wife of Dereck Gordon, a leader in WPJ, concluded that as VPI, WPJ women were playing a role that was open to women in a way it was not to men (because of perceptions of women that would conceivably protect them from public violence). She reports that in their confrontational demands to see what was held in storerooms, they would face resistance from storekeepers and the "food that they were seeking to secure for the people was sometimes destroyed" (Interview with Author 2016). Such practices acknowledged violence as a dimension of struggle even though they were women facing more powerful forces. The right to eat was attached to the affordability and availability of food, and the CWP was intent on addressing both concerns through direct challenges to distributors' practices of creating scarcity and through supporting the government's use of price controls.

The private result of VPI and other such activities was the stigmatization of CWP women. Gordon recalls that they were seen as polarizing viragos who promoted trouble in the society. She suspects the view of them was inherent in the nature of what they were doing (Interview with Author 2016). Beverly Manley-Duncan recalls that the PNP and the society at large viewed WPJ/CWP women as "hostile" (Interview with Author 2016). Reflecting on the women of the WPJ, Trinidadian Maureen Warner-Lewis, scholar and wife of WPJ leader Rupert Lewis, says they "came out of a different formation than herself." They seemed "prepared to give up stable domestic life" and "had a different kind of vision" that took women into the public sphere. They shaped her view of Jamaican women as "not sentimental." They "didn't linger and pine" and were not "romantic about private life"; they were, she says, tough and militant, not the swooning type (Interview with Author 2016).

After the defeat of the PNP in 1980, the context shifted for VPIs. In their November–December 1980 report, VPIs recorded increased hostility toward volunteers (CWP 1980d). In response to an incident where they had been refused entry and verbally abused by the managers at the distribution company, Seprod Jamaica Ltd., the responsible government minister, Douglas Vaz, defended Seprod's refusal to admit the VPI, arguing, "These are different times and there will be changes" (CWP 1978a). The defeat of the PNP and the political movement that had ascended in the 1970s coupled with the rise of a government aligned with global capitalism and the United States limited the possibilities for the consumer rights struggle to continue as it had developed through the CWP.

Struggle for Maternity Leave: Women's Private Lives and Anti-Capitalist Politics

Maternity leave with pay was one of the major struggles of the CWP on behalf of Jamaican women. This particular struggle was solidarity-building, pro-motherhood, and anti-capitalist. It accorded with the CWP's broader focus on working-class women as the group most negatively impacted by the absence of protections for mothers in capitalism. Their emphasis is of historical import given that for Black women on Caribbean slave plantations, pregnancy did not protect them from racist violence, nor did it diminish their workload. Postpartum, they could neither protect their offspring nor protect themselves. Women were not given any special time for childcare, having to take their newborns to work in the fields, sometimes left on the ground and at risk from the elements. Further, they faced the constant threat of losing their children to the market as slaves (see Bush 2010). Maternity leave with pay could right historical wrongs and improve women's conditions in the present. The CWP was specifically pushing the state to make concessions for women that would directly impact their capacity to maintain families and their agency as reproductive and productive beings. The bid for maternity leave was attached to the CWP's concerns around housing, women's status as heads of households, establishment of minimum wages, standardization of school uniforms for children to reduce costs to parents, and food crises. Strategically, the CWP approached maternity leave as a health issue for mothers and children—they argued that it would facilitate the government's nutrition program for mothers and children given that women could not breastfeed if they had no leave (JCWR 1980, 1).

Former CWP member Dacia Brown-Davis points out that though these were women's issues, they were also class conflicts that put the CWP against the business and upper classes on the issues (Interview with Author 2016). The CWP noted that business interests campaigned against maternity leave even while they had benefited from a 50 percent increase in prices in 1978 (JCWR 1980, 2–3). Opposition to the provision of maternity leave also came from the Jamaica Teachers Association in relation to unwed mothers, the Gleaner newspaper, the IMF, the Chamber of Commerce, and the Jamaica Employers Federation (CWP n.d.c). The IMF demanded that maternity leave be treated as a fringe benefit, as consistent with its demand for a 45 percent devaluation of the Jamaican dollar, an end to price controls, and a guarantee of 20 percent profit to businesses and wage restraint in response to the economic crisis of the period (CWP n.d.c, 2).

Success came after two years of struggle by the women's movement, which included the formation of a Joint Committee for Women's Rights (JCWR), with the passing of the Maternity Leave Act (1979). The women held demonstrations and public meetings, distributed pamphlets, and collected over 9,000 supporting signatures to petition the cause.[12] Its success was important not only for women's private lives but also for energizing the women's movement. Linnette Vassell argues that Michael Manley was pushed to take a favorable position on maternity leave given the public and mass nature of their struggle including within the PNP, which he led. He had wavered in his promises to the women's movement, at points delaying announcement of the law and seeking to turn back efforts (Vassell, Interview with Author 2019). Vassell's assessment that Manley's position on maternity leave was responding to the mass women's movement is consistent with the view that Manley was radicalized and energized by the national movement, the breadth of which Lewis describes as characterized by "a lot of independent activity taking place in the communities" (2019, 137).

In the struggle for maternity leave, Beverly Manley functioned as part of the embodied politics of the women's movement in that the women's movement could exploit her relationship with Michael Manley in favor of the causes of women. Vassell recounts that in one of their meetings, a pregnant Beverly Manley blocked Michael Manley from leaving without making concessions for women (Interview with Author 2016). Beverly Manley's standing in the way exemplifies the struggle for women's rights and the methods they were required to use to achieve them. According to Manley-Duncan, "We were courageous and feisty, we faced Michael Manley down" (Interview with Author 2016). She said of the PNP women that they raised the consciousness of men in the party. And that she personally "made sure that Michael understood why the women's struggle was important for the country's development" (Manley 2008, 148). It is important when studying political leadership to appreciate those who influence people in power. We could imagine a different outcome if Beverly and Michael Manley were not married. Beverly Manley-Duncan's subjectivity is important because she was able to bring her life experience, which differed from that of mainstream power-brokers, into the consciousness of Michael Manley and the politics of the PNP. She understood that women mattered to national development and that the prime minister needed to understand this. Further, her political leaning to the left connected her leadership of the PNPWM with the CWP and with a specific interpretation of women's rights and needs beyond liberal politics to the socioeconomic well-being of those women and their families.

The CWP did not see its legislative victory in 1979 as the end of the battle. It correctly anticipated that employers would try to deny women the benefit (Brown 1978). In the Seaga years (1980–1989), the CWP recorded attacks on maternity leave. Employers reportedly refused to pay women for leave or refused them a return to duty after their period of leave had ended (CWP 1983). Some women themselves resisted the use of the benefit in the initial period after the law was passed. Manley-Duncan recalls that women at the bottom of the social hierarchy had to be convinced that they had the right to maternity leave (Interview with Author 2016). In this phase of struggle, the CWP held public broadcasts educating women on the right to maternity leave and on how to agitate if they were denied leave. They undertook public announcements in their program of political action that included announcements on the law and its connections to the struggle for women's rights and provided reporting mechanisms to pursue cases for women who were deprived of the benefit. Announcements declared,

> The Maternity Leave Law is now a reality after 2 years of struggle. More struggle means more benefits;

> The Maternity Leave Law is now a reality. Let's now struggle for a fairer distribution of basic food;

> The Maternity Leave Law protects all women from being fired because of pregnancy, even if they have not worked for 52 weeks. Report difficulties.[13]

These announcements are important statements of the politics of the CWP. First, the CWP demanded that women deploy their agency to receive benefits. Second, the CWP rooted maternity leave in a communist vision of social equality over individual rights. As with other agendas pursued by the CWP, maternity leave was seen as part of establishing a social order that gave people the right to eat. Third, and more profoundly for Black women, the CWP connected maternity leave to the human desire to be pregnant, to have children, and to live in a society that allowed them to protect their offspring—conditions historically denied to Black women since the period of slavery and thereafter because of poverty or their positions at the bottom of the social hierarchies of the societies they live in across the Americas.

Conclusion

I wish to conclude with a return to Lambert's questions: "What would it mean to reimagine [*sic*] revolution with women at its center? How do [women] shape the ideology of revolution, and how do they make themselves the beneficiaries of political power?" While the Workers Party of Jamaica made room for women's political action, the ways in which the Committee of Women for Progress women shaped their own agendas, carved their own alliances, undertook popular mobilization, and built a movement must be seen as revolutionary. They sought emancipation for people at the bottom of the social hierarchy, especially Black women. Many of the issues highlighted by the CWP and their mobilization for and of women and the working class are not only historically significant. The oppression of ordinary people within capitalism and imperialism remains a reality. The struggles of the CWP are a lens through which to consider women's political practices and the potential for revolutionary change today. Even at the present moment when neoliberal capitalist victory in the Caribbean and much of the world gives the impression that the potential for revolution seems lost, the CWP evidences political possibility. As the women of the CWP were "communists wearing panties," the CWP's type of revolution meant and continues to mean turning the world around for those who are most exploited by it, including in their private worlds.

In this chapter, I intend to offer an alternative to the male-centered, leader-centric, analytical framed scholarship on political change in the postcolonial Caribbean. This means rethinking the legacies of the political parties, movements, and their leaders in regional politics. By highlighting the work of the CWP, this chapter demands that we rethink the Michael Manley–centric analysis of Jamaican politics in this era, the legacies of the PNP, the WPJ, and most critically, the place of Black "communist" women in revolutionizing the world. Here I presented those women as full participants and leaders of the movements that brought change, and I sought to fill in knowledge gaps regarding Black women's radical contributions to politics.

Acknowledgments

I wish to thank Linnette Vassell and Rupert Lewis for giving me access to their WPJ and CWP papers, which facilitated this research. I accessed the papers at their homes, but they are now located at the University of the West Indies Library (Mona) and the Institute of Jamaica respectively. I also wish to thank the women who struggled in the movement and those who sat with me to share their knowledge.

Notes

1. See Stephens and Stephens for an explanation of social change that privileges charisma over social movement. They argued that the low density of civil society gave space for Manley's charisma to direct policy (1986, 324).
2. Interview with Amy Thame, CWP/WPJ member. Thame reports, for instance, that the ethnically Lebanese Faye Tortello, the sister of Edward Seaga, then leader of the JLP, was a regular caller to talk shows who was allowed to spout racial vitriol against Vassell.
3. See David Scott's (2001) interview with Rupert Lewis for a discussion of the competition between elements of the Left including the PNP.
4. French et al. (1987) demonstrate a clear relationship between the WPJ and OWP. Their assessment focuses on the way women's emancipation was dealt with "within the Party and by Party members in mass organizations, *particularly the OWP*" (my emphasis).
5. Ingrid Munroe, president of the later outgrowth of the CWP, the Organization of Women for Progress, argued that the CWP was against and had never been affiliated with any political party. She posited that since its inception, it was felt that in a situation where parties are dominated by male leadership, the independence and priority of women's issues would likely be subordinated in any affiliated women's arm. She argued that the CWP supported women's need to be more

politically active, their right to independent political viewpoints, to support, criticize, or oppose political parties or party positions in the interest of women and the people. She described its membership of between 60 and 200 women as largely middle class, Kingston based, university educated, mainly "non-communist, but left leaning and pro-WPJ" (I. Munroe 1988).
6   See also CWP (n.d.g).
7   Reflecting on the party after "almost 20 years since these issues were raised in pre-party formations," party women complained they were "still fighting against accusations of dividing the struggle, being bourgeois feminist, being anti-male or even being lesbian" (French et al. 1987, 6 and 10).
8   CWP members and associates provided feedback for a paper I presented on the CWP at the Institute for Gender and Development Studies, UWI, Regional Coordinating Unit, October 7, 2020.
9   For a discussion of Black women's lives and labor in anti-capitalist, postrevolutionary Cuba, see Crumdy, in this volume.
10 For a discussion of Black Brazilian women activist scholars' (Lélia Gonzalez and Luiza Bairros) work on Black women's labor and rights, see Sotero, in this volume.
11 The CWP noted that since March 1980, there was a practice among some distributors, wholesalers, and supermarket operators of giving special favor in food distribution when other customers had been told there was no rice or flour available (CWP 1980c).
12 JCWR groups included the YWCA, Jamaica Association of Social Workers, Junior Doctors Association, the WPJ, the PNP Women's Movement, Voluntary Organization for Uplifting Children (VOUCH), Methodist Women United, and National Union for Democratic Teachers.
13 The CWP ran a telephone line for reporting cases and for follow-up on problems accessing maternity leave (CWP, n.d.e).

References

Boyce Davies, Carole. 2008. *Left of Karl Marx: The Political Life of Black Communist Claudia Jones*. Durham, NC: Duke University Press.

Brown, Judith, 1978. *Maternity Leave Law: Statement to the Jamaica Broadcasting Corporation*, June 29. Committee of Women for Progress (CWP) Papers. National Library of Jamaica.

Bush, Barbara. 2010. "African Caribbean Slave Mothers and Children: Traumas of Dislocation and Enslavement across the Atlantic World." *Caribbean Quarterly* 56, no. 1–2: 69–94.

Campbell, Horace. 1985. *Rasta and Resistance: From Marcus Garvey to Walter Rodney*. London: Hansib Publications.

CWP (Committee of Women for Progress). 1978a. *Contribution of CWP to Teach-In Discussion*, November 27. CWP Papers. National Library of Jamaica.

———. 1978b. *Report of CWP Evaluation and Planning Meeting*, October 7–8. CWP Papers. National Library of Jamaica.

———. 1980a. *1980 Elections*. Pamphlet. CWP Papers. National Library of Jamaica.

———. 1980b. *Newsletter of the CWP*. No. 25, October 24. CWP Papers. National Library of Jamaica.

———. 1980c. *The VPI Programme—A Programme for the People*, December 9. CWP Papers. National Library of Jamaica.

———. 1980d. *VPI Report*, November–December. CWP Papers. National Library of Jamaica.
———. 1983. "More Politics Not Less." *WFP Newsletter* 2, no. 3 (April 29). CWP Papers. National Library of Jamaica.
———. 1984. "Women for Progress." *CWP Newsletter* 3, no. 6 (September 25). CWP Papers. National Library of Jamaica.
———. 1985. *Critical Review and Appraisal of Progress Achieved and Committee of Women for Progress: Obstacles Encountered in Attaining the Goals and Objectives of the UN Decade for Women: Equality, Development and Peace in Jamaica (1976–1985)*, August. CWP Papers. National Library of Jamaica.
———. n.d.a. *The CWP and How It Is Different*. CWP Papers. National Library of Jamaica.
———. n.d.b. *The CWP and the National Plan for Women: Women and the Struggle for National Liberation, Democracy and Socialism in Jamaica*. CWP Papers. National Library of Jamaica.
———. n.d.c. "Maternity Leave in the Year of the Child." CWP Papers, Institute of Jamaica.
———. n.d.d. *Note on Its Aims*. CWP Papers. National Library of Jamaica.
———. n.d.e. Paid announcements. CWP Papers. National Library of Jamaica.
———. n.d.f. *Report on Campaign to Encourage Women to Vote for Progress*. CWP Papers. National Library of Jamaica.
———. n.d.g. "Women—Step Up the Struggle for Progress, Fight against the IMF." *Newsletter of the CWP*. CWP Papers. National Library of Jamaica.
———. n.d.h. "Women—Vote for Progress." Pamphlet. CWP Papers. National Library of Jamaica.
Fixmer, Natalie, and Julia T. Wood. 2005. "The Personal Is *Still* Political: Embodied Politics in Third Wave Feminism." *Women's Studies in Communication* 28, no. 2: 235–257.
Ford-Smith, Honor. 2019. "The Body and Performance in 1970s Jamaica: Toward a Decolonial Cultural Method." *Small Axe* 23, no. 1 (58): 150–168.
French, Joan, Marion Bernard, Joan Ross-Frankson, Shirley Campbell, Paulette Chevannes, Lucy Brown-Hutton, Nancy Anderson, and Jenny Jones. 1987. *Women's Emancipation, Socialism and the Party*. CWP Papers. National Library of Jamaica.
Gray, Obika. 2012. "Imagining Freedom: Afro-Jamaican Yearnings and the Politics of the Workers' Party of Jamaica." In *Caribbean Political Activism: Essays in Honour of Richard Hart*, edited by Rupert Lewis, 171–198. Kingston: Ian Randle.
JCWR (Joint Committee for Women's Rights). 1980. "The Maternity Leave Struggle in Jamaica." January 14. CWP Papers. National Library of Jamaica.
Kaufman, Michael. 1985. *Jamaica under Manley: Dilemmas of Socialism and Democracy*. London: Zed Books.
Lambert, Laurie R. 2020. *Comrade Sister: Caribbean Feminist Revisions of the Grenada Revolution*. Charlottesville: University of Virginia Press.
Lewis, Rupert. 1998. *Walter Rodney's Intellectual and Political Thought*. Barbados: Press University of the West Indies.
———. 2019. "The Jamaican Left: Dogmas, Theories, and Politics, 1974–1980." *Small Axe* 23, no. 1 (58): 97–111.
Manley, Beverley. 2008. *The Manley Memoirs*. Kingston: Ian Randle.
Mars, Perry. 1998. *Ideology and Change: The Transformation of the Caribbean Left*. Detroit: Wayne State University Press.

Munroe, Ingrid. 1988. "Can Women Bring Mutual Respect, Fair Play to Political Life?" *The Gleaner*, May 8, B12.

Munroe, Trevor. 1988. "The Left and the Question of Race in Jamaica." In *Garvey: His Work and Impact*, edited by Rupert Lewis and Patrick E. Bryan, 283–298. Kingston: Africa World Press.

Quinn, Kate. 2015. *Black Power in the Caribbean*. Gainesville: University of Florida Press.

Scott, David. 2001. "The Dialectic of Defeat: An Interview with Rupert Lewis." *Small Axe* 5, no. 2: 85–177.

Soares, Judith. 1991. "Women and Revolutionary Politics: The Case of the WPJ." In *Forging Identities and Patterns of Development in Latin America and the Caribbean*, edited by Harry Diaz, 157–167. Toronto: Canadian Scholars' Press.

Stephens, Evelyne, and John Stephens. 1986. *Democratic Socialism in Jamaica: The Political Movement and Social Transformation in Dependent Capitalism*. Hampshire: Macmillan Higher Education.

Vassell, Linnette, 1980. Letter from CWP Coordinator to Organizations to sit on Platform of Mass Rally, September 19. CWP Papers. National Library of Jamaica.

4

Exercising Diversity

• • • • • • • • • • • • • • • • • • • •

From Identity to Alliances
in Brazil's Contemporary
Black Feminism

JULIA S. ABDALLA

In October 2019, Angela Davis spoke to an audience of about 15,000 people in Ibirapuera, an urban park in São Paulo, Brazil's largest city and its most important financial center. At the event named "Freedom Is a Constant Struggle," the title of one of Davis's recent books, the intellectual activist discussed central issues in Brazilian politics and chanted its most widespread progressive mottoes with the crowd. The large number of people from all corners of the country who went to see and listen to Davis one year after far-right presidential candidate Jair Bolsonaro's election, which broke with the country's democratic consolidation trend established in the 1980s, was no surprise. Public participation in other recent Black feminist events and protests, such as the Black Women's March in 2015, brought approximately 50,000 women to the capital city, Brasília. The Latinidades Afrolatinas festival is another example of such events. Patricia Hill Collins and Sirma Bilge's (2016) account of Latinidades's fourth edition in 2014 depicts the festival as overtly political: "its expressed purpose lay in promoting 'racial equality and tackling racism and sexism'" (7). It was attended by important Brazilian and foreign intellectuals and activists and inclusive of a large sum of people from various age groups, professions, racial and ethnic backgrounds, and nationalities. According to the authors, Latinidades had elements of an academic symposium, a political organizing event, an African cultural heritage event, and a mass-music festival and represented the different connections to the Black feminist agenda in the region (Hill Collins and Bilge 2016, 7).

These events attest to the dimension, connections, and expanding visibility and impact of present-day Black feminism in Brazil, the second-largest Black country in the world, in a period of growing social conservatism. Black women compose about 27 percent of the country's population and 18 percent of the active labor force.[1] Despite recent improvements in the living conditions of Afro-Brazilian populations, however, they are still the majority among paid domestic workers, earn less than white women and Black men for the same jobs, are more prone to be victims of violence, are deprived of public services, and are hypersexualized in Brazilian culture. Black women's activism started long before the 2010s with origins that can be traced back to the antislavery struggle and long-standing engagements and intellectual and political exchanges with Black liberation movements in the African diaspora.[2] Nonetheless, the magnitude and heterogeneity displayed at these events is unprecedented.

Much of this expansion relates to the constitution of new generations of Black feminists, beginning in the early 2000s, in close relationship with public policies that targeted long-standing inequalities in the country such as affirmative actions for Black and Indigenous populations, the extension of labor rights for domestic workers, and the democratization of access to the internet. Notably, this expansion refers not only to the movement's visibility and cultural relevance but to the transformation of its practices, strategies, agendas, and discourses as it becomes more massive and diverse. Circulating in a vast field of collective actions that exceed national boundaries and differ from traditional social movements—such as the Slut Walk, the Latin American marches against gender violence, international youth and women's strikes, spontaneous manifestations, occupations, and others—these Black feminist activists defy the established grammars and boundaries of a politics of contestation. With significant expression over consumer markets and reaching increasingly larger publics, their manifestations point to an expanded and transformed notion of activism (Figueiredo 2018).

A central argument in this chapter is that the movement's transition and growth since the early 2010s have influenced conversations regarding differences among Black women (including class, age, sexuality, access to education, and region, among others). Previously a nuisance for a movement that sought unity, differences have become a central, perennial, and even a welcome element of Black feminism's politics. In other words, there has been a shift from a robust identity-based organization to a coalitional approach, with reconfigured practices that welcome alliances among different organized movements and marginalized subjects. This modification of the movement deepens and safeguards some of the previous generations' achievements in validating social-movement-designed political subjects, which are currently being discussed in the public sphere.

This chapter seeks to shed light on the ways intersectionality operates within the practices and routines of social movements and to contribute to the documentation of present-day Black feminism in Brazil and its complexity. The first section presents a concise historical overview of contemporary Black women's movements in Brazil, which dates back to the struggle for democracy in the late 1970s. It highlights the transformations in their structures and agendas that follow social and political shifts beginning in the 2000s. In the second and third sections, I examine contemporary activists' conflicts and negotiations of difference and coalition-building processes. Relying on qualitative data from research carried out between 2016 and 2018, I present two initiatives that display the characteristics, challenges, and potential of the current moment of Black feminism in Brazil—an enormous national march in 2015 and a local activist group formed by many collectives and movements to attend this march. Taking these initiatives as privileged sites to observe Black Brazilian women's movements and feminisms, I consider a few of the ways in which differences are dealt with and alliances operate within and among recent movements.

Black Brazilian Women's Movements in Historical Perspective

The contemporary expression of Black women's mobilization in Brazil blossomed in the late 1970s among the broader framework of popular resistance to the military dictatorship. As part of a stage of political debate and resistance, Black women's collectives were initially formed to articulate an autonomous agenda. Thus, the early constitution of contemporary Black feminist movements questioned the Black movement's and feminist movement's lack of Black women's participation in political debates, their blockages against the collective organization of Black women's agendas and the suppression of their issues, and most strikingly, the connections between Black women's oppression and Black men's or white women's liberation (Lemos, 1997).

During the 1980s and early 1990s, as these Black women collectives and organizations grew, solidified their actions (Rios, 2017), and sought alliances with housing, anti-violence, religious, and popular movements, they started confronting their own inner divisions. In local, national, regional, and transnational feminist and anti-racist meetings and events (Ribeiro, 1995; Roland, 2000), the organizational diversity among activists challenged the movement's main goals—developing unified programs of action, a political identity, and one single instance of national representation (Rodrigues 2006). The first National Black Women's Meeting (I Encontro Nacional de Mulheres Negras), in 1988, is a case in point. Considering the movement's complex and diverse base of activists and political groups—women from different regions of the country; maroons, Afro-Brazilian religions, cultural heritage groups, and other traditional communities; popular community-based groups, trade unionists, and middle-class collectives formed in universities; organizations connected with different religious affiliations and with different relations with other movements and perspectives toward the state; and others—numerous activities were put in place to allow the sharing and incorporation of the needs and realities of all in the resulting joint platform.[3] Even so, there were relevant conflicts between different perspectives of the movement, predominantly those regarding its connections with other movements and political parties. Important analyses of this encounter relate the quarrels to the diversity of the women and their forms of political organization, which most activists then perceived as a problem (Cardoso 2012; Silva 2014).[4]

Controversies intensified in the 1990s as reduced institutional spaces for dialogues between the state and organized civil society at the national level led to the growth of nongovernmental organizations, especially in the southeastern and southern regions of the country (Rodrigues 2006; Santos 2008). As these specialized and professionalized organizations disputed the Black women's agenda in transnational meetings and sought partnerships and resources from international organizations and agencies (Caldwell, 2009), the various perspectives within the movement made its internal divisions starker. Núbia Moreira (2007) and Sônia Santos (2008) point to class divisions as the main source of these conflicts. They highlight that besides their concentration in wealthy urban regions, nongovernmental organizations (NGOs) accumulated more financial resources and their activists more educational attainment than grassroots organizations. Also relevant were the debates on the place of sexuality within the movement's discussions and identity. These issues resulted in the constitution of two national representing entities, the Articulação de Mulheres Negras Brasileiras (National Black Women's Articulation, AMNB), an NGO-centered articulation founded in 2000 to intervene in the preparation for the World Conference against Racism, Racial Discrimination, Xenophobia and Related Intolerance in 2001, and the Fórum de Mulheres Negras (Black Women Forum), created in 2003 and associated with the movement's grass roots (Rodrigues 2006).

These disagreements took place in a moment in which social movements were being centralized and in which singular identities and spaces were fought for by various forces (Alvarez 2014; Facchini, Carmo, and Lima 2020). They can thus be understood as disputes for *the* Black women's movement, as well as for the content, meanings, and limits of the category "Black woman." Class, region, formal education, political trajectory, and sexuality would play an important part. Then, in the process of being construed as a public interest group, the "Black woman" political identity would grow into a relevant marker for building social policy from the mid-1990s onward, a period of "democratic stabilization" (Rios and Maciel 2018).

The reopening of dialogues between the state and civil society, starting in the late 1990s, led to the formation of councils, working groups, and the first racial equality policies. That trend intensified in the first decade of the twenty-first century with the creation of the Special Office for Policies for the Promotion of Racial Equality (SEPPIR) and the Office for Policies for Women (SPM), both constituted in 2003 and led by relevant activists.[5] Councils and conferences at different levels and for various social groups (women, Black and Indigenous populations, LGBTQA+, and youth, among others) integrated a participative structure that funneled civil society's claims and ideas to state entities and branches charged with policy-making (Matos and Alvarez 2018), with relevant effects for social movements. Policies like the National Comprehensive Health Policy for the Black Population (2007), the Statute of Racial Equality (2010), the expansion of public universities and affirmative action (2003/2012), and the regulation of domestic labor (2013), among others, conceived in these spaces and meetings, led to significant changes in the lives of low-income and Black populations.[6]

Important activists and scholars of the movement see these shifts as driving different conversations. In a 2018 paper, Ângela Figueiredo argues that a new epoch is on course for the Black movement in Brazil, marked by the beginning of affirmative action for Black students in universities, the expansion of debates on social and racial inequality, and a boom of Black feminist debates (Figueiredo 2018). In a 2012 interview, activist, scholar, and former SEPPIR minister Luiza Bairros expressed a similar perception, describing this "boom" as a period marked by the "specification" of "other identities among Black women," which allowed "multiple possibilities of political organization for Black identity" (Alvarez 2012, 840–841).

Social scientists Flávia Rios and Regimeire Maciel (2018) argue that more than a new phase, there is a new generation of Black feminists with a specific set of concerns, experiences, and political styles. Based on the I Encontro de Negras Jovens Feministas (First Young Black Feminists Meeting), which took place in Salvador in 2009 and can be traced back to articulations during the tenth Encuentro Feminista da América Latina y del Caribe (EFLAC), Rios and Maciel reflect on the formation of a "young feminist" political identity within feminist debates and spaces of representation, which soon led to a specifically "young Black feminist" identity. Formed by many of the first beneficiaries of affirmative action, this generation directs their critique and demands to the state, seeking to participate and influence institutional arenas. Their interventions usually privilege reflections on education, with courses and trainings focused on nonacademic, informal, or traditional knowledge adding to the participants' various educational trajectories. Festivals and academic events are also common forms of mobilization among this group. Along with the broader access to the internet, social media, and smartphones that led to a pronounced and complex online presence, they considerably amplified the movement's publics and participation. Despite these important changes, such as these activists' self-identification as Black *feminists*, remarkable given the term's rejection in the previous generation, the NGO format and general focus of the actions is very similar to the previous generation's strategies.

Another remarkable transformation of Black women's movements' practices and agendas began in the 2010s, as the country's social and political climate changed drastically. Corruption scandals, rampaging demonstrations, economic crises, and the world's growing social conservatism contributed to a deteriorating political climate that culminated in the deposition of President Dilma Rousseff in 2016 and, later, in Jair Bolsonaro's election in 2018. In this context, overtly racist manifestations against social policies and the murder of councilwoman Marielle Franco and her driver Anderson Gomes in 2018 compose a scenario characterized by Black feminist scholar and activist Sueli Carneiro as "the end of cordial racism's hegemony in social relations" in Brazil (Santana 2017).[7]

Self-identified "intersectional feminists," a third generation to coexist in present-day Black Brazilian feminism, emerged in the public sphere in this context of exacerbated social conflict (Rios and Maciel 2018). "Intersectionality" is one of the key terms this generation of the movement employs, testifying to the activists' concentration on topics seen as neglected by previous generations, such as transfeminism and sexuality, and marking their heated debates with feminists. As collectives proliferate in various social spaces, different affiliations express the generation's multiple perspectives toward politics. Besides the now-consolidated "Black feminism," the emerging "intersectional feminist," "womanist," "Africana womanist," "hip-hopper," and many others add to the series of political definitions that thrive in this period. Importantly, "intersectionality" has also expanded beyond Black feminism, reclaimed by other social movements in their struggles for amplified social representation, and frames a shared orientation toward a "fight against all kinds of oppression" (Zanoli 2020).

As a part of this generation's growing activism, influencers, YouTubers, bloggers, and women in debate groups and forums have become references of Black feminism, which expands beyond traditional social movement definitions and strategies (Bringel, 2018; Carmo 2018; Gomes 2018; Rios and Maciel 2018; Lima, 2020). They engage in less established forms of protest like soirées, slams, interventions, and other noninstitutional forms of political participation and announce different pedagogies and political languages marked by the "suspension of society's values, codes, and practices, replaced by collective experimentation of new social conventions" (Carmo 2018, 18). These renewed political languages focus on the bodies and markers of various identities that characterize the "transgressive choreographies" of bodies put forward in these actions (Facchini, Carmo, and Lima 2020; Gomes 2018). Their ability to reach large publics and their proficiency in issues like self-esteem, esthetics, day-to-day experiences, and subjectivity are connected to the unprecedented influence they have acquired over consumption markets and cultural products.[8] Also, their political formation commonly begins in urban peripheries and neighborhoods, a shift from the previous almost exclusively university-based collectives, which also helps explain its diffusion in the public sphere (Rios and Maciel 2018).

Differences and Alliances in Contemporary Brazilian Black Feminism

In the last several decades, Black women's organizations and feminisms grew in complexity and connections. As anthropologists Regina Facchini, Íris do Carmo, and Stephanie Lima (2020) point out, the "significant enlargement" of collective actions and organizations by Black women, lesbians, workers, and rural women, among other political subjects that disputed and complexified the feminist identity, made it so that "the 'others' of feminism became 'other feminisms'" (20). In this sense, representations based on strategic essentialism give way to a plural and expanding set of political subjects that coexist in the current scenario. Within Black feminism, this process of "decentralization" (Alvarez 2014; Facchini, Carmo, and Lima 2020) leads to the inner pluralization of the "Black woman," with "domestic workers, maroon women, lesbians, women from traditional communities, [and] young women/hip-hoppers/graffiti artists/b-girls/*capoeira* players, among others" (Alvarez 2014, 41) sharing an increasingly complicated scene marked by the affirmation of complex and coalitional identities.

In the current outlook of Black feminist mobilization, generations and various political subjects coexist and differences come to occupy a prominent—and profitable—space within its internal dynamics. As stated by Jurema Werneck, a veteran of the movement, in a text that quickly became a classic,

> Black women don't exist. Or yet: concerning their identities as political subjects, Black women are the outcome of an articulation of heterogeneities resulting from historical, political, and cultural requirements to confront the adverse conditions set by Western Eurocentric domination through centuries of enslavement, colonial expropriation, and the racialized and racist modernity in which we live.... Articulations that progressed despite (and considering) the ambiguities and limitations of our identities, themselves based on strongly

phenotypical (visual) external attributes imposed by the dominating gaze, whose destruction extends to genocide and epistemicide. Thus, the processes by which different "Black women" identities are construed must contain the elements for their own transcendence, allowing new and unstable concepts of "Black women," more adequate to what we need, want, and must be in different political scenarios. (Werneck 2010, 16; my translation)

Werneck's position models the shift within the Black women's movement in relation to its political subject: from a single identity and a set of disputes for its content to a complex and unstable articulation of heterogeneities driven by political needs and scenarios.

I now turn to the analyses of two initiatives: the Black Women's March, a massive demonstration that gathered a vast scope of initiatives within the movement, and, more centrally, the Black Women's Front in Campinas and the Surrounding Region, a local organization of activists and political groups that raised funds for traveling to the march and remained active until 2018. The study is based on ethnographic fieldwork carried out from August 2016 to July 2018, including participant observation and fifteen in-depth semistructured interviews with members of the Front, as well as archival research. I report on findings related to differences as they appeared in the movement's organization and routine and discuss the recent emergence of debates surrounding diversity.

The Black Women's March

One of the most expressive episodes in the history of Black women's mobilization in Brazil, the Black Women's March, took place in November 2015, a couple of days before National Black Awareness Day, a national date established as a result of Black movements' struggles. It gathered about 50,000 Brazilian and foreign marchers in the capital Brasília. "Innovative methodologies" and creative formats such as that of the march were developed by the movement to "deal with" diversity within the movement and produce spaces where its various forces would congregate and be recognized (Alvarez 2014). The march's organization provides an arena to understand recent Brazilian Black feminism, where conflicts within the movements have become visible and older controversies have been brought to the table.

According to Lemos (2016), the idea for the march originated at the first Latin-American and Caribbean Women's Meeting (I Encontro de Mulheres Afro Latino-Americanas e do Caribe) in the Dominican Republic in 1992. However, plans for the march only started in 2011, when Nilma Bentes and Maria Malcher, two experienced activists, presented the idea in the Fórum Afro XXI, an event that took stock of anti-racist policies in Latin America ten years after the Conference of Durban, at which several heads of state, officials, international agencies, and civil society representatives were present. A series of negotiations and debates followed in Black women's movements, including pressure for the National Black Women's Articulation to embrace the idea. The project was officially launched in 2013, during the III Nacional Conference for Promoting Racial Equality (Conferência Nacional de Promoção da Igualdade Racial, CONAPPIR), with the support of and direct actions of activists Luiza Bairros, minister of the Special Office (SEPPIR) and an experienced activist of the Black and Black women's movement, and Regina Adami, a SEPPIR adviser.

Counting on a dynamic and renovated scenario within Black women's movements, the march's success might be credited to the movement's institutionalization—both the civic processes of professionalization and specialization of its activities and the increase of its relations with the state (Rios 2019). First, activists interviewed by Lemos claim that Bairros and other activists working in the state provided crucial resources and assistance for the idea to take off. Second, the movement's relations with the state and its policy-oriented focus are clear in the march's platform—the documents are directly addressed to the state, even as they discuss deeply socially and culturally entrenched issues. They regain a discursive strategy cemented by the Black movement which challenges the "minority" vocabulary, stressing the populational magnitude of Black women ("We are 49 million Black women—in other words, 25 percent of the Brazilian population"). Finally, by claiming the commitments and international agreements to the elimination of racism and sexism signed by the Brazilian state, the documents invoke their own trajectory of state-movement relation (Abdalla 2020), linked to the actions and triumphs of NGOs, which championed earlier processes of institutionalization in civil spheres.

However, institutionalization also had its costs. Even though the articulation around the country's political crisis lightened these frictions, the different positions activists held toward the government and transnational spheres regained potency as one of the main challenges to the movement's cohesion. Producing unity meant dealing with an internally plural movement, in which varied political perspectives as well as generational, regional, and organizational differences were more than circumstantial, reflecting unequal trajectories and resources. An example is the fallout between young and more experienced activists regarding the use of the term "Black feminism" in the march's communication. Preferred by younger activists without institutional affiliation, who constituted at least one-third of the event's organization teams, versus more experienced activists who defended the term "Black women's movement," the absence of the term "Black feminism" testifies as much to the power held by the more seasoned activists as it does to the fragmented organization of the younger ones (Lemos 2016). Lemos mentions both the proliferation of political denominations and the "lack of maturity" around the "discussion on Black feminism" as contributing to this scenario (230).

Another relevant matter was the national organization for the protest, especially the distribution of the limited public funds made available to the march. Though most activists evaluated the actions of the national committee positively, they also reported a lack of attention to regional specificities in the attribution of resources. This led to difficulties for maroon and other rural communities, who had specific needs of the organization, as well as problems for activists in larger states, who struggled to ensure their participation. Lemos's interlocutors claimed that some regions received more resources from the march's central organization. The division privileged well-known activists from larger cities, who actually could have gathered these resources themselves. This trend contributed to logistical and financial hardship for smaller local organizations which, given the distance and challenges of traveling to the capital, both needed to raise larger sums to participate and had limited opportunities for doing so. In Malcher's words, "we have to break bread, but the bread was not broken as equally as we wanted" (Lemos 2016, 259). While these quarrels and divisions were taken by activists to symbolize the distance between the central organizers and the grass roots, the conflicts may also be seen as effects of a growing and pluralizing field of social movement action, defined by its divergences and connections as much as its common grammars. In that context, despite eventual tensions, the march worked as a generator, propelling the field's enlargement and enriching its connections and networks.

The Black Women Front in Campinas and the Surrounding Region

The Black Women Front was one of the local initiatives to raise funds for activists to travel to the Black Women's march that flourished during the event's organization. It started in 2015 with a series of debates between activists who lived in Campinas, a large city in the countryside of São Paulo, the wealthiest state in Brazil and the birthplace of some of the country's largest Black liberation movements. Campinas is also known as the last Brazilian town to effectively abolish slavery and for its segregation and violence against Black people. The city also has many long-standing and varied anti-racist and activist groups.

The initial debates included activists from different movements, experiences, classes, sexualities, ages, and levels of access to formal education. Their perspectives converged on a few points. As the women organizing in other parts of the country, such as Lemos's interlocutors, the activists in Campinas felt a lack of adequate support in the local preparation for the event from the larger movement, which offered its resources to well-known activists to the detriment of grassroots activists. They also criticized the sources of funding, the state or financing agencies or NGOs, which represented what they understood as "institutionalized" forms of protest. These perceptions of the movement as "institutionalized" and "hierarchical" had driven their rejection of former attempts to organize for the march in the region. Former attempts had been organized by two sets of social-movement networks connected to political parties, the government, or the state: Agentes de Pastorais Negros (Black Pastoral Agents, APNs), a progressive section of the Catholic Church very active in low-income communities during the 1970s and 1980s' resistance against the dictatorship, and the Central Única dos Trabalhadores (CUT), the largest trade union central in the country. Though the activists were not equally critical of these factors, most wanted to attend the march *as an independent movement*.

The Front's activities included fundraisers—soirées, lunch parties, and similar events—that gathered local movements, authorities, and the larger public to draft a fully consensual local Black women's platform. With the collective decision to make the articulation permanent, one month before the march, the Front's larger project became that of constituting a local forum of political groups and a network that connected militants who worked on various social justice issues and initiatives around a Black feminist collective agenda.

Drafting that platform meant connecting the collectives' agendas and stitching together Black women's various social positions as workers, poor people, LGBTQIA+, activists, students, youth, and others. The activists negotiated their groups' participation in the Front and their agreement with the resulting manifesto, which oriented their actions from then on. These groups had varied histories and sizes and focused on different issues: Black movements (cultural groups, most long-standing and traditional ones, and more recent collectives focused on anti-racist education), domestic and sex workers' labor organizations, popular feminist movements, and intersectional collectives (a Black feminist group and a Black LGBTQIA+ collective from the outskirts of the city). It implied working closely with the groups and frequently discussing agendas and strategies specifically in terms of political formation, with both sides pledging to get familiarized with the other's debates and struggles. Platforms circulated in the network of groups and were presented, discussed, connected, and rethought from various perspectives. The Front and the collectives also committed to publicizing and attending one another's activities, leading joint actions, and exchanging material resources like headquarters or megaphones. This increased their audience, their chances of self-funding their projects, and their agendas' outreach. These partnerships circulated material resources, political capital, agendas, and knowledge. In the words of thirty-two-year-old lawyer and radical Left activist Cristiane Anizeti, the Front represented the construction not of "a single event [or] an autonomous front," but of "a process in which one movement looks at what the other is doing and, even if that is not my primary platform or action, I will contribute to it" (Interview with Author 2018).

With the support of around twenty relevant local political groups, the Front collected considerable political capital from the start. Each group was represented by activists who intermediated political and organizational decisions and the relations between the Front and the group. Thus, the network prompted the representatives to a more frontal position in their collectives and in politics and assisted them in accumulating political capital and negotiating their terms, both forming and supporting them to dispute politics. As fifty-five-year-old anti-racist and feminist activist Magali Mendes explained, collective representation was meant to push the activists to relevant positions in their organizations, speaking not only for themselves, but *on behalf* of these organizations and movements, something the Front recognized that women, especially Black women, were not taught or given space to do:

> The Front potentialized our actions, if I was irrelevant in my original organization, when I represent it in the Front . . . , [I stand out as saying] "I am the Black woman who represents the Worker's Party in the Front," "I represent the Socialist Party in the Front." . . . Thus, even if people took us for granted, we resumed power. And we need to be mature to perceive that and not get lost in things that men don't get lost . . . : I am not here to dispute for the party, I am here to find out that the party doesn't talk about me and to talk about myself in it. (Interview with Author 2018)

Thus, the Front served a set of purposes in the activists' formation, participation, and gathering of power resources within the organizations they were involved in.

Fostering these intermovement conversations required careful attention and thoughtful disposition for dialogue. Though relations were mostly harmonious, these encounters highlighted former unresolved issues, particularly with the Black movement. One controversy came from the LGBTQIA+ collective, which frequently brought up activists' misfortune in Black and LGBTQIA+ movements, both noninclusive to Black and poor LGBTQIA+ people. Misrepresentation and lack of space in these movements led the group to self-define as a *Black LGBTQIA+ movement from the peripheries* and to take up an intersectional framework of action that sought to establish connections between different platforms of action (Zanoli 2020). Another strained relation was between the Black movement and the organization of sex workers in the city. This conflict was never as open and exposed as the one with the LGBTQA+ group. However, through listening to the perspectives of both groups regarding the city's history, a political and historical hiatus was made clear, namely, that as slavery ended and Black women continued to be forced into precarious work, predominantly as domestic and sex workers, the domestic worker eventually came to be the paradigmatic figure on which the Black movement relied to defend the interests of Black women. Meanwhile, sex workers were left to their own devices.

Differences among the activists also became more salient after 2016 as their goals turned to richer local engagements and issues with outside movements. At a period of confidence in its political resources, which included the successful participation in the Black Women's March and the support of twenty local collectives and movements, the Front intensified activities and set to dispute the characteristics and inclusivity of regional politics, including local councils and other institutions with policy-making powers, as well as social movements and the civil society.

A relevant case refers to the protests on March 8, International Women's Day, organized yearly by local feminist groups. Despite their willingness to dispute the "face" and the agenda of the feminist movement, the Front's participation in the protest was rediscussed every year to exhaustion. As twenty-four-year-old affirmative action activist Taina Santos explained, participating in those events "meant arguing all the time": activists felt exotified, feared, and ostracized by the comments on topics like affirmative actions and suggestions that Black feminists come to the protest wearing traditional garments of Afro-Brazilian religions to spruce up the demonstration. Exhausted and enraged with the demands to constantly prove themselves capable of participating in political deliberation, they needed a space to "withdraw" and to "think calmly . . . and feel stronger to dispute these psychologically exhausting political spaces," as twenty-six-year-old political scientist Sidélia Silva explained.[9] They also had issues with the decision processes that they saw as centralizing and hierarchical, and the power division that privileged long-standing groups with more resources and whose relations with political parties, the state, or the church resulted in rigid and bureaucratic politics with needless rules and little space for making creative alliances and rethinking categories and strategies. Younger activists found these spaces particularly inaccessible and were more resentful of these problems. Joining forces with other groups excluded from the feminist protests, like transsexual women and sex workers, the Front continued to participate in the joint protests but expanded its own activities on March 8 to include activities in a local women's prison, an experience that placed incarcerated women's concerns and needs at the top of the articulation's agenda. Eventually, the organization began separate activities on the date.

Many activists often claimed that they had learned their most valuable lessons in feminism from women who never understood themselves as feminists like their mothers, aunts, or grandmothers. Such women had fought hard for their families and defied the social norms of their times to care for their children and communities in the face of all adversities and hardship. Most of the older women became feminists during their life experiences and struggles. By challenging the limits of what being a feminist means, they particularized these meanings and repositioned difference. In other words, by building a definition of feminism on the grounds of their own experience, they revealed the race, class, religion, and sexuality subtexts in the previous definitions and took possession of a self-defined modality of feminism; as a result, what was understood as "feminism" came to be framed as "traditional" or "white feminism."

As the objectives in the Front's manifesto were further elaborated and developed in practice, they constituted another source of controversy. For instance, while younger activists commonly reflected on the "discovery" or "uncovering" of their identities as Black women, women in their fifties or older had been educated on their racial identity from early on and had a strong perception of racism and the overt segregation that their parents and relatives had lived through. Contraposing common conceptions of a lack of racial identification in the country, these activists are "far from confused about the validity of Blackness as a social category, which is often debated among Brazilian and Brazilianist scholars alike" (Perry 2016, 106). Activists in their late thirties and forties, also familiar with their racial identities from early on, resented the co-optation and depoliticization of modes of expression like hip-hop that had assisted the constitution of their political subjectivities. Despite shared perceptions of stereotypes and how these limited Black women's social experiences, political interpretations of these issues were also varied. More experienced women rejected a vocabulary of suffering and mobilized images of themselves as self-sufficient and warriors. Younger women, in turn, located their identities within episodes of pain and loneliness, framing the individual-society entanglement from a subjective, almost psychoanalytic perspective. Finally, in other situations, like the debates on class and work, clashes were related to the movement's strategies, priorities, and alignments. One of the most experienced activists, Magali Mendes, explored these issues when speaking to an audience of Black university students:

> We cannot think about *the Black woman,* about us, without considering a category of 8 million women, the domestic workers.... So, since they are organized, we need to think about how we as Black women can collaborate with their struggle and their agenda.... This is our struggle.... So, we must take this struggle and incorporate it as our own! It is a historical struggle, and it hasn't ended, it has its contradictions—because you're talking about affirmative action, the university, but 8 million women are still domestic workers and a big part of them is illiterate. So, how do we join these two things? This is our challenge as Black women.[10]

As her speech indicates, activists from previous generations and especially women in trade unions opposed what they perceived as a lack of support for the needs of poor workers and the prioritization of middle-class educated women's agendas, which depoliticized Black feminism and served capitalist markets.

The changing demographics of the university places it at a crossroads where various divergences meet, leading to new research agendas (Lima 2010), as well as demands for "purposeful research" and a "stimulus against intellectualism" on the part of movements. The more experienced activists in the Front were intensely critical of some of the work performed by young researchers, which they saw as disconnected from the grass roots and too focused on the aesthetic, affective, and psychological aspects of Black women's experiences. However, younger activists' experiences in the university—being discriminated against by colleagues and teachers, institutional disadvantage, bureaucratic persecution, and the liminary position they came to occupy within their communities after going to the university—were constitutive of such psychological suffering and pessimism and were explained and understood alongside these reflections. This division was also clear in activists' self-reference as "domestics and doctors" in good-humored but suggestive description of their alliance. During the period that the articulation lasted, some activists formed spaces to unite their experiences in the university and as activists—such as an activist graduate course in African heritage—and partnerships in research and teaching.

Other forms of taking up this "permanent exercise of dealing with diversity," as the activist frequently described the Front's challenges and richness, included dynamics with participative methodologies and extensive debates. Each monthly meeting was oriented by a theme question that built on previous meetings or on recent discussions or events, like "Why do we march?" and "Why is our march permanent?" These questions demarcated the moments and priorities of the Front's actions, provided a starting point for collective reflections, and structured the conversation. "We know what separates us. What unites us as Black women?" became a milestone and was often brought to the conversation, helping activists regroup and reorganize. When intergenerational conflicts seemed excessive, for instance, the question helped to recall their fruitful cooperation counting on the experience and reputation of older activists and the younger generation's ability to mobilize large audiences, which together had worked to legitimate their activities in the eyes of more traditional political actors in the city.

The Front also built on the ideas of "alliances" and "shared responsibilities," conveying an intersectional politics of producing encounters and agendas between different groups. These ideas are synthesized in the general commitment expected from all to learn about the social struggles involved in the organization and take responsibility for dismantling different forms of oppression, regardless of being directly affected by them. It implied both debating their shared circumstances and forming solidarity to overcome limitations in social transformation in a "prefigurative" mode, that is, by "[anticipating] or [enacting] some feature of an 'alternative world' in the present, as though it has already been achieved" (Yates 2015, 4). As thirty-three-year-old anthropologist Mariana Morais explained, that meant breaking with conventional patterns of socialization and relations to stimulate cultural and social transformation through their own present actions:

> We have been fighting this silly sexist idea that women compete and don't help one another.... All the allies who come here come to add something, to participate, knowing that they come *as allies* and this entails responsibilities: if we need to go to Brasília, the allies are on call to keep things going with the kids, ensuring backstage work during our meetings. They work the kitchen all day long and take care of the kids. Otherwise, we are always faced with the same question, divided.... If you're in the kitchen, you can't be in the meeting talking.[11]

As sixty-one-year-old popular educator and trade unionist Regina Teodoro described them, such practices can be thought of as a "construction of equality in practice," implicating the larger political community in an experimental fashion. By doing so, they overcome the usual limitations the activists—and a great number of Black women—face when participating in politics. Mentioning "white" and "academic" feminists alongside Black activists, institutional actors, and communities, Mariana went on to explain that anyone can become an ally, as the crucial element for alliances is the political commitment to disturbing deep-seated behavior and interactions that reproduce inequality and sharing accessed spaces of power and resources.

Conclusion

This chapter presents a transversal perspective on Brazilian Black feminist movements, arguing that the movements' pluralization and heterogeneity in the last decades led to new understandings and forms of "dealing with" difference that have important implications for the movement's political subjectivity and, as I discussed in more detail, for the relations among activists and organizations, in which commitments, pacts, debates, and other "diversity exercises" prevail.

Building on the victories and experiences of previous political cycles, the strategies of various Black feminist and Black women's movements in recent times constitute forms of opposing conservative state violence. They do so by reaffirming and connecting different political identities—feminists, Black activists, LGBTQIA+ and working-class activists, and others—that are in contradiction with and confront homogenizing conservative discourses and the country's traditional heterophobic racism (Guimarães 1995), that repudiates difference and affirms the full equivalence between the lives of white and Black people in Brazil, overlooking enormous inequality and violence.

Experiences like the Black Women's Front, marches, and recent collective candidatures and mandates (Rodrigues and Freitas 2021) not only testify to the growth and pluralization of Black women's movements but set up different forms of experimenting and doing politics. In these forms, the discursive and effective repositioning of difference both within and outside the movement works to radically expand representation. With differences taken as starting points for spaces of formation, histories, struggles, and problems can be shared and readdressed as exercises of alignment that invigorate, complicate, and democratize the movements' inner dynamics.

Notes

1 Calculation based on 2015 data from the website *Retrato das Desigualdades de Gênero e Raça*. https://www.ipea.gov.br/retrato/
2 See T. Santos (2008); Perry and Sotero (2019); and Sotero, in this volume.
3 Maroons (*quilombolas*) are rural Black communities formed by slaves who ran away from the plantations in the colonial period, a large number of which remain. Given their original purpose as escape-and-hiding places for fugitives, *quilombos* (maroonages) are usually located in remote places, especially in vast regions such as the states in the Amazonian region.
4 A notable exception is Lélia Gonzalez, who wrote of the meeting and conflicts in it, "If we are committed to a project of social transformation, we cannot concede to ideological postures of exclusion that privilege only one aspect of our lived realities. When we claim our difference as Black women, as amefricanas, we do so with bodies that are marked by economic exploitation, as well as racial and sexual subordination. For that reason, we carry everyone's freedom with us" (1988, 363).
5 Only in SEPPIR, three important activists of the Black woman's movements, Matilde Ribeiro (2003–2008), Luiza Bairros (2011–2015), and Nilma Lino Gomes (2015), acted as ministers.
6 The national law of affirmative action was sanctioned in 2012, but the first public universities to enact such policies in their selection processes did so in 2003. Many others followed soon. See Sotero (2013).
7 For more details and a discussion, see Caldwell et al. (2019).
8 See Pereira and Rodrigues, in this volume; see Silva (2019).
9 Formation I, October 10, 2016.
10 Conference Day on the Rights of Black Women, Universidade Estadual de Campinas, 2017.
11 Mariana Morais, Sarau das Aliadas, October 2016.

References

Abdalla, Julia S. 2020. *Alianças, Encontros e Margens: Feminismos Negros e Interseccionalidade na Frente de Mulheres Negras de Campinas e Região*. PhD diss., University of Campinas, Brazil.

Alvarez, Sonia. 2012. "Feminismos e Antirracismo: Entraves e Intersecções; Entrevista com Luiza Bairros." *Revista Estudos Feministas* 20, no. 3: 833–850.

———. 2014. "Para Além da Sociedade Civil: Reflexões sobre o Campo Feminista." *Cadernos Pagu* 43: 13–56.

Bringel, Breno. 2018. "Mudanças no Ativismo Contemporâneo: Controvérsias, Diálogos e Tendências. In *A Luta Popular Urbana por seus Protagonistas: Direito à Cidade, Direitos nas Cidades*, edited by FASE, 20–29. Rio de Janeiro: FASE.

———. "Transnational Black Feminism in the 21st Century." In *New Social Movements in the African Diaspora: Challenging Global Apartheid*, edited by Leith Mullings and Manning Marable, 105–121. New York: Palgrave Macmillan.

Caldwell, Kia L., Wendi Muse, Tianna Paschel, Keisha-Khan Y. Perry, Christen Smith, and Erica Williams. 2019. "On the Imperative of Transnational Solidarity: A U.S. Black Feminist Statement on the Assassination of Marielle Franco." *The Black Scholar*, March 23. www.theblackscholar.org/on-the-imperative-of-transnational-solidarity-a-u-s-black-feminist-statement-on-the-assassination-of-marielle-franco/.

Cardoso, Claudia P. 2012. *Outras Falas: Feminismos na Perspectiva de Mulheres Negras Brasileiras*. PhD diss., Universidade Federal da Bahia, Brazil.

Carmo, Íris N. do. 2018. *O rolê Feminista: Autonomia, Horizontalidade e Produção de Sujeito no Campo Feminista Contemporâneo*. PhD diss., University of Campinas, Brazil.

Facchini, Regina, Íris do Carmo, and Stephanie Lima. 2020. "Movimentos Seminista, Negro e LGBTI no Brasil: Sujeitos, Teias e Enquadramentos." *Educação e Sociedade* 41: 1–22.

Figueiredo, Ângela. 2018. "Perspectivas e Contribuições das Organizações de Mulheres Negras e Feministas Negras contra o Racismo e o Sexismo na Sociedade Brasileira." *Direito & Práxis* 9, no. 2: 1080–1099.

Gomes, Carla C. 2018. *Corpo, Emoção e Identidade no Campo Feminista Contemporâneo Brasileiro: A Marcha das Vadias do Rio de Janeiro*. PhD diss., Federal University of Rio de Janeiro.

Gonzalez, Lélia. 1988. "A Importância da Organização da Mulher Negra no Processo de Transformação Social." *Lélia Gonzalez. Primavera Para as Rosas Negras* [2018]. São Paulo: UCPA Editora.

Guimarães, Antônio S. A. 1995. "Racismo e Antirracismo no Brasil." *Novos Estudos* 43 (November): 26–44.

Hill Collins, Patricia, and Sirma Bilge. 2016. *Intersectionality*. Cambridge: Polity Press.

IPEA (Instituto de Pesquisa Econômica Avançada). 2021. "Retratos das Desigualdades de Gênero e Raça." www.ipea.gov.br/retrato/apresentacao.html.

Lemos, Rosália. 1997. *Feminismo Negro em Construção: A Organização do Movimento de Mulheres Negras do Rio de Janeiro*. Master's thesis, Federal do Rio de Janeiro.

———. 2016. *Do Estatuto da Igualdade Racial à Marcha de Mulheres Negras 2015: Uma Análise das Feministas Negras Brasileiras Sobre Políticas Públicas*. PhD diss., Universidade Federal Fluminense, Niterói, Brazil.

Lima, Márcia. 2010. "Desigualdades raciais e políticas públicas: ações afirmativas no governo Lula". *Novos Estudos CEBRAP*, no. 87: 77–95.

Lima, Stephanie. 2020. *A Gente não é Só Negro! Interseccionalidade, Experiência e Afetos na Ação Política de Negros Universitários*. PhD diss., University of Campinas, Brazil.

Matos, Marlise, and Sonia Alvarez. 2018. *Quem são as mulheres das políticas para as mulheres no Brasil?* Porto Alegre, Brazil: Zouk.

Moreira, Núbia R. 2007. *O Feminismo Negro Brasileiro: Um Estudo do Movimento de Mulheres Negras no Rio de Janeiro e São Paulo.* Master's thesis, University of Campinas, Brazil.

Perry, Keisha-Khan. 2016. "Geographies of Power: Black Women Mobilizing Intersectionality in Brazil." *Meridians* 14, no. 1: 94–120.

Ribeiro, Matilde. 1995. "Mulheres Negras de Bertioga a Beijing." *Revista Estudos Feministas* 3, no. 2: 446–457.

Rios, Flávia. 2017. "A Cidadania Imaginada pelas Mulheres Afro-brasileiras: Da Ditadura Militar à Democracia." In *50 anos de feminismo: Argentina, Brasil e Chile*, edited by Eva Blay and Lucia Avelar, 227–255. São Paulo: Edusp.

———. 2019. "Antirracismo, Movimentos Sociais e Estado (1985–2016)." In *Movimentos Sociais e Institucionalização: Políticas Sociais, Raça e Gênero no Brasil Pós-transição*, edited by Adrian G. Lavalle, Euzeneia Carlos, Monika Dowbor, and José Szwako, 255–285. Rio de Janeiro: Editora da Uerj.

Rios, Flávia, and Regimeire Maciel. 2018. "Feminismo Negro Brasileiro em Três Tempos." *Labrys, études Féministes/ Estudos Feministas* 1 (June): 120–140. www.labrys.net.br/labrys31/black/flavia.htm.

Rodrigues, Cristiano. 2006. "As Fronteiras entre Raça e Gênero na Cena Pública Brasileira: Um Estudo da Construção da Identidade Coletiva do Movimento de Mulheres Negras." Master's thesis, Universidade Federal de Minas Gerais, Belo Horizonte, Brazil.

Rodrigues, Cristiano, and Viviane G. Freitas. 2021. "Ativismo Feminista Negro no Brasil: Do Movimento de Mulheres Negras ao Feminismo Interseccional." *Revista Brasileira de Ciência Política* 34: 1–54. www.scielo.br/j/rbcpol/a/NFdhTdVVLSRPHzdDzVpBYMq/?lang=pt.

Roland, Edna. 2000. "O Movimento de Mulheres Negras Brasileiras: Desafios e Perspectivas." In *Tirando a Máscara: Ensaios Sobre o Racismo no Brasil*, edited by Antonio Sérgio Guimarães and Lynn Huntley, 237–256. São Paulo: Paz e Terra.

Santana, Bianca. 2017. "Sobrevivente, Testemunha e Porta-voz." (Interview with Sueli Carneiro). *Revista Cult*, May 9. https://revistacult.uol.com.br/home/sueli-carneiro-sobrevivente-testemunha-e-porta-voz/.

Santos, Sonia B. 2008. "Brazilian Black Women's NGOs and Their Struggles in the Area of Sexual and Reproductive Health: Experiences, Resistance, and Politics." PhD diss., University of Texas.

Silva, Gleicy M. 2019. "Corpo, Política e Emoção: Feminismos, Estética e Sonsumo entre Mulheres Negras." *Horizontes Antropológicos* 25, no. 54: 173–201.

Silva, Joselina. 2014. "O I Encontro Nacional de Mulheres Negras: O Pensamento das Feministas Negras na Década de 1980." In *O Movimento de Mulheres Negras: Escritos sobre os Sentidos de Democracia e Justiça Social no Brasil*, edited by Joselina da Silva and Amauri Mendes Pereira, 13–41. Belo Horizonte, Brazil: Editora Nandyala.

Sotero, Edilza C. 2013. "Transformações no Acesso ao Ensino Superior Brasileiro: Algumas Implicações para os Diferentes Grupos de Cor e Sexo." In *Dossiê Mulheres Negras: Retrato das Condições de Vida das Mulheres Negras no Brasil*, edited by Mariana Mazzini Marcondes, Luana Pinheiro, Cristina Queiroz, Ana Carolina Querino, and Danielle Valverde, 35–53. Brasília: IPEA.

Werneck, Jurema P. 2010. "Nossos Passos Vêm de Longe! Movimentos de Mulheres Negras e Estratégias Políticas contra o Sexismo e o Racismo." *Revista da ABPN* 1, no. 1: 8–17.

Yates, Luke. 2015. "Rethinking Prefiguration: Alternatives, Micropolitics and Goals in Social Movements." *Social Movement Studies* 14, no. 1: 1–21.

Zanoli, Vinícius. 2020. *Bradando Contra Todas as Opressões! Ativismos LGBT, Negros, Populares e Periféricos em Relação*. Salvador, Brazil: Editora Devires.

5

"This Isn't to Get Rich"

• • • • • • • • • • • • • • • • • • • •

Double Morality and Black
Women Private Tutors in Cuba

ANGELA CRUMDY

"Pretty. I teach that a lot. Pretty is '*bonito*,' but it can also be used for many things. Pretty soon to say *muy pronto*. Pretty near *muy cerca*. Pretty far *muy lejos*." Elena was a thin, seventy-eight-year-old, dark-skinned woman with an obvious knack for the English language. During our interview, she riffed off a list of idioms and book titles, crisscrossing between English and Spanish. Despite being retired, she spent most of her time tutoring English, caring for her sick older sister, and chasing after food and medicine once she was alerted that they were available in a certain part of the town—looking for "everything under the sun. *Todo pero en goticas*." Elena belonged to Cuba's burgeoning elderly population, and her example confirms that many of those who meet Cuba's retirement threshold must continue to bring in additional income to maintain their livelihoods and that of those around them.

In this chapter, I use a Black feminist anthropological lens to analyze the work behaviors of elderly Black women *repasadoras* (private tutors) in Cuba who subvert state laws while still upholding revolutionary values. These women demonstrate what is commonly referred to as *doble moral* (double morality), contradictory logics often motivated by dire socioeconomic constraints that lead Cubans to engage in behaviors that go against the official rhetoric about what is considered lawful and acceptable. It is not clear whether clients know if their tutors are unregistered with the Cuban state; however, given the ubiquity of double morality, it is likely that clients do not care. Scholars of Cuba have documented double morality in studies with communities ranging from Cuban youth (Blum 2011) to religious leaders (Wirtz 20014). Private tutoring is an ideal space to explore double morality because while education is one of Cuba's most lauded institutions, the system is known to be increasingly more corrupt in recent years due to the highly competitive college entrance exams (Castro Ruz 2013). I argue that to further understandings of double morality, rather than just document that double morality exists, scholars should attend to the mechanisms Cuban people use to mitigate the contradictions they experience. In doing so, studies can reveal more about how double morality manifests at the individual level in relation to subjective identities. The logic expressed by Black women tutors regarding their work in the informal sector reflects the ideologies of Cuba's Black aging population: although these women are engaging in unauthorized tutoring, they still uphold socialist, revolutionary, community-oriented values that are informed by their experiences coming of age during the Revolution initiated in 1959. Despite not being officially authorized to tutor, Black women tutors reconcile their work status by expressing reverence for the revolution, emphasizing their need to meet their necessities, using fair pricing, and demonstrating a commitment to future generations.

Understanding Double Morality within the Context of Post-Special Period Cuba

In the early 1990s, the near-decade-long span of economic hardship known as the Special Period in Times of Peace fundamentally changed Cuban society and made double morality a common way of life. The dissolution of the Soviet bloc meant that Cuba lost one of its main trading partners and the country's ability to sustain itself economically. Basic food supplies disappeared from shelves (Garth 2020) and fuel shortages caused massive blackouts and forced people to find alternative sources of transportation including bicycles and horse-drawn carriages. Anthropologist Kristina Wirtz writes that because of the economic hardships, Cubans of all parts of society coped "by 'inventing' (their word) often morally dubious or illegal private, entrepreneurial activities to generate income in dollars, often by offering services to tourists: operating private taxis, offering unlicensed rooms-for-rent, opening speakeasy-like private restaurants, and even engaging in *jineterismo* (hustling and prostitution)" (2014, 414). These activities, while unauthorized, allowed people to earn some type of income when the state could no longer provide for them. Alongside these challenges, there was also a resurgence of race- and class-based cleavages in

Cuban society reminiscent of prerevolutionary times, when racial segregation was common and social mobility for people of color was limited. The Special Period made financial stability particularly precarious for Cubans of color, who were largely excluded from work in the tourist sector and who receive only one-third of the remittances sent to their white counterparts (Sawyer 2006). The Special Period undoubtedly caused a countrywide calamity; however, it had an especially acute impact on the Black community that brought forth historically rooted inequities.

In 1993, amid the Special Period, the government legalized 135 self-employment (*cuentapropismo*) options primarily in repair, agriculture, and transportation to allow citizens to meet the demands that state institutions could no longer fulfill. Income-generating opportunities corresponding with the opening of the country to foreign tourism (to attract much-needed income) grew to encompass an array of jobs like private taxi driver, home restaurant operator, and artisanal craft vendor. The state also included private tutoring as an approved type of entrepreneurship for the first time in 2010, after having outlawed it during the 1959 Revolution.[1] In exchange for the ability to work, *cuentapropistas* (self-employed individuals) are expected to pay taxes on their earnings, pay license fees, and purchase their supplies from the Cuban government. Registered cuentapropistas are required to pay a set tax every month irrespective of whether they have brought in any income that month. Scholar of social mobility and women's labor in the Global South Daliany Jerónimo Kersh (2019) suggests that while these fees are a way for the state to recuperate monies that would otherwise be lost to the underground economy, they can also be a deterrent to licensure. It was commonplace for people, especially those with small enterprises, to work informally to avoid additional fees and maximize their profit.

Initially, as private enterprises were authorized, there was an especially strong stigma associated with being a cuentapropista because it countered socialist logics condemning making an earning off of one's fellow country person. One of the women participants in Jerónimo Kersh's (2019) study of Cuban women's work practices during the 1990s noted, "I didn't take money from anyone: they gave it to me voluntarily.... It wasn't classed as an immoral thing. It would have been illegal if I robbed from the state and sold things.... Many people got rich doing things they shouldn't have been doing" (142). As a result, Jerónimo Kersh's respondents often described their work as legal even if it technically was not and emphasized that this work was neither unethical nor lucrative, which are characteristics of typically associated with cuentapropista work.

However, private enterprise has become more commonly accepted as an increasing number of people work as private taxi drivers, private bed-and-breakfast hosts, and artisans. According to Cuban feminist economist

Teresa Lara Junco (2021), women make up approximately one-third of registered cuentapropistas, but they are more likely to be hired by others, whereas men are more likely to own their own business. Women who work as cuentapropistas, whether registered or not, often take on feminized, domestic work such as sewing, cleaning, beauty, cooking, cleaning, and caring for children and elders. Tutoring is just one of the many ways Cuban women have pursued entrepreneurial efforts beyond the traditional jobs provided by the state.

Studying Black Women Tutors in Cuba

In this chapter, I present the results from ethnographic research, including participant observation and open-ended interviews, conducted from 2018 to 2019 with four Black women repasadoras aged seventy years and older. In Cuba, like much of Latin America, racial identification is quite complex, and even within the broad categories of white, Black, and mestizx (mixed race), there is great variation depending on multiple physical characteristics including skin tone, hair texture and color, and others. The women I interviewed consented to participate in a study about the experiences of *mujeres negras* (Black women) and thus self-identified as such. The most recent census data collected in 2012 documented the Cuban population as follows: white 64.1 percent, Black 9.3 percent, and mestizo (mixed race) 26.6 percent (*Oficina Nacional De Estadística e Información* 2014, 81). However, given suggestions that the published demographic information is an attempt by the government to whiten the nation, other sources estimate the non-white population to be at least half if not the majority of the population (Moore 2019; Booker and Daché 2021).

My introduction to my research participants was facilitated by my Spanish teacher, whom I came to know over the course of the three years that I visited Cuba for dissertation research. Through snowball sampling, I met other Black women whom my instructor knew intimately or by casual acquaintance. Elena (seventy-eight), from the introduction, was my Spanish teacher's sister-in-law and a retired receptionist who taught English. Regina (seventy-three) was my Spanish teacher's former colleague who was a retired, university-trained foreign language instructor with a command of Russian and English. They were longtime friends who studied Russian together in the Soviet Union after participating in the 1961 Literacy Campaign. Gladys (seventy-three), a neighbor from across the street, was a full-time primary school teacher who tutored students in the evenings. Finally, Susana (seventy), the only woman in the study who did not reside in Havana but in Guantánamo, was a retired primary school teacher introduced to me by one of my Spanish teacher's former students. The last two women provided lessons in all core subjects (Spanish, history, math, and social studies) much like they would during formal classroom instruction at the primary level. Two of the women were in long-term relationships, which aligns with the national average rate of pairings: 49.9 percent of women aged sixty to seventy-four are either married or in conjugal unions (*Oficina Nacional De Estadística e Información* et al. 2019, 41). By the year 2025, when nearly 25 percent of the country's population will be over sixty years of age, Cuba is projected to be the country with the highest population of elderly people in Latin America (Bautista et al. 2020, 1). Relevant to this study is that women make up the greater share of those over sixty; in 2016, women made up 53.4 percent and men 46.8 percent of the country's elder population. At the time of my research in 2019, the national average for the monthly pension was 362 pesos or $14 USD (*Oficina Nacional De Estadística e Información* 2021).[2] All the women came to private tutoring work in different ways and had various levels of formal training; however, the animating factor shared among all of them was a desire to earn extra income. Despite their being well over sixty, the state's minimum retirement age for women, this study shows how income-generating work was justified for these women to maintain a decent quality of life in their old age.[3]

This chapter employs a Black feminist anthropological lens to understanding Black women's experiences as unauthorized tutors. Succinctly put, "Black feminist anthropological theory asserts that by making the complex intersection of gender, race, and class the foundational component of this scholarship, followers gain a different and ... fuller understanding of how Black women's lives (including our own) are constituted by structural forces" (McClaurin 2001, 19). This chapter is specifically informed by scholarship that emphasizes the context that shapes how and why people work, including their social networks, education levels, and environment, all of which influence the socially reproductive realities of Black working women (Barnes 2015; Mullings and Wali 2001). Regionally specific ethnographies are instructive because they consider the ways that women define the meaning of their work and locate the instances of agentive action even within oppressive working circumstances (Bolles 2021; Freeman 2000; Prentice 2015; Ulysse 2007). Black women are historically more likely to work outside of the home in Cuba and elsewhere in comparison to their white counterparts (Davis 1983; Stoner 1991). Further, Cuban anthropologist María Ileana Faguagua notes that Black Cuban women have a long history not only of working but also of holding multiple jobs (Center for Democracy 2013, 52). Thus, critical feminist ethnography can reveal *how* these women understand their labor and the negotiations they make on a daily basis. The Black women in this study utilized four specific means to reconcile their double morality: expressing reverence for the revolution, emphasizing that earnings go toward meeting personal needs, using a sliding scale for payment, and investing in future generations.

Reverence for the Revolution

Despite knowingly subverting state laws, the Black women I interviewed expressed reverence to the 1959 Cuban Revolution for providing them with the skills that are now sustaining them at this later stage in life. People who came of age in the wake of the reforms instituted by the revolutionary government were likely influenced by its ideologies about the significance of work. Revolutionary values praised a socialist work ethic, which paired work with education and emphasized individual effort for the collective good. Attributed to key figures in the Cuban Revolution, Che Guevara's 1965 concept of the *hombre nuevo* or the "new man" envisioned that Cubans would develop the proper political and social dispositions described as *"conciencia"* (consciousness) to advance the revolution (Blum 2008, 206). The new woman ideology "encouraged women to work outside of the home, study, and participate in political organizing to be deemed a productive member of society. She would replace her predecessor, who was often depicted as being "the older housewife, the woman who neither studied nor worked, who defended her own family's interests against those of the collective" (Chase 2015, 168). Having been exposed to this rhetoric for most of their lifetime, it makes sense that Black women tutors would derive a strong sense of identity and worth from their work. As such, the decision to retire would not be taken lightly. Jerónimo Kersh (2019) found that respondents associated their work with a sense of usefulness and identity and that they often worked far beyond the retirement age. Being the first generation of professionalized women encouraged to work outside of the home, these women also had a unique social reproductive burden in that they had to simultaneously care for ailing parents and children while also maintaining a job (Andaya 2014; Núñez Sarmiento 2010).

Given their awareness of the inequities that preceded the revolution, the women in my study expressed deep admiration for Fidel Castro, the national leader from 1959 to 2011 who died three years prior to my fieldwork period. Their memories and reverence for him were evinced not only in their words but in their tone, with some even being on the brink of tears as they spoke about how drastically their lives were changed by his leadership. Given their age, the women had an awareness of the limited work possibilities that were previously available to people like their parents and how inaccessible education was for people of their race and class before the revolution. Susana, a retired primary school teacher with over forty years of experience, began her teaching career at the age of twelve as a *brigadista* (youth volunteer) in the 1961 Literacy Campaign, a countrywide effort that brought together youth and trained professionals to eradicate illiteracy on the island.[4] She came from a working-class family with four children. Her father sold flowers, but the family lived off of her mother's earnings as a dressmaker. Reflecting on her own career, Susana stated,

> I am extremely grateful to the revolution since before the revolutionary triumph no president had taken care of improving the standard of living of the population. I also thank Fidel Castro Ruz very much for all his efforts, and it hurt a lot when he passed away. I think we will never have another president like him. He worried about the poor even though he had no need because his family had money. In fact, if Fidel had not sacrificed himself and fought for the people until he achieved the triumph of the revolution, neither I, nor the Blacks of Cuba, nor the poor, would have had any right. Before the triumph of the revolution, the people suffered from unemployment, poverty, exploitation and abuse, but the leaders and the well-off lived well.

Susana expressed a deep appreciation for the ways that the revolution, and Fidel Castro in particular, took an interest in the most disadvantaged of Cuban society. Castro was a trained lawyer, and for this reason, she appreciates his ability to act on the behalf of those who had less social standing. Early in the revolution, reforms were made to address some of the social inequities that disproportionality impacted poor and people of color such as nationalizing private schools, desegregating recreational facilities, and creating a national registry of anonymous job seekers which took the decision-making power away from unions and employers (de la Fuente 2001). For Susana, she seemed exceptionally grateful to Fidel Castro and the revolution for changing her life and that of generations to follow.

This reverential sentiment was echoed by Gladys, a seventy-three-year-old woman with a combined earning strategy wherein she worked as a full-time primary school teacher *and* private tutor during the week.[5] Gladys understood the significance of her career within the broader span of racial oppression in Cuba over the course of the last century. Although too young to teach prior to the revolution, Gladys witnessed firsthand how the rampant graft and nepotism of prerevolutionary times kept poor people and people of color from obtaining employment in the public school system. Gladys's aunt was denied a teaching position in the public school system, although qualified, because it was sold to a politician's daughter.[6] Subsequently, she opted to teach in a neighborhood school outside of the formal school district's jurisdiction. As a young person, Gladys participated in the 1961 Literacy Campaign and then started her teaching career as an assistant before becoming a credentialed classroom teacher. She acknowledged that her early experiences were an asset to her throughout her career. Speaking on the early stages of her professional life, she noted,

> The pedagogical assistants of that time were not like those of now. We were given dance, theater, etc. That is why besides being a teacher, I am prepared to do many more things. I told the school principal that I no longer wanted to be an assistant but a teacher. The director helped me and sent me to follow up with the community members as a kind of training to get to know how classes were taught. At that time, I met my current husband, who was an engineer. When he finished engineering, he had to perform his social service in Motembo, Corralillo, and I accompanied him. I already had two daughters. There, I worked in a rural school where all grades were taught. Thanks to that experience, I can now tutor students of different grades at the same time.

Gladys expressed gratitude for the various opportunities she had to learn and teach during the early years of the revolution. The professional position that was unfairly denied to her aunt was a position that Gladys excelled in thanks to the support offered by the revolution and her fellow educators. She credits her earlier experiences teaching in a rural school with multiple grades for her ability to do the same as part of her repasando work.

Unlike the other women in this study, Elena did not have formal training in teaching. She spent the majority of her professional life working as a receptionist, but she still credits the revolution with helping her to have marketable skills that she now used as a private tutor. Elena came to private tutoring as someone with a penchant for the English language—especially idioms. She began giving lessons approximately three years before we met and was currently tutoring one student who attended the Lenin School, a boarding school for academically gifted students.[7] Prior to the revolution, Elena worked as a maid in her late teen years, a position that was held by many women of color at the time. When Fidel Castro and the revolution came to power, this type of domestic work was outlawed along with other occupations, like prostitution, for being considered undignified and outside of women's full potential. Cuban education ethnographer Denise Blum notes that by 1962, approximately 20,000 former domestic servants were taking night classes at schools established in the capital city of Havana and nearby districts. These courses generally included shorthand, typing, administration, commercial secretary, and driver training (Blum 2011, 65).[8] As a result of these reforms, Elena began work as a receptionist in Central Havana for a law firm, which she retired from at the age of fifty-eight. She stated, "There are many things that the revolution has achieved, and I am one of them. I spent a year on scholarship at the Hotel Nacional when I was studying to work in the bank, and I didn't have to pay anything. Where does that happen? In what country does that happen? Much less for Black women." She viewed herself as the embodiment of the revolution's exceptionalism because someone like her benefited from the reforms without having to do anything in return. Free

English training was also something that she appreciated and pursued with enthusiasm. For three years, Elena finished her work at the office at 5 P.M. and then traveled fifteen minutes to her classes at the Julio Antonio Mella language school. She felt certain that she was now benefiting from that sacrifice she made many years ago.

> The only thing that you have to do is be a good student. Be disciplined, but you don't have to pay, the education doesn't cost [anything]. . . . Those three years that I was at Antonio Mella didn't cost me a cent. I didn't pay absolutely anything, including for the books they gave me, but when I finished, I had to give them back for those that were coming after me. Those three years, I didn't have to pay absolutely anything for English classes. It's like medicine here in Cuba, here the medicine doesn't cost [anything]. I'm going to inject my sister [or] I need a shot, if the nurse has to go to the home, they go to the home. In other countries that costs.

The revolutionary reforms coupled with her persistent will and curiosity enabled Elena to transform her life from a maid to office personnel to private English tutor. Her acknowledgment that these offerings make Cuba distinct from other countries in the world shows the extent of how highly she regards these opportunities and her pride in her country. Collectively, these women expressed a strong reverence for the revolution because it afforded them monetizable skills and resources. These are the very skills that they now use to earn additional income that goes unreported to the state. Even though private tutoring work was not authorized, these women demonstrated that they had a work ethic that was still very much tied to the revolution and its values.

Teaching to Meet Personal Needs

Another way that Black women tutors made sense of their double morality was by emphasizing that their earnings went toward meeting their personal needs rather than extravagances. Many of them needed additional income because their retirement payments were not enough to meet their needs. In 2008, the national average monthly pension was 235 pesos/$10 USD (Mesa-Lago 2017, 113) and in 2013 it was approximately $20 USD (2017, 118), which was hardly enough to cover the basic needs of women and their households. Women commonly referenced food and transportation (to visit family members and to attend doctor visits) as the main ways they spent their earnings. Susana, a seventy-year-old "retired" primary school teacher in Guantánamo, stated that she kept up her teaching activities to fill in the shortcomings of her state retirement pension. When I interviewed her, she had nine tutoring students and jokingly noted that she had no interest in running a school and therefore did not want to take on any more students. Sitting at her dining room table, she assured me, "Actually, I didn't retire because I need to survive. Although my husband, and I are already retired, the checkbook is not enough, and we have to continue working in order to live. I give review sessions here in my house, and he is dedicated to cleaning industrial cooking machines and appliances." Susana understood herself to be in a pseudo-retirement not by choice but out of necessity.

This was similar to the situation of Regina, who also gave lessons as a way to mediate financial gaps. On the day that I interviewed Regina, she also had a doctor's appointment nearby. Transportation to appointments like this one were paid for through her private tutoring earnings. She stated, "[I tutor] in order to maintain myself, for my necessities.... This 2 CUC [Cuban convertible pesos] goes toward food... the bus sometimes... I'm very tired... and the collective taxis. If I have to go to the doctor like today, [my earnings] are for day-to-day expenses. This money is gone in a day. It's not that I'm going to become rich with this money." Her asking price for her tutoring services, 2 CUC, was a direct reflection of the market and price of goods at the time. Two CUC may not have been a fortune, but it still served a very important purpose. Arguably, being of retirement age did not signal the end of remunerated work but rather necessitated that people continue to work to supplement their monthly retirement pension. When women's private tutoring work is contextualized within a broader conversation about Cuba's economic state, it becomes clearer why these women would pursue additional sources of income at their age.

"This Isn't to Get Rich": An Ethical Approach to Determining Tutoring Rates

Double morality was also reconciled through Black women tutors' ethical approach to determining pricing, which was influenced by the deep disdain they expressed for the capitalist exploitation of the Republican period (1902–1958), as well as the economic turmoil caused by the economic embargo imposed by the United States. That the women took a less market-driven approach to setting their tutoring rates demonstrates a socialist orientation even within the context of entrepreneurial work. In practice, women upheld their ideals by setting a fair, fixed price or offering a sliding scale based on the financial standing of the student's family. The precarity of tutors' income did not encourage women to increase their prices even though the number of students they had could fluctuate depending on the point in the school year. Susana told me that with her students she charged "depending on the economic situation of the child. For example, if the child comes from a family with financial difficulties I charge twenty-five pesos, but if your family has possibilities, I charge forty."

For her, it was important to determine her pricing on an individualized basis by accounting for what she thought the family could comfortably afford. Both Regina and Elena, however, had a fixed rate of 2 CUC per session.[9] They generally taught older students and subjects that were more directly related to college admissions and/or attaining a job, so this may explain the fixedness of the price. Still, there were ethical considerations at play. Regina, after being told that most other people were charging 10 CUC, doubled down to say, "Two CUC. I can't charge any more or any less. . . . If a pound of meat costs 50 MN [moneda nacional, or Cuban pesos], why [charge less] if I'm going to give you knowledge that is for your entire life? I can't charge more because here. . . . Why am I going to charge 3 or 4 CUC? Two CUC because I have to give them photocopies, and furthermore, it's a specialty not a core subject. English is a specialty; Italian is a specialty as well as Russian." Although tutors took up this extra work to offset the rising cost of living, Regina felt that her rates fairly reflected the price of goods and materials at the time, and she wasn't interested in increasing them.

While there was an economic drive behind tutoring work, women did put limits on what they were willing to do for money. Some implemented boundaries, like in the case of Susana, who limited the number of students she was willing to work with. Others were willing to discontinue working with certain clients and forfeit their earnings altogether because they felt that their integrity as an educator was being compromised and their overall love for the topic was infringed upon by the working conditions. Several of the women spoke about the need to stay mentally active to ward off Alzheimer's disease and recognized it would be counterproductive to take on stressful work that would exacerbate already existing health issues. In light of the results of the "National Survey of Aging", which revealed that 80 percent of the elderly suffered from a chronic illness and that women suffered more so than men (Oficina Nacional de Estadísticas e Información, in Acosta 2017), the boundaries and limits women set for their tutoring work made sense. Elena provided a pointed example of how she decided to forgo a high-paying job to maintain her peace of mind. After being asked what qualities an exemplary tutor should have, she shared the following anecdote:

> The first thing, is what I told you, is that one likes what they are doing, that they are formal. By any means that they can see that the student is interested because if the student is uninterested. . . . I don't like to teach that way.
>
> Why am I telling you this? Because I started teaching classes with a little boy over there in Reparto Kohly. I would go to the house, he would come and the mother would say "Doni"—that's what she would call the boy: "Doni, here is the professor." He would come disenchanted, coming to the table and throwing his notebook. They paid me 10 CUC to go to his house. I preferred to

lose that 10 CUC, and I told the mother . . . "I'm going to lose the money that I use for my monthly 5 CUC bill, but I won't give classes to Doni, your son, because he isn't interested in English." . . . I was explaining something to him, "Look, Doni, it's like this," and he was sleeping. I was explaining, but his mind was somewhere else.

In this case, although she needed the money, Elena was willing to forgo the stress of working with a disinterested student. She did not intend to get rich but to make a modest income while sharing her expertise on a subject she genuinely enjoyed. These examples show that even though there is a tangible need for additional money, Black women tutors still wanted to maintain their dignity. They did so by charging ethical prices and refusing to compromise themselves to earn more irrespective of how much a client offered. Although they were pocketing the money that could have gone toward maintaining their credentials to work as official cuentapropistas, they still upheld socialist ideals, thereby maintaining a rather balanced approach to their double morality.

"This Can Help You Too": Private Tutoring as an Investment in Future Generations

Black women tutors also rationalized their entrepreneurial work as an investment in the future generation of Cuban professionals. Given that many of the women viewed their formal training as a pivotal offering of the revolution, they seemed eager to give that same type of long-term benefit to their students. This is demonstrated by Regina, who taught her two children English, and they now work in the tourism industry. She explained:

My children? I take the reins with my children. The oldest finished secondary and went to technical school as a technician in transportation operations and he completed his service, and he learned to drive. He matriculated to the university and passed the entrance exam, but at the same time I was giving him English classes at home, and he attended English classes. He passed the English exam. When he passed the exam, he went on to work on various jobs. . . . It's not necessary to go into those stories because they are very long . . . because there was a lack of people that spoke English and he had a good mastery of it. Afterward, he went to work as a taxi driver, as a chauffeur for Cuba Taxi, because he knows English.

My daughter, the same thing happened to her. She finished secondary, went to technical school and graduated with a degree in gastronomy. I gave her English classes, and now she is working in tourism. She's waiting to see if they call her to work in another hotel.

Regina used her own language skills to help support and guide the career paths of her children even though they each had training in technical fields. She felt that it was her responsibility to "take the reins" and ensure that her language skills were used to better herself *and* her family members. Tourism is a highly lucrative sector that largely relegates darker-skinned people to more menial and low-paying positions (Roland 2011), so her efforts to provide them with private language training was an investment into a professional future that might otherwise be unattainable. This investment could also benefit Regina when she is no longer able to work and is fully reliant on her children to take care of her, especially considering that state resources for the elderly (e.g., nursing homes and daily activities for the elderly) are scarce and the work of caring for elderly relatives often falls on the women in a family (Andaya 2014; Núnez Sarmiento 2001; Destremau 2018).

Elena was not as successful in getting some of the young people in her life to understand the value of learning English and broadening their career possibilities. One potential student shirked off private English lessons and the possibility of a new job that required a general knowledge of the language. Elena recounted their conversation:

> That's what I always [say], to everyone, to young women, "Look, study my dear, study. Study so that later when you are older . . . it's going to weigh on you." Not long ago, I saw a young woman, she was white, and she said that she couldn't get a job that they were offering at a hotel because she didn't know English and they asked her . . . I believe that she was twenty-three years old, yes, twenty-three. They asked her if she had an understanding of the English language. A while ago, I said "Girl, why don't you take English class?" [The girl responded,] "No, I'm not into that" [and I said,] "If you had taken English with me starting at the time that I told you, now you would be able to get that job."
> The youth have to take advantage of it. You have the fresh mind. I, with my age, have it—the students tell me, "Teacher, how is it that you remember all of this?" First, is because I like it. Second, is because I learned it well.

This recounting is significant because Elena drew a direct connection between the young woman's ability to speak English, her future job prospects, and long-term benefits. The perceived shortsightedness of the girl was disappointing because Elena knew that the possibilities for learning a new language become more onerous as someone ages. For this reason, she implored the girl to avail herself of the opportunity to learn a new language while she was still young.

Both Elena and Regina expressed a deep community-oriented commitment in their pedagogical practices, asserting that they want their students to walk away with practical skills that would equip them to communicate effectively in English, whether while engaging with tourists at a hotel or while driving a taxi. As such, Black women tutors did not merely view their students as customers but instead took a more profound interest in their professional wellbeing. In the same way that women tutors developed their language skills early on in life and were now using it to sustain them in their later years, they also wanted the same possibilities for the youth they encountered through their classes. Double morality thereby became more palatable because they were offering a service that would directly benefit their clients in the foreseeable future.

Concluding Remarks and Broader Implications

Attending to how Black women reconciled their contradictory orientations toward revolutionary values in a difficult socioeconomic atmosphere allows scholars to better understand double morality as an effective coping strategy. As Black women are part of Cuba's ever-growing elderly population, their decisions to engage in entrepreneurial work were informed by political, economic, and social circumstances, including the U.S. trade embargo, the aftermath of the Special Period, and racialized employment practices, that made meeting their basic needs difficult despite the monthly retirement pension they received from the state. The four Black women private tutors I interviewed exhibited a double morality, knowingly eluding the state's legal measures but doing so in a way that expressed gratitude toward the revolution, met personal needs without excess, charged clients in an ethical way, and expressed an interest in future generations. The experiences of these elderly Black women private tutors in Cuba speaks to broader conversations about double morality and Black women's work practices in Latin America and the Caribbean.

The study of double morality must attend to the heterogeneity of the Cuban population to understand how a conflicted morality manifests differently depending on the individual. The significance of the 1959 Cuban revolution for the Black women in my study suggests that in evaluating the meaning of work and the deployment of double morality, the historical context into which these women were born should also be taken into consideration when analyzing their ideologies surrounding work. The women I interviewed, born in the aftermath of the Cuban Revolution, perceived their tutoring activities as fitting into a broader socialist work ethic that benefited the collective community, even though they bypassed some of the legal parameters outlined by the state.

A focus on retirement-aged individuals is an opportunity to foreground the importance of age and generational differences within already-existing conversations about Black women and work in the region.[10] Age can influence what type of labor opportunities are available, one's physical ability to perform certain tasks, ability to travel, and so on. As such, what forms of economic employment do Black women in the Americas engage in when options are extremely limited but financial needs are still unmet? More research is needed to help answer this question. Furthermore, a focus on older women is a call to consider the protracted arc of Black women's work practices throughout their lifetime and not just when they are presumed to be of "working age." Retirement age is a recommendation that may not align with the lived realities of individuals who do not have the social or economic capital to rely on savings, remittances, the state, or family members to address their day-to-day needs. Only focusing on the labor of workers pre-retirement leads to the erasure of a key population who by the fact of their age, and the *expectation* that they are not working, are overlooked by scholars.

Black women like Elena, Regina, Gladys, and Susana used tutoring as a means to make ends meet but not to get rich. They aspired to help others develop marketable skills that would help them get jobs and to sustain themselves knowing intimately what it was like to struggle financially as an elder in Cuban society. They leveraged their instructional skills in a way that allowed them to embody parts of a revolutionary work ethic but also bypass state-mandated requirements so that they could keep the entirety of their earnings. The way that these women rationalized their double morality illustrates the extent people are willing to go, whether *muy lejos* (very far) or *muy cerca* (very close), to sustain their livelihoods.

Notes

1 In the early 2000s, private tutoring was described as a "world megatrend" (Baker and LeTendre 2005) and increases in this form of employment have been documented in other Post-Soviet states. See: DeYoung Alan J., et al 2006, Niyozov and Shamatov 2010, Silova 2009.
2 At the time of research, 2019, the exchange rate was approximately $1 USD to 1 Cuban convertible peso (CUC) to 25 Cuban pesos (CUP).
3 The official minimum retirement age in Cuba for women is sixty for women and sixty-five for men as determined in the 2009 Social Security Law 105/08 (Ponce-Laguardia 2020, 1).
4 The 1961 Literacy Campaign was a nationwide effort to eradicate illiteracy. Nearly 1.1 million people including youth and adults volunteered their time to teach Cubans in the countryside, in urban areas, and in the workplace. It is projected that they reduced the rate of illiteracy from 23.6 percent to 3.9 percent through this concerned effort (Blum 2011).
5 To read more about Cuban women's combined earning strategies, see Núñez Sarmiento (2001); Jerónimo Kersh (2019); and Center for Democracy in the Americas (2013).
6 In the 1940s, corruption was especially pervasive in the public education system according to professor of Comparative and International Education Rolland G. Paulston: "Because Cuban teachers held life tenure as government officials and

received full salary whether they taught or not, teacher appointments became a major focus of patronage. Not infrequently, appointments were purchased outright at prices ranging from $500 to $2,000" (1971, 382).
7   To read more, see Mette Louise Berg (2015).
8   To read more on government-sponsored job training programs that sought to "rehabilitate" domestic servants, prostitutes, and the rural poor, see Chase (2015) and Jerónimo Kersh (2019).
9   Cuba began utilizing two currencies at the height of the Special Period, and the Cuban Convertible peso (CUC) was valued roughly at 25 Cuban pesos (CUP). Vázquez (2018) notes, "The CUC, basically equal in value to the dollar, was introduced by then-President Fidel Castro (prime minister 1959–76, president 1976–2008) in 1994 to create a stable currency and was initially used by foreign tourists. Since then, the CUC has been seen as an allegory of inequality: over the years, as social differences have deepened in Cuba, the more privileged have access to CUCs and receive remittances from abroad." At the time of my fieldwork, the convertible peso was still part of the country's dual currency system; however, as of January 1, 2021, the country had moved to a single currency.
10 For a historical discussion of Black women's activism surrounding workers' rights in Jamaica, see Thame and in Brazil, see Sotero, in this volume.

References

Acosta González, Elaine. 2017. "Más Viejos y Desprotegidos: Déficits y Desigualdades En El Cuidado Hacia Las Personas Mayores En Cuba." *Cuba Posible*. https://cubaposible.com/cuidados-personas-mayores-cuba/.
Andaya, Elise. 2014. *Conceiving Cuba: Reproduction, Women, and the State in the Post-Soviet Era*. New Brunswick, NJ: Rutgers University Press.
Barnes, Riché J. Daniel. 2015. *Raising the Race: Black Career Women Redefine Marriage, Motherhood, and Community*. New Brunswick, NJ: Rutgers University Press.
Bautista Sánchez Oms, C. Alberto, Y. Rodríguez Alfonso, Jesús Ríos Garit, and E. Ramírez de Armas. 2020. "Relationship between Systematic Physical Activity and Cognitive Functions in the Third." *EC Orthopaedics* 11, no. 5: 01–05.
Benson, Devyn Spence. 2016. *Antiracism in Cuba: The Unfinished Revolution*. Chapel Hill: University of North Carolina Press.
Berg, Mette Louise. 2015. "'La Lenin Is My Passport': Schooling, Mobility and Belonging in Socialist Cuba and Its Diaspora." *Identities: Global Studies in Culture and Power* 22, no. 3: 303–317.
Blum, Denise. 2008. "Socialist Consciousness Raising and Cuba's School to the Countryside Program." *Anthropology & Education Quarterly* 39, no. 2: 141–160.
———. 2011. *Cuban Youth & Revolutionary Values*. Austin: University of Texas Press.
Bolles, A. Lynn. 2021. *Women and Tourist Work in Jamaica: Seven Miles of Sandy Beach*. Lanham, MD: Rowman & Littlefield.
Booker, Brakkton, and Amalia Daché. 2021. Afro-Cubans on the Brink, July 30. https://www.politico.com/newsletters/the-recast/2021/07/30/amalia-dache-afro-cubans-justice-493788.
Cabezas, Amalia L. 2009. *Economies of Desire: Sex and Tourism in Cuba and the Dominican Republic*. Philadelphia: Temple University Press.
Center for Democracy in the Americas. 2013. "Women's Work: Gender Equality in Cuba and the Role of Women in Building Cuba's Future." Washington, DC, 2013.

https://thecubaneconomy.com/wpcontent/uploads/2013/03/CDA_Womens_Work1.pdf.
Chase, Michelle. 2015. *Revolution within the Revolution: Women and Gender Politics in Cuba, 1952–1962.* Chapel Hill: University of North Carolina Press.
Davis, Angela Y. 1983. *Women, Race & Class.* New York: Knopf Doubleday.
de La Fuente, Alejandro. 2001. *A Nation for All: Race, Inequality, and Politics in Twentieth-Century Cuba.* Chapel Hill: University of North Carolina Press.
Destremau, Blandine. 2018. "Population Aging in Cuba: Coping with Social Care Deficit." In *Contextualizing Health and Aging in the Americas: Effects of Space, Time, and Place*, edited by Jacqueline L. Angel, Luis Miguel F. Gutiérrez Robledo, and Kyriakos S. Markides, 311–336. Austin, TX: ICAA/Springer.
DeYoung, Alan J, Madeleine Reeves, and Galina K Valyayeva. 2006. *Surviving the Transition? Case Studies of Schools and Schooling in Kyrgyz Republic.* Greenwich, CT: Information Age Pub.
Freeman, Carla. 2000. *High Tech and High Heels in the Global Economy.* Durham, NC: Duke University Press.
Garth, Hannah. 2020. *Food in Cuba: The Pursuit of a Decent Meal.* Stanford, CA: Stanford University Press.
Jerónimo Kersh, Daliany. 2019. *Women's Work in Special Period Cuba: Making Ends Meet.* Cham, Switzerland: Palgrave Macmillan.
Lara Junco, Teresa. 2021. "Feminist Economy, a Contribution for the Cuban Social Model." https://capiremov.org/en/analysis/feminist-economy-a-contribution-for-the-cuban-social- model/.
McClaurin, Irma, ed. 2001. *Black Feminist Anthropology: Theory, Politics, Praxis, and Poetics.* New Brunswick, NJ: Rutgers University Press.
Mesa-Lago, Carmelo. 2017. "The Cuban Welfare State System: With Special Reference to Universalism." In *The Routledge International Handbook to Welfare State Systems*, edited by Christian Aspalter, 106–121. New York: Routledge.
Moore, Carlos. 2019. "Silence on Black Cuba." In *The Cuba Reader*, edited by Aviva Chomsky, Barry Carr, Alfredo Prieto, Pamela Maria Smorkaloff, and Carlos Moore, 380–384. Durham, NC: Duke University Press.
Mullings, Leith, and Alaka Wali, eds. 2001. *Stress and Resilience: The Social Context of Reproduction in Central Harlem.* New York: Springer.
Niyozov, Sarfaroz, and Duishon Shamatov. 2010. "Teachers Surviving to Teach: Implications for Post-Soviet Education and Society in Tajikistan and Kyrgyzstan." In *Globalization, Ideology and Education Policy Reforms*, 153–74. Dordrecht: Springer Netherlands.
Núñez Sarmiento, Marta. 2001. "Cuban Strategies for Women's Employment in the 1990s: A Case Study of Professional Women." *Socialism & Democracy* 15, no. 1: 41–64.
———. 2010. "Cuban Development Strategies and Gender Relations." *Socialism & Democracy* 24, no. 1: 127–145.
Oficina Nacional de Estadística e Información. 2014. "Censo de Población y Viviendas 2012 Diciembre 2012." La Habana: La Oficina Nacional de Estadística e Información, 2014. www.onei.gob.cu/sites/default/files/informe_nacio nal_censo_0.pdf.
———. 2021. "7.13-Cantidad de Beneficiarios de La Seguridad Social Vigentes, Pensión Media y Altas Concedidas." Series Estadísticas Empleo y Salarios 1985–2020 Enero-Diciembre 2020. República de Cuba, February 12. www.onei.gob.cu/node/15870.

Oficina Nacional de Estadística e Información, Centro de Estudios de Población y Desarrollo, Ministerio de Salud Pública, and Centro de Investigaciones sobre Longevidad, Envejecimiento y Salud. 2019. "Encuesta Nacional de Envejecimiento de La Población." La Habana, September. www.onei.gob.cu/sites/default/files/0.enep-2017_documento_completo_0.pdf.

Paulston, R. 1971. "Education." In *Revolutionary Change in Cuba*, edited by Carmelo Mesa Lago, 375–97. Pittsburgh: University of Pittsburgh Press.

Ponce-Laguardia, Tania Maité. 2020. "Educational Program for Retiring Persons: A Community Experience in Cienfuegos Province, Cuba." *MEDICC Review* 22, no. 1: 28–32.

Prentice, Rebecca. 2015. *Thieving a Chance: Factory Work, Illicit Labor, and Neoliberal Subjectivities in Trinidad*. Boulder: University Press of Colorado.

Roland, Kaifa. 2011. *Cuban Color in Tourism and La Lucha: Ethnography of Racial Meanings*. New York: Oxford University Press.

Sawyer, Mark Q. 2006. *Racial Politics in Post-Revolutionary Cuba*. New York: Cambridge University Press.

Silova, Iveta. 2009. "The Crisis of the Post-Soviet Teaching Profession in the Caucasus and Central Asia." *Research in Comparative and International Education* 4, no. 4: 366–383.

Stoner, K. Lynn. 1991. *From the House to the Streets: The Cuban Woman's Movement for Legal Reform, 1898–1940*. Durham, NC: Duke University Press.

Ulysse, Gina. 2007. *Downtown Ladies: Informal Commercial Importers, a Haitian Anthropologist, and Self-Making in Jamaica*. Chicago: University of Chicago Press.

Vázquez, Daniel. 2018. "After More than Two Decades, Cuba May End Dual Currency System." University of New Mexico Digital Repository. https://digitalrepository.unm.edu/noticen/10506/.

Wirtz, Kristina. 2014. "Performance: State-Sponsored Folklore Spectacles of Blackness as History." In *Performing Afro Cuba: Image, Voice, Spectacle in the Making of Race and History*, 219–256. Chicago: University of Chicago Press.

6

A "Bundle of Silences"

Untold Stories of Black
Women Survivors of the War
in Colombia

CASTRIELA E. HERNÁNDEZ-REYES

Since 2012, Colombia has commemorated the National Day for Memory and Solidarity with Victims of the armed conflict on April 9. On that day in 2019, I was invited to participate in a regional event to remember the victims of armed violence. There, I met Doña Luz, a seventy-year-old Black woman who is one of the 9 million victims of war registered by the Unit for the Attention and Integral Reparation for the Victims (Unidad para la Atención y Reparación Integral para las Víctimas) in Colombia. The meeting took place at a public university located in Barranquilla, on Colombia's Caribbean Coast and the city where my mother, a *palenquera* woman, migrated in the early sixties to work within the domestic and informal labor market.[1] During that meeting, Doña Luz stared at me and asked, "*¿Eres víctima?*" (Are you a victim?). I replied, "Yes, I am." Immediately, she asked me, "*Tú no pareces del Pacífico, ¿lo eres?*" (You are not from the Pacific region, are you?). "No, Doña Luz," I replied. "I'm from Barranquilla." Later, I invited Doña Luz to assist with my ethnographic research, through which I gathered Black women's embodied stories and critical accounts of armed and state violence. In that conversation, Doña Luz smiled and with a sweet-toned voice said, "Of course, I am going to share my story with you":

"The first time I experienced violence was in 1971 when I lived in Chocó. My husband was murdered, and his body was thrown into the river. One of my daughters, who was five years old, disappeared that day. After many years, I am still looking for her. I would like to know if she is alive or not."

Due to the growing armed and state violence, Doña Luz and her relatives vacated their lands in the early 2000s looking for a safe place to live in the Caribbean region. As is the case for thousands of similar gut-wrenching stories, her family's story has been unwarrantedly silenced and forgotten within the national rhetoric of Colombia's five decades of armed conflict, which claimed at least 220,000 people's lives (GMH 2013). This armed conflict is considered one of the longest-lasting ones in the Western hemisphere and the one with the highest number of internally displaced people (IDPs), with more than "8.3 million according to Government statistics" (UNHCR 2020, 24). Doña Luz became one of the thousand mourners of "the land of graves without bodies" (Hartman 2007, 70). In other words, she is one of many Black and racialized women mourners of an emptied land where her husband was killed and her daughter is still missing.

In Colombia, armed and state violence has disproportionately been directed against Black and negatively racialized women living in resource-rich territories. They have been victims of various forms of violence that have compelled them to vacate their land and live as displaced people inside and outside the country. Official data contend that approximately 1 million IDPs belong to Black communities. More than 500,000 are Black women and Black girls, many of whom are victims of land dispossession, sexual slavery, servitude, and sexual violence in the armed conflict. In the "afterlife" of the war, most Black women are still struggling with social and racial inequalities (e.g., the informal economic market, care labor, domestic labor, etc.) and structural and institutional violence as a result of the reproduction of what Perry (2015) calls "systemic gendered anti-Black racism" (168) as part of the daunting legacy of colonialism.

A critical and intersectional understanding of how race, gender, class, and racism interlock in Colombia's armed and state violence is very undertheorized. Hegemonic scholarship on the armed conflict disregards the voices and lived experiences of Black women (and Indigenous) survivors. What is surprising is that despite the economic, cultural, environmental, and social impacts of the war over racialized bodies, communities, and spaces, scholars appear to view these impacts of the armed conflict as expected consequences of confrontation, that is, as something given rather than the product of the historical process of racialized dispossession and colonial-state racism that merits investigation. Thus, in this chapter I ask, (1) what do Black women survivors' everyday lived experiences tell us about the intersections of race, gender, class, the body, and racism in Colombia? and (2) how do they contest and disrupt hegemonic knowledge production and discourses of Colombia's war? Neglecting Black women's subjective experiences constitutes practices of epistemic racism and forms of exclusion within historical records and knowledge production. Epistemic forms of exclusion ignore that race and racism are critical dimensions for comprehending armed violence dynamics in ethnoracial territories as well as how they impact Black women's lives and bodies as an ongoing process of violent colonial repression.

Following Sueli Carneiro (2005), I propose to darken and subvert armed/state violence and transitional justice studies by bringing Black women's subjective experiences and voices to the center of their analysis. First, I offer a brief background on the impacts of the armed conflict on Black women and communities. Drawing from a Black/decolonial feminist approach and methodology, I examine testimonies of three Black women survivors of the war: Doña Luz, Antonia, and Juana. I situate their unique embodied experiences at the center of the analysis by showing how they co-construct the notions of race, gender, the body, and class while rendering colonial patterns of racism within the armed conflict visible. Then, I critique the colonial practices of epistemic racism by showing how Black women's collective and political strategies of resistance contested those practices by building what I call "alternative spaces for racial healing, reconciliation, and transformation." Black women, as survivors of armed and state violence, face multiple forms of gendered and racial inequalities, social marginalization, and economic exclusion that keep them at the bottom of a hierarchical society that is racist, classist, and sexist. Thus, finally, I examine how the armed conflict and the colonial legacies of racism interlock and impact Black women's bodies, demonstrating how slavery lives on in modern times (Hartman 1997) through what I theorize as *the colonial/modern racial project of war*. The ways the armed conflict impacts Black and negatively racialized people's lives and territories are rooted in systemic exclusion, violence, and racism. This chapter contributes to a global political strategy of claiming historical reparations that are able to disrupt more than four centuries of silencing, racial injustices, and structural and epistemic racism that keep Black women's herstories hidden.

Methodology

This chapter is part of a more extensive collaborative and multisited activist ethnography conducted in Colombia, in which contributors shared their racial, class, and gender identities (Perry 2015).[2] It draws from participant observation, formal and informal meetings, and semistructured and in-depth interviews. I carried out this ethnographic research in collaboration with incredible Black women who agreed to share their stories and embodied experiences as survivors of the war. As a Black woman and victim of the violence myself, I often employ the preposition "our" to index my felt personal connection to this Black/decolonial feminist ethnography.[3]

I analyzed testimonies I gathered in conjunction with my research participants (Battle-Baptiste 2010; Perry 2015; Smith 2016). The chapter centers on three stories of Black women survivors who faced devastating experiences of structural exclusion, institutional racism, land dispossession, gender-based violence, and forced migration: Doña Luz, a Black seventy-year-old woman whose heartbreaking story took place in Rio Sucio, a small village in the department of Chocó in the Pacific region; Antonia, a Black forty-nine-year-old woman from San Basilio de Palenque; and Juana, a forty-eight-year-old woman from Mampuján. The last two stories took place in two different towns in the Caribbean subregion known as the Montes de María. Montes de María and Chocó are primarily inhabited by Black, Indigenous, and poor peasant people. Both territories have a long history of violent processes of dispossession and resistance practices, in which local and global armed and civil actors utilize violence to exploit, exclude, and control populations. Like thousands of other survivors, these Black women collectively had the strength to resist violent repression linked to colonial legacies of racism that continue to shape and structure their bodily existence.

Afro-Colombians and the Ongoing Armed and State Violence

In 2016, and after various failed peace processes to end sixty years of armed conflict, the Colombian government and the Revolutionary Armed Forces of Colombia (FARC-EP) signed a ceasefire and peace accord considered a historical landmark agreement internationally because of the inclusion of considerations of gender and ethnicity. The peace agreement created the illusion that the longest-lasting armed conflict in the Americas would soon be ending. However, five years later, armed and state violence persists in Colombia, including in many of the racialized territories inhabited by Black and Indigenous people. Thus, the agreement did not bring the desired peace to many rural towns overnight.

As I stated earlier, more than 500,000 IDPs are Black women and girls, and 25 percent of Afro-Colombians are impacted by guerrillas, paramilitary groups, state-military forces, organized drug criminal organizations, and the so-called emergent bands. Paramilitary groups, for example, not only constructed and reinforced a particular social regime where colonial patriarchal power, sexism, and racist oppressions were exerted against racial-ethnic people (GMH 2011); they also instituted a violent hypermasculinization that utilized sexual slavery as a coercive and dominant weapon to control Black and racialized women's bodies. They did so while encouraging the exploitation of resource-rich territories, making them accessible to local and transnational racial capitalism.

Some Afro-Colombian scholars offer a critical understanding of how settler-colonialism, land dispossession, and economic politics of deterritorialization operate within the armed conflict and how they are tied to violence as part of the political economy of war inserted into global capitalism (Arboleda-Quiñonez, 2019; Hernández-Reyes 2018, 2019; Lozano 2016). Elsewhere I contend (2018) that in Latin America, a racialized and colonial/modern gender system reconfigured power relations of domination, oppression, and marginalization, fostering the punishment of Black women's bodies. Latin American governments instituted a patriarchal colonial power that endorsed Black women's reproductive labor and the control and regulation of their sexuality in the nineteenth century through this racialized gendered system. It turned Black women's bodies into disposable "commodities" in the slavery market and the colonial matrix of racialized/modern capitalism.

I argue that the armed and state violence in Colombia has turned into "the functional surrogate of slavery" that determines "the social and physical death" (Dillon 2012, 114) of Black and Indigenous people in racialized territories. The social and physical death is made visible through forced displacement, gender-based violence, deterritorialization, and sexual violence, as well as through the forced disappearance, murders, environmental racism, and dispossession of Black and Indigenous people. Therefore, structural and embodied violence against Black communities cannot be delinked from the long durée history of slavery and colonization or the impacts of systemic inequalities (Arboleda-Quiñonez 2019; Hernández-Reyes 2018, 2019; Lozano 2016; Vergara-Figueroa 2017). Instituted mechanisms of colonial violence have fostered the reconfiguration and production of Black territories. Most poor people occupying the Colombian Pacific region bear witness to myriad forms of genocide, ethnocide, and ecocide that foster the eviction and elimination of Black and Indigenous cultures and communities (Arboleda-Quiñonez 2019).

The Need for an Intersectional Analysis of Armed and State Violence

The Black intellectual Santiago Arboleda-Quiñonez builds the notion of "eco-ethnogenocide" as an analytical tool to best explain the violence impacting Black lands and culture as part of the "neo-colonial reshaping of the territory" (Arboleda-Quiñonez 2019, 94). However, Arboleda-Quiñonez's analysis fails to include the category of "feminicide" (defined in the Colombia Criminal Code as the killing of a woman because of her gender), excluding Black and Indigenous women's survivors and limiting our understanding of how their everyday experiences of armed and state-sponsored violence reveal how systems of oppression, racism, and patriarchy intertwine within war. The reconfiguration of the social order in Black and racialized territories due to drug trafficking, social-racial inequalities, and state and armed violence make Black women and girls the primary targets of feminicide (Sinisterra-Ossa and Valencia 2020; Abello-Hurtado-Mandinga 2020).

Excluding Black women's perspectives from the analysis of armed and state violence undermines the ability to investigate the complexities of how systems of power, oppression, and domination interlock and operate within a war. As Black and decolonial feminist intellectuals assert, race, gender, sexuality, and class are not isolated categories but mutually constituted mechanisms of domination and oppression visible and legible through Black women's lived and embodied experiences (Alexander 2014; Crenshaw 1990; Davis 2003; hooks 2014 [1982]; Hernández-Reyes 2019; Hill Collins 2000; Lugones 2010; Smith 2016).

In the Americas, Black women are continually dispossessed, disenfranchised, and "constructed as pawns in the national discourse and not as key players" (Alexander 2014, 9). Black women "have assumed the task of writing into history their experiences, incorporating their roles as workers, mothers, and activists" (Mullings 2004, 19). Black women's stories and needs are minimized and utterly discounted in service of hegemonic narratives that overlook embodied experiences that shape our understanding of the world. Exploring what happened to Black women survivors in Colombia contributes to the production of collective narratives that shed light on historical and contemporary forms of exclusion and marginalization within the study of armed and state violence. Drawing from this standpoint, I assert that Black women survivors' voices and lived experiences contribute to theorizing anti-Black violence and deconstructing white/mestizx dominant scholarship on the armed conflict and state violence.

Disturbing Epistemic Racism through Black Women's Testimonies of Armed Violence

Revisting Doña Luz's Testimony

In 1999, the armed violence returned to Río Sucio, Chocó. Doña Luz, afraid of being killed, vacated her house and territory. Along with her, some relatives and neighbors fled to protect their lives. Once again, many homes and neighborhoods were vacated because of the war:

> Violence has haunted us, "Mami." In the late 1990s, armed men forced us to abandon our homes and vacate our lands. My sister and her children were also forced to flee. To protect their lives, they migrated to Turbo, Antioquia. However, Turbo was not a safe place for my sister and her family. Three of her children were killed by paramilitary groups in just one year of living there. I still cry a lot when I remember and share my family's story. It is hard to remember and keep our memory alive because the pain is still here [Doña Luz touched her chest] and I know it will always be the same.

Lived experiences offer an intimate perspective on the war through which the voices and bodies of Black survivors became channels to narrate the anti-Black violence in Colombia. Doña Luz lost her husband, daughter, and livelihoods. Her sister left her house with her children to safeguard their lives. However, paramilitary violence killed three of her boys in just one year. Doña Luz's story makes visible the harms and the economies of Black pain and suffering (Smith 2016) tied to the legacies of state-sponsored-abandonment.

According to the Special Unit for the Search for Persons deemed missing in the armed conflict, more than 50,000 persons disappeared during the war in Colombia. Doña Luz's daughter is part of this worrying data on missing people. The missing body of her daughter warns about the risks Black girls and Black boys face in their territories and places where the armed violence never ends and state and everyday violence persists. Doña Luz and her family were forced to vacate her homeland, bringing only their family's memoirs, clothes, and nothing else.

Shared Stories of Harm, Pain, and Loss: "They Made Us Captives of Pain"

On March 18, 2021, I met with Antonia after canceling our first meeting because I had the flu and was frightened that my symptoms were associated with COVID-19. Antonia came to my home at 10 A.M., and I offered her a cup of coffee. Later, I shared with her the purposes of my ethnographic fieldwork, inviting her to collaborate with me on my research. She asked me to keep her data secure and I agreed to do so. Antonia is a forty-nine—year-old woman from San Basilio de Palenque, a nurse practitioner, and a survivor of gender-based violence and forced displacement. Our interview lasted ninety-four minutes. I started by asking her, "Antonia, based on your experience as a Black woman survivor of the armed violence in Colombia, what can you tell me about your lived experience in the framework of the armed conflict?" Antonia breathed, looked at me, and started sharing her story:

> The truth is that before I began to have such negative experiences that, unfortunately, many Colombians lived through without being directly or indirectly part of the conflict, I was suspicious that these horror events could happen in my place. I was a person who used to say: "No, these problems don't occur anywhere; how and why could they [armed actors] come to a village and kill members of the community if the people never affected them?" So, I thought those facts were not accurate. But, just at the moment, I had to live through them; when I was forced to flee to protect my life, I said: this is real; these violent events happen anywhere in Colombia. When I felt so much fear for my life and the lives of the people around me, I suddenly wanted to be in Africa and be one of the women in chains who arrived on a boat.... On a ship where

maybe I would have died in chains and never been shot. Or [to live in a country] where I would probably not be a victim of so many humiliations to which victims are still subjected.

Antonia's voice cracked. After more than twenty years since the first violent event happened in Palenque, she continues to feel hurt remembering what happened. For a Palenquera survivor, crying while recounting her experience was a way of healing the still-open wounds. I remained silent, waiting for her to recover. She calmed herself down and then continued narrating her story:

We are victims of the state because when you knock on the Office of the Victims Unit doors, you must repeat the drama you have already lived through every time. The best thing for the officials would be for you to underline what happened to you, how it happened to you, where you were that day, and what you did. They victimize us when they ask us which side we belong to. The truth is that it is very heartbreaking to have to remember those experiences. Sometimes I feel it would be better if I had never been born.

C: Why do you say that the state was responsible for what happened in Palenque?

A: Why can I say it was the state? Because in the case that happened in Palenque in 1999, when two victims: Alfonso, a mestizo man from Santander, and my compadre, named Orlando, were killed, it was the state that caused the loss. I am sure of it. . . . Within that group of men, the presence of a man of medium height, with a white shirt and gray shorts, stayed with me. They entered my house; they locked us in. They threatened us with weapons of all sizes, and I said, oh my God, could this be a nightmare?

Antonia could not forget that Palenquera people "were trapped, cut off, and humiliated":

I remember we lived moments of anguish when we were forced to move, to leave our houses to sleep in the cemetery because we thought we would be protected there. Palenque became a ghost town. The joy that characterized the Black people, for being Black, Afro, and Palenqueros, disappeared. Why did it disappear? Because of the shots fired by the state. In its eagerness over the loss of the struggle against illegal armed actors, the state has subjected the people to a battle of which they are not guilty, to a war in which we have not participated. If the great Benkos Biohó fought against the Spanish Crown to set us free and build this territory . . . to live in peace. So, we should not be forced to participate in a fight where we do not know the causes.

Antonia's experience demonstrates the harm produced by the violent loss that Palenqueros survivors experienced. Her story travels back to the past and present, looking for our ancestors. She told me that a couple of hours before the tragic event happened, she was braiding her hair and re-creating the paths to freedom and reunions weaved for our ancestors. The history of enslaved rebellion tells us that Black women's freedom strategies were essential for acquiring free land in South America and the Caribbean. Our *ancestras* braided their hair, crafting strategic maps representing the paths toward freedom. They also secured seeds of corn, bananas, and other foods necessary to preserve life after slavery in the new free territories known as Palenque (Navarro and Rebolledo 2017). *Cimarron* women resisted slavery and became owners of land in the "new world."[4] Thus, Antonia's remembrances accounted for the heartbreaking history of slavery and colonization. They evoked how Black women's bodies were utilized in instituting a gendered, racialized, and sexualized system that characterizes Latin American racial states (Hernández-Reyes 2018). Additionally, her narrative reveals how paramilitary groups and the Colombian army were not two independent forces but the same armed troops who executed crimes and human rights violations against civilians in her town.

My meeting with Antonia was also a space for me to reconnect with and retrieve parts of my family's untold story of harm and suffering. The war impacted several of my family members in Palenque. Kidnapping, murder, forced displacement, and eviction shaped the set of devastating acts of violence my family experienced. After the capture of one of my youngest uncles, my grandmother's health was compromised. Tia's (as everyone in the family and in the town called her) body gradually became weaker. She began to forget names, places, and dates. The armed violence facilitated my grandmother's journey and her early meeting with our ancestors. No one in my family associates my grandmother's soul and body pain with the violent events that affected our family.

While paramilitaries tortured and killed hundreds of Black, Indigenous, and poor peasants in many rural territories, such as Palenque and the towns of the Montes de María, I was an undergraduate student at a public university in Barranquilla, Colombia. I served as a member of the student organization Alma-Mater. Between 1998 and 2006, paramilitary groups killed more than a dozen leaders at the Universidad del Atlántico. Para-state violence killed several of my friends. For many years, those not killed by paramilitary gangs had to flee and live as internally displaced persons first before being forcedly exiled to survive. As Palenquera women, Antonia and I form part of an extended family. Our stories share a mourning and healing journey. We must cope with the trauma of the armed and state violence and the prevailing structural, institutional, and everyday racism in Colombia.

Weaving over Quilts to Move through the Pain: Building Collective and Diasporic Memories Resistance

It was a sunny morning when I started my trip to Mampuján. First, I arrived at Cartagena's bus terminal. Then, I took another bus to go to Mampuján Town, where I met Juana. Mampuján is a small village located in the Caribbean subregion of Montes de María. The weather suddenly changed during the journey to Juana's home. The rain started, and thunderstorms and lightning became part of the journey. The agricultural landscape contained vast crops of oil palms. I was perplexed because I did not see traditional yam, cassava, corn, or banana crops but instead large extensions of oil palm crops belonging to the "new" owners of the land. Land-grabbing mestizx families benefited from paramilitary violence and control in the Montes de María subregion.

It was 2:00 p.m., and my husband and I exited the bus in front of a small store. In the corner of the store was a peasant man from the region selling some yams and cassava. I asked him if he knew Juana, and he immediately replied, "Of course, her house is very close to here." He kindly told us the shortest route to Juana's house. Upon our arrival, Juana greeted us with a welcome hug. It was like arriving at the home of an old friend or relative. Juana told us, "You must be hungry. I cooked fish and stewed chicken with coconut rice and cassava. You haven't had lunch, so eat, and then we can talk about whatever you want." We ate everything. The food was delicious. Juana's house's walls were beautified with quilts made by Black women weavers and survivors of the war. Juana is a Black woman survivor and leader of a grassroots organization called Tejedoras de Sueños de Mampuján (Weavers of Dreams of Mampuján).

I started my interview. Juana began telling me that she and her *sistas* decided to narrate their stories through quilt needlework:

> We wanted to show that violence is nothing new to us but a cycle that must be understood and broken. So that it does not continue to affect us. The first, the most significant, and the strongest displacement experienced by Blacks and our ancestors happened when we were forced and brought from Africa to this land. That is why we wanted to weave our stories into the quilts. History tells us that the slavers have taken the land from us many times, many times they have displaced us, many times they have threatened us and tried to exterminate us, and many times we have survived. And that cycle ... has not been broken. So, we must recognize it and stop it.

Juana's powerful narratives articulate remembrances that warn about the transatlantic slave trade and colonial legacies of racism still present and relevant in Colombia's armed and state violence, impacting Black people's bodies and everyday lives. Through the quilts, Black women's experiential and bodily dimensions reveal the "dehumanizing effects of racism" (Smith 2016, 33), the persistence of silencing practices, and the maintenance of racial and social injustices that Black women often contest. Anthropological and sociological works focused on memory assert that memory is transmitted through sociocultural practices that incorporate symbolic and material elements that are embedded in performed rituals, religious practices, landscape, artifacts, remains, and nondiscursive language (Battle-Baptiste 2010; Connerton 1989; Rappaport 1990; Taylor 2008). While memory is a personal and cognitive experience and a habit inscribed in the body and social practices, lived experiences work as collective practices of remembrance to produce a set of situated knowledge that makes sense of the world. Black women weavers keep enslaved people's memory in the Caribbean alive through their narratives and the ritual performances of remembering the past.

For Black women survivors, their bodies become a powerful device to recreate and explain social rules of remembrances by evoking a shared past. Juana and many Black women from Mampuján use the quilts as a pedagogical tool to preserve their memory and heal the armed conflict's pain. Thus, quilts as creative art and material culture (Figueroa-Vásquez 2020) render Black women's "unwritten" stories visible. When Juana says that the first displacement, the most significant and severe one Black people and our ancestors experienced, ensued when we were forced and brought from Africa to this land, she demonstrates how and why Black women survivors struggle and want to weave our stories into the quilts.

According to Juana, strategies of eviction and marginalization against Black people are systemic mechanisms of exclusion: "As you know, during the bipartisan war, the town was displaced and burned. Then, the guerrillas came here, and people were also displaced. Then, paramilitaries also displaced Black people, and now we are fighting to avoid our children being forced to move away from here. So that is why we are showing how this violent cycle is not new, that it continues to hurt us and continues to affect us." According to the National Center for Historical Memory, paramilitary fighters executed more than twenty massacres in this region. Black women from Mampuján assert that paramilitary gangs' terror strategy forced the eviction of their people in the Montes de María. Paramilitary groups constructed and imposed "a particular social order" in which being white was considered "synonymous with stepping up in the social ladder in a predominantly Afro-descendant territory" (GMH 2011, 37). They instituted a specific regime, regulating lives and controlling women's and LGBTQ bodies and sexuality. They also determined who could live or be killed and who should be forcedly displaced or disappear.

Massacres, land dispossession, forced migrations, and death became visible in what I call the "modern/colonial racial project of war." The racial project of war in Colombia has kept the white/mestizx hegemonic power in the country by controlling and subjugating the lives, nature, bodies, and territories of Black, poor peasants, and Indigenous people. As part of a long-lasting colonial system, the racial project of war and its capitalist strategies of accumulation by dispossession, masculine domination, and gendered and racialized exclusion keep Black women and bodies as commodities, "disposable" and "killable."

Connecting to Historical Experiences of Silencing and Epistemic Racism

The political legitimacy of Black women survivors' stories rests on how their voices and embodied experiences unveil historical mechanisms of exclusions and oppressions exerted on their lives, bodies, and lands. As Hartman says, erasing "all evidence of existence before slavery" was a tactic carried out by colonial society and slaveholders (Hartman 2007, 155) to keep Black women silenced. This strategy of erasing our history initiated centuries of erasing the history of Black women in the Americas. In response to this erasure, women like Juana argued that projects such as the Weavers of Dreams collective disrupt institutional politics of forgetting in the making of the Colombian racial state: "We wanted to show that violence is nothing new to us but a necessary cycle that must be understood and broken.... The first, the most significant, and the strongest displacement experienced by blacks and our ancestors happened when we were forced and brought from Africa to this land.... History tells us that the slavers have taken the land from us many times. And many times, they have displaced us, threatened us, and tried to exterminate us."

Juana's testimony reflects on Colombian independence history. In 1851, when the Colombian state declared the end of slavery, white/mestizx landowners and elites led a slaveholder rebellion demanding to keep slavery or receive monetary compensation to protect their wealth. They claimed that "property without Negroes to cultivate it was worthless" (López-Alves 2000, 108). Black enslaved people were property but not individuals with property rights. They were part of the colonial capitalist logic of accumulation but not owners of the means of production. This logic of appropriation and exclusion measured Black people as commodities in the agricultural market. Thus, while before abolition having Black people in white/mestizx productive settlements increased the value of the property, conversely, in the twenty-first century and afterlife of slavery, Black people who cultivate their land, practice ancestral mining, and create strategies to protect life and nature are undervalued under the logic of racial capitalism.

Antonia's testimony demonstrates how the violence Black women survivors experienced through war and state violence reproduces colonial patterns of racism, patriarchal domination, and exclusion that are less visible within the hegemonic production of knowledge. Her narrative makes the loss of relatives, friends, livelihoods, and happiness visible. Her lived experience reveals the steadiness of colonial violence and assigns the state responsibility for armed violence:

> I remember that we lived moments of anguish when we were forced to move, to leave our houses to sleep in the cemetery because we thought we would be protected there. Palenque became a ghost town. The joy that characterized blacks as Black, Afro, and Palenqueros disappeared. Why did it disappear? Because of the shots fired by the state. In its eagerness to lose the struggle against the illegal armed actors, the state has subjected the people to a battle of which it is not guilty, to a war in which we have not participated.... Therefore, we should not be forced to participate in a struggle where we do not know the causes.

Antonia bears witness to how death seemed to become the only condition of possibility for Black people in her town. Contrary to the scholarship of many white/mestizx scholars, I argue that a *colonial/modern racial project of war* endures in Colombia. This racial project of war accounts for structural and institutional mechanisms of exclusion, oppression, and marginalization reconfigured through different means of violence. In doing so, the practices of epistemic exclusion and epistemic racism constitute the epistemological dimension of the colonial/modern racialized project of war.

Black people's strained living conditions in the landscape of racialized dispossession are exacerbated by ongoing violent processes of evictions, forced displacement, gender-based violence, and structural inequalities. Thus, the racialization of Black bodies and territories within the underlying logic of state racism safeguards colonial rule over Black people's lives and bodies. The expansion of the war in Black and Indigenous territories, the gendered violence against Black and racialized women, and the strengthened politics of death reflect how the colonial/modern racial project of war and its patriarchal mode of production operate. In this racial project, Black territories are seized as a product of violence and displacement, appropriated by white/mestizx actors, leading to the increase in the lands' value, all while fostering the commodification and devaluation of racialized bodies within the global political economy of the war. Thus, the racial project of war facilitates economic accumulation for some through the dispossession of Black communities, the conception of their land as pollutable commodities (a product of environmental racism), and the construction of racialized people and Black women's bodies as killable.

Reparation through Collective Remembrance

Doña Luz, Juana, and Antonia's experiences, like thousands more racialized survivors' stories, expose the cruelty of armed violence and structural exclusion in Colombia throughout its history. The everydayness of the war created a never-ending stream of worries over how survivors would protect themselves, safeguard their relatives' lives and their lands, or find a new secure home to sleep in. When a Black woman survivor touches parts of her body to show where she hurts, she makes visible and legible the painful stories and traumas produced by the armed conflict. Their embodied experiences, inflicted with harm, loss, and hurt, situate them as victims of the war and survivors of state violence and its racialized capitalist mode of production. Their reembodied and ritualized lived experiences illustrate what they have lost and what they would like to see, touch, and feel again, but are unable to do so, except through their collective remembrances. From my perspective, Black women always remember what they have lived through, even while their experiences are often marginalized and excluded from dominant accounts of history. Centering the voices and experiences of Black women such as Doña Luz, Juana, and Antonia in research and discourses surrounding the armed conflict would significantly alter how the national history, collective memories, and truth about the armed conflict are conveyed, informing a process of historical reparations grounded in social, gendered, and racial justice.

For example, Doña Luz's husband was killed, and his dead body was thrown into the Atrato River in Chocó; the Atrato River still bears witness to pain and devastation in Chocó. For Black and Indigenous people, this river represents a living space and a vehicle for the transportation, preservation, and celebration of communities' livelihoods. Nevertheless, armed conflict, state-sponsored and illegal extractivism, and drug production have notably changed the meanings of rivers such as the Atrato. Due to the armed conflict, the Atrato has become a mourning place for innumerable "disposable" corpses. In 2017, the Colombian Constitutional Court "issued a ground-breaking judgment recognizing the Atrato River as a legal subject with rights to increase its protection" (Calzadilla 2019, 3). This legal decision would not have been possible without Black, Indigenous, and environmental social leaders' resistance and collective struggle to protect lives and nature.

In another example, Juana's and Antonia's testimonies evoke our ancestors and the violence they experienced in the past. They make visible and legible how the harms remain and continue to shape our everyday lives. Thus, the past and the present experiences of violence overlap and are inseparable for Black people. When Antonia's accounts brought into light the struggles of the Cimarrónes, people led by Benkos Biohó against the Spanish Crown, she reaffirmed that in the afterlife of slavery and colonization, Black people still struggle to obtain their freedom and recover their humanity. On the other hand, when Juana remembered the cycle of violence in her town, she recounted our struggle and resistance practices. Our embodied experiences as Black women survivors resonate and work as an "antidote to oblivion" (Hartman 2007) even though, as Toni Morrison (2004) writes, "coming back dead to life hurts." Raising our voices and rejecting being silent is a way to rewrite the stories of what happened to us and defeat heteropatriarchy-dominant narratives.

Following Simone Alexander (2014), I assert that Black women survivors' alternative practices of racial healing, reconciliation, and transformation work as strategies of racial empowerment and reclaiming of joy and Black spirituality. Black women survivors in Colombia create living archives and graphic testimonies focused on their lived and embodied experiences. Their archives dispute epistemic racism while working as counterhegemonic narratives and feminist Afro-epistemologies. I believe that the creative artwork of the Black women from Mampuján (Juana's Weavers of Dreams collective) is, in one way, the first community-based archival project of historical reparation made by Black women. Black women's creative work, including that of the collective, could be considered a turning point in constructing truth, reconciliation, and historical reparations within the transitional justice efforts in Colombia.

Conclusion

Conducting feminist anthropological and ethnographic work as an insider activist within my community underscores the need to create anti-racist epistemic spaces able to make visible and legible untold stories of Black women in the Global South. At this point, to countervail the erasure of Black women's experiences, I have examined and theorized Colombia's armed and state violence as a colonial/modern racial project of war that reproduces and reinforces "geographies of racial dispossession" (Schmidt 2013, 213) and racial capitalism through the seizure of territories, gender-based violence, and environmental racism.

Armed and state violence and structural racism are not independent forms of violence. They intertwine to maintain social and racial hierarchies in our society. In this chapter, I argue that hegemonic accounts of the Colombian armed and state violence have not concerned themselves with how Black women victims are trapped within coexisting patterns of patriarchal colonial power and structural racism, that is, how they are captives of a long durée violent process of colonization that informs and shapes their everyday lives. Black women's bodies speak and exhibit the pain and harm they have experienced historically. Afro-Colombian women are producers of counterhegemonic narratives that demand historical reparations and racial justice from the state to dismantle structural patterns of domination, racism, and exclusion.

Drawing from Doña Luz, Juana, and Antonia's lived experiences as survivors of the Colombian armed and state violence, I argue that Black women's subjective experiences work as reservoirs and channels for liberation and appropriation of Black historicity. They contest the reproduction of racialized and gendered structural amnesia within historical records. A racialized and gender-structural amnesia is understood as the process through which Black women and Black people's storytelling are nameless and unwritten because they supposedly do not matter for the dominant knowledge production.

I contend that Black women's narratives are cultural and political strategies for processing pain, mourning, and devastation. By underlining how forced displacement, exclusion, and dispossession work over their bodies, Afro-Colombian women make visible colonial patterns of racism and exclusion reproduced by the war. Their embodied languages are political acts of resistance that constitute what I call *alternative space for racial healing, reconciliation, and transformations*. Alternative forms of racial healing imply comprehending the role history and systemic exclusions play in reproducing racial stereotypes, everyday racism, and anti-Black violence. They challenge gender and racial prejudices and injustices, disrupt the "bundles of silences," and undo epistemic racism. They also serve as alternative politics for mourning and intimate collective wellness.

Given the resounding and unwarranted silencing of Black women's stories, I argue that when Black women survivors touch their hands, heart, face, or legs to show where their body hurts, they make visible painful stories, harm, and trauma experienced within the war. Black women's spirituality, cosmogony, ancestral wisdom, and love bear witness to myriad resistance and collective political projects to re-create, protect, and care for their life (Lozano and Peñaranda 2007). Protecting life and nature is part of anticolonial and diasporic collaborative projects that promote the recovery of dispossessed humanity. When telling and sharing our untold stories, our voices work as an insurgent political practice and a vehicle of resistance to confront the hidden rules of silencing Black people's history. Our collective voices become a tool to bridge our struggles and resistance and demand historical reparations and racial justice.

Notes

1 A *palenquera* is a Colombian woman of African descent from Colombia's Caribbean Coast; the term also indexes Afro-Colombian women who historically wore colorful dresses and sold fruit and have become a symbol of the Caribbean Coast.

2 This chapter is part of a more extensive collaborative and multisited activist ethnography conducted between 2019 and 2022 in Colombia, examining the intersections between race, gender, class, and body within the armed conflict and transitional justice discourse. My special gratitude and love to the Black women who collaborated in this research sharing their lived experiences. I thank the

Department of Anthropology of the University of Massachusetts Amherst for the Pre-Dissertation Award Sylvia Forman Third World Scholarship (2017), the Sylvia Forman Graduate Fellowship (2019), and the 2022 Johnnetta Betsch Cole Award, which recognizes the contribution of my work in writing, creating a public scholarship project, and commitment to inclusive social justice.
3   This ethnography was restricted by the COVID-19 pandemic and ongoing violence in Colombia.
4   *Cimarrónes* (maroons) were enslaved people who escaped slavery and lived together in rural communities.

References

Abello-Hurtado-Mandinga, Maria Ximena. 2020. "Black Girl Bodies: Notes on the Legacy of Colonialism in South America and the Urgency of a Black Liberation Project for Black Girls." *The Black Scholar* 50, no. 4: 18–29.

Alexander, Simone A. James. 2014. *African Diasporic Women's Narratives: Politics of Resistance, Survival, and Citizenship*. Gainesville: University of Florida Press.

Arboleda-Quiñonez, Santiago. 2019. "Rutas para Perfilar el ecogenoetnocidio Afrocolombiano: Hacia una Conceptualización desde la Justicia Histórica." *Nómadas (Col)* 50: 93–109.

Battle-Baptiste, Whitney. 2010. "Sweepin' Spirits: Power and Transformation on the Plantation Landscape." In *Archaeology and Preservation of Gendered Landscapes*, edited by Sherene Baugher and Suzanne M. Spencer-Wood, 81–94. New York: Springer.

Calzadilla, Paola Villiavicencio. 2019. "A Paradigm Shift in Courts' View on Nature: The Atrato River and Amazon Basin Cases in Colombia." *Law, Environment and Development Journal* 15: xiii.

Carneiro, Sueli. 2005. "Ennegrecer el Feminismo." *Nouvelles Questions Feministes: Feminismos Disidentes en América Latina y El Caribe* 24, no. 7: 21–22.

Connerton, Paul. 1989. *How Societies Remember*. Cambridge, UK: Cambridge University Press.

Crenshaw, Kimberle. 1990. "Mapping the Margins: Intersectionality, Identity Politics, and Violence against Women of Color." *Stanford Law Review* 43: 1241.

Davis, Angela. 2003. "Racism, Birth Control and Reproductive Rights." In *Feminist Postcolonial Theory:–A Reader*, edited by Reina Lewis and Sara Mills, 353–367. New York: Routledge.

Dillon, Stephen. 2012. "Possessed by Death: The Neoliberal-carceral State, Black Feminism, and the Afterlife of Slavery." *Radical History Review* 2012, no. 112: 113–125.

Figueroa-Vásquez, Yomaira. 2020. *Decolonizing Diasporas: Radical Mappings of Afro-Atlantic Literature*. Evanston, IL: Northwestern University Press.

GMH (Grupo de Memoria Histórica). 2011. *La Guerra Inscrita en el Cuerpo: Informe Nacionalde Violencia Sexual en el Conflicto Armado*. Bogotá: Centro Nacional de Memoria Histórica.

———. 2013. *¡Basta ya! Colombia: Memorias de Guerra y Dignidad*. Bogotá, Colombia: Imprenta Nacional.

Hartman, Saidiya. 1997. *Scenes of Subjection: Terror, Slavery, and Self-making in Nineteenth-century America*. Oxford: Oxford University Press.

———. 2007. *Lose Your Mother: A Journey along the Atlantic Slave Route*. New York: Farrar, Straus and Giroux.

Hernández Reyes, Castriela Esther. 2018. "Aproximaciones al Sistema de Sexo/género en la Nueva Granada en los Siglos XVIII y XIX." In *Demando mi Libertad: Mujeres Negras y sus Estrategias de Resistencia en la Nueva Granada, Venezuela y Cuba, 1700–1800*, edited by Aurora Vergara Figueroa and Carmen Luz Cosme Puntiel, 29–76. Cali, Colombia: Editoral Universidade Icesi.
———. 2019. "Black Women's Struggles against Extractivism, Land Dispossession, and Marginalization in Colombia." *Latin American Perspectives* 46, no. 2: 217–234.
Hill Collins, Patricia. 2000. "Gender, Black Feminism, and Black Political Economy." *The Annals of the American Academy of Political and Social Science* 568, no. 1: 41–53.
hooks, Bell. 2014 [1982]. *Ain't I a Woman? Black Women and Feminism*. New York: Routledge.
López-Alves, Fernando. 2000. *State Formation and Democracy in Latin America, 1810–1900*. Durham, NC: Duke University Press.
Lozano, Betty Ruth. 2016. "Asesinato de Mujeres y Acumulación Global: El Caso del Bello Puerto del Mar, mi Buenaventura." In *Des/DIBUJANDO EL PAIS/aje: Aportes para la Paz con los Pueblos Afrodescendientes e Indígenas; Territorio, Autonomía y Buen Vivir*, edited by Sheila Gruner, Melquiceded Blandón Mena, Jader Gómez Caicedo, and Charo Mina-Rojas, 73–86. Medellín, Colombia: Ediciones Poder Negro.
Lozano, Betty Ruth, and Bibiana Peñaranda. 2007. "Memoria y reparación ¿y de Ser Mujeres Megras qué?" In *Afro-reparaciones: Memorias de la esclavitud y Justicia Reparativa para Negros, Afrocolombianos y Raizales*, edited by Claudia Mosquera Rosero-Labbé, 715–724. Bogotá, Colombia: Universidad Nacional de Colombia.
Lugones, María. 2010. "Toward a Decolonial Feminism." *Hypatia* 25, no. 4: 742–759.
Morrison, Toni. 2004 [1987]. *Beloved*. New York: Vintage.
Mullings, Leith. 2004. "Race and Globalization." *Souls* 6, no. 2: 1–9.
Navarro, Erelis, and Angelica Rebolledo. 2017. *Los Turbantes y Peinados Afrocolombianos: Una Aalternativa Pedagógica*. Publisher unidentified. ISBN 958482323X, 9789584823236.
Perry, Keisha-Khan Y. 2015. "State Violence and the Ethnographic Encounter: Feminist Research and Racial Embodiment." In *Bridging Scholarship and Activism: Reflections from the Frontlines of Collaborative Research*, edited by Bernd Reiter and Ulrich Oslender, 151–170. East Lansing: Michigan State University Press.
Rappaport, Joanne. 1990. *The Politics of Memory: Native Historical Interpretation in the Colombian Andes*. Durham, NC: Duke University Press.
Schmidt, Heike Ingeborg. 2013. *Colonialism & Violence in Zimbabwe: A History of Suffering*. Rochester, NY: Boydell & Brewer.
Sinisterra-Ossa, Lizeth, and Inge Helena Valencia. 2020. "Orden Social y Violencia en Buenaventura: Entre el Outsourcing Criminal y la Construcción de Paz desde Abajo." *CS* 32: 103–129.
Smith, Cristen A. 2016. *Afro-paradise: Blackness, Violence, and Performance in Brazil*. Champaign: University of Illinois Press.
Taylor, Ula. 2008. "Women in the Documents: Thoughts on Uncovering the Personal, Political, and Professional." *Journal of Women's History* 20, no. 1: 187–196.
UNHCR. 2020. "Global Trends: Forced Displacement in 2020." www.unhcr.org/statistics/unhcrstats/60b638e37/global-trends-forced-displacement-2020.html.
Vergara-Figueroa, Aurora. 2017. *Afrodescendant Resistance to Deracination in Colombia: Massacre at Bellavista-Bojayá-Chocó*. New York: Springer.

7

The Burden of *Las Bravas*

• • • • • • • • • • • • • • • • • • •

Race and Violence against
Afro-Peruvian Women

ESHE L. LEWIS

One cold afternoon, I sat in a café in Lima across from my friend, an Afro-Peruvian activist with strong ties to the feminist movement and years of experience working on racial justice. I was interested in women's issues in the Afro-descendant community and had been thinking about interpersonal violence. I had never seen or heard mention of Black women in public discussions on gender violence or in the six years I had spent working with Afro-Peruvian communities.

"What do you think about a project about intimate partner violence among Afro-Peruvian women?" I asked hesitantly.

My friend paused and looked up at me over the rim of her teacup. "I think it's a great idea. You should do it. Someone needs to do it."

I breathed a sigh of relief. "I thought you were going to say it wouldn't be worth it. I never hear anyone talk about it," I added.

She nodded, reaching for her sandwich. "That's probably true. Women don't like to talk about it in general, and Black women, well . . . they think they can't say it."

I stayed silent, inviting her to say more.

"We're supposed to be strong; everyone expects Black women to be strong. So they assume it doesn't happen to us, and we come to believe it shouldn't because we are strong. So we keep quiet. It happens to us, but we say nothing."

Her statements and strikingly similar remarks from other Afro-Peruvian women activists led me to focus my ethnographic research on intimate partner violence (IPV) among women of African descent.[1] I wanted to understand the interlocking structures of oppression that create and sustain these beliefs, which are contradicted by the violence that shapes the lives of Afro-Peruvian women. Those statements, I would learn, are the social manifestation of the systemic violence that fuels the calculated social and political exclusion of Afro-descendant women in Peru.

I set out to learn more about women's experiences as they reported and took legal action through state services. In 2015 the Ministry of Women and Vulnerable Populations (Ministerio de la mujer y poblaciones vulnerables), or MIMP, began to collect data on the ethnicity of women who use Women's Emergency Centers (*Centro emergencia de la mujer*), or CEM, services by including an identity question on the standard intake form. This is one of several efforts headed by the Peruvian government to acknowledge ethnic diversity and to collect disaggregated data in accordance with international documents that have been ratified by the state.[2]

For twenty-one months, I interviewed Black and Afro-Peruvian *usuarias*, women who received support to process their IPV cases through CEM across metropolitan Lima and the constitutional province of Callao to the north of the city. I conducted ethnographic research consisting of interviews with CEM staff, admissions workers, and usuarias across eight different CEM. I also engaged in conversations and activities with Afro-Peruvian social activists, state workers, and members of the feminist movement. I use pseudonyms for members of Presencia y Palabra, a Black feminist collective I cofounded, but include the real names of other activists. I champion Black women as critical analysts of their circumstances, exceedingly capable of and best suited for providing insight into the sociopolitical problems they face. Their voices and experiences are frequently dismissed and devalued. I seek to rectify that on a minor scale through my writing by centering them as knowledge producers worthy of note.

I begin by addressing stereotypes about Black women to demonstrate that the absence of their experiences from local and national narratives of IPV is a result of sociopolitical silencing. I identify and deconstruct the stereotypes that form the basis of accepted understandings about Black women and bar their stories of violence from public view. I then provide a record of different kinds of violence Afro-descendant usuarias reported and show how anti-Black racism contours their experiences. I conclude by considering approaches to support Black women through understanding gender-based violence (GBV) and strategies for its eradication.

Black Women's Aggression

In Peru, stereotypes about Black women's aggression and their sexual prowess are used to support the false belief that they do not endure IPV. These ideas constitute what Patricia Hill Collins calls "controlling images," which she defines as "images designed to make racism, sexism, poverty, and other forms of social injustice appear to be natural, normal, and inevitable parts of everyday life" (1990, 69). Much like Afro-descendant women in other parts of the diaspora, Black women in Peru are subjected to specific kinds of degrading stereotypes that perpetuate reductive and discriminatory ideas about their racial and gender identities to justify their oppression (Walker 2017; Hill Collins 1990; Harris-Perry 2011). To be recognized as both a woman and Black is to be perceived as angry and aggressive. This distances Black women from being viewed as submissive, a stereotype widely associated with Indigenous women from the Andean region (CEDET 2008; Alcalde 2017). Both in terms of physical attributes and demeanor, Black women are deemed more masculine due in part to their historical subjection to grueling labor (Zamudio 1995; Hill Collins 1990; Muñoz Flores 2014). This has also been used as justification for controlling Black women with the use or threat of physical violence.

In the media, Black women also appear larger than Indigenous and *mestizo* men, which further supports the presumption that they are more than capable of causing bodily harm. This idea is also reinforced linguistically through the frequent use of the Spanish word *brava* to describe Black women, which, when used in this context means "strong" or "fierce" and constitutes a warning. However, the essence of the word *brava* relates to fear of Black women's voices, which are thought to be proof of their aggressive nature. During my research, Afro-Peruvian women—activists and usuarias—repeatedly signaled that those around them perceived them as aggressive or intimidating because of the sound of their voices, which serves as one exemplification of their "controlling image" (Hill Collins 1990). Their voices were described as "grating," "scary," "deep," and "loud," even when they were speaking in their normal or quiet tones.

Afro-descendant Women's Experiences

Afro-Peruvian women's experiences offer stark contrast to the stereotype of Black women as one-dimensional, inherently aggressive people. Claudia, an elderly usuaria who was a mother of four, lived with her husband who had abused her for decades and whom she reported for the first time when we met. She had short, curly hair and light skin—so light that one of the CEM workers refused to believe she was Afro-descendant. Claudia described herself as *trigüeña*, or wheat-colored, but identified as Afro-descendant because her father is Black. During our interview, in a small windowless room of the CEM in her district, she told me that she didn't get yelled at in the street for being Black because of her features, but she noticed that this happened to women who were identifiably Black because of their skin tone, hair, and other features. "You see it happen all the time with men on the street. A Black woman walks by, and she's bigger than the other women, and the men lower their voices and say "Cuidado, esa negra 'ta brava" (Be careful, that Black woman is fierce), like they are afraid of her." Claudia's comment provides a clear understanding of the way the word *brava* is used to describe Black women but also emphasizes the fact that this belief is so commonplace, it is discussed openly in public spaces and readily understood by society.

Angelina, a young, quiet usuaria, was living at home with her parents in a poor neighborhood when we spoke. Until shortly before our meeting, she had been living with her boyfriend in his family home, but her mother and aunts came to move her out once they realized she was being abused by her partner. Angelina then reported her boyfriend for physical violence at her mother's insistence. During our interview, I asked her how she self-identified and whether she believed there were common perceptions of Black women. She recalled being chastised by her mother, whom she described as white on different occasions due to her voice: "We would be talking, and she would suddenly cover her ears and say, 'Shut up, you're screaming like a *negra* (Black woman)!' and I wasn't screaming! Maybe I was a little excited, but I certainly wasn't screaming." Her account, like those of many others, demonstrates how social beliefs that Black women are loud and intimidating even permeate familial relationships.

In Presencia y Palabra (or Presencia) meetings, members used similar personal examples to highlight the ways in which Black women's voices signify aggression to the public. Almost everyone could recall encounters with people who told them their voices were loud or grating. One member, Flor, told us that in an office setting, she was asked to lower her voice so many times that she ended up speaking in a whisper. The members collectively agreed that their lived experiences served as proof that they are viewed as more masculine and less docile than Indigenous women and are believed to have bad tempers or to be intimidating. They also pointed out that these stereotypes beget violence from others who feel the need to control them and force Black women to constrict themselves. These experiences left them feeling angry and embarrassed about being treated like living caricatures.

Black Women's Aggression in IPV Discourse

In the context of IPV discourse, it becomes clearer that attempts to deny Black women's humanity form the foundation upon which violence against them is justified. Because Black women are characterized as aggressive and having an innate ability to physically fight, they are only socially legible in the context of violence as women whom no one would dare to hit or as aggressors themselves (Davis 1981; Davis 2006; Hautzinger 2007). One afternoon, at the beginning of my research period, I visited a friend and his cousin, Marco, both of whom are Afro-Peruvian, and mentioned my new research project. Marco wanted to know when I planned to start working.

"As soon as the MIMP gives me the data on Afro-Peruvian women," I answered.

"You mean Black women?" he asked, frowning.

I nodded.

"But whom are you going to speak to?"

It was my turn to look confused.

"Afro-Peruvian women. Black women who have been abused," I said slowly.

Marco leaned toward me. "That's going to be impossible," he murmured apologetically. "Black women don't get hit."

Marco wasn't the only one convinced that Black women are not—and cannot be—victims or survivors of violence. I grew accustomed to hearing comments like "¿Quién se atrevería a pegar a una negra? (Who would dare to hit a Black woman?)," when I wasn't speaking with Black and Afro-descendant women about their experiences of violence.

Afro-Peruvian women are also expected to be complicit in upholding the illusion that they are not subjected to violence. "Failing" to do so, they may be faced with disbelief and shaming. "Tremenda mujer, ¿cómo te va a pegar a ti? ¡Tremenda mujer que se deja pegar! (You're a fierce woman; how could they hit you? A fierce woman who lets people hit her!)" Sofia Carrillo, an Afro-Peruvian journalist and public health specialist, shouted, imitating common public sentiments. These reactions stem from the inability to reconcile the commonplace image of a large, fierce Black woman with that of the victim of domestic violence, often portrayed as a downtrodden, broken shadow.

This pattern of comments and interactions reveals what it means to be a Black woman in the context of intimate violence. In a country where it is estimated that most Black Peruvians are in interracial relationships, women of African descent are likely to be partnered with men of *mestizx* or Indigenous backgrounds—men stereotyped as physically smaller than Black women.[3] This provides further "proof" that these women would not suffer violence or abuse. Therefore, the question "Who would dare to hit a Black woman?" should be understood as "Who would dare hit a strong woman who clearly embodies the threat of violence?" In this way, stereotypes of aggression silence Black women's stories of abuse because they exist outside the scope of what is socially conceived as possible for them—violence against Black women becomes an "unthinkable act" (Trouillot 1995) which perpetuates invisibility. This is mirrored in the lack of political will to bring this issue to the fore and the resource allocation necessary to correct it.

Afro-Peruvian Women's Reactive Aggression

Afro-Peruvian women face the stress and pressures that result from poverty, frequent acts of interpersonal racism, and systemic discrimination as they interact with the government and other institutions. Both the realization of and opposition to their own denigration are grounds for upset: it is logical to feel anger amid such a hostile environment. Yet, since racist thought and practice have been normalized and Black women are hypervisible and viewed as disruptions, their negative reactions to racist comments are often more noticeable to onlookers than the offending actions or comments (Portocarrero 2009; van Dijk 2007; Ames 2011). Susana Matute, a veteran activist involved with Afro-descendant organizing through one of the oldest nongovernmental organizations in the country and an experienced teacher, had plenty to say about this problem in social and professional environments. She spoke about being perceived as having an intimidating presence because of her height—she is roughly five feet, ten inches—and her deep voice. Susana talked about the frustrations of advocating for herself when her body and reaction to offensive behavior become the focal point rather than the inflammatory actions:

> If you're bothering me, why are you surprised that I get aggressive? "Oh, Black women are so aggressive!" Don't be ridiculous. They are hiding the aggression of their actions against us. My aggression is the result of their actions. You provoke me and *I'm* the bad one! Explain that to me. I'm the only one speaking up, so of course I'm scandalous, I'm dramatic . . . ¡soy una negra, pues!/[I'm a Black woman]. . . . You can treat me any way you want but I can't respond in kind. Then on top of all of that I'm tall, I have this face and this [strong voice], *papacito*, of course I'm not going to look like Miss Universe when I retaliate!

Susana's comments describe her views on responding to microaggressions (Solórzano, Ceja, and Yosso 2000; Sue 2010; Sue et al. 2007). Sue et al. (2007) define racial microaggressions as "brief and commonplace daily verbal, behavioral, and environmental indignities, whether intentional or unintentional, that communicate hostile, derogatory, or negative racial slights and insults to the target person or group" (273). These acts induce adverse effects on the mental health of marginalized people, leading, in some cases, to outbursts and anger in response that is reasonable rather than irrational (Sue 2010), which is how the reactions of Susana and many other Black women are perceived. In similar fashion, Patricia Hill Collins (1990) homes in on Black women's aggression as a response to microaggressions, not a predisposition. She demonstrates that these covert acts of racism are insidious because they frequently go unseen by white (and in this case, mestizx) audiences, so reactions to this hostile behavior is interpreted as signs of mental instability and poor character. Susana's comment illustrates the difficulties and frustration of advocating for oneself in a context of normalized violence and a society that expects docility in the face of constant racist and misogynistic rhetoric and actions.

Sexual Stereotypes

The second central stereotype to discussions about Black women and intimate partner violence revolves around their sexuality. Black women are portrayed throughout the diaspora as sexually insatiable (Caldwell 2007; Carneiro 2003; Carrillo and Carrillo 2011; Hill Collins 1990; Crenshaw 1991; Cuche 1975; hooks 1981; Gordon-Ugarte, this volume; Muñoz 2014; Williams 2013). The supposed perpetual willingness of Black women to engage in sexual activity has its roots in the enslavement period, when it was conceived as a justification for sexual assault perpetuated by enslavers, and it continues to be reinforced through media and society today. This discourse warps assault into logical and normalized behavior by characterizing women of African descent as unrapable because their bodies are public property. Since they do not have bodily autonomy, Black women are not able to offer or withdraw consent (Crenshaw 1991; Carneiro 2003; Davis 1981). This myth continues to encourage society to use and control Black women's bodies freely.

In Peru, there are many well-known examples of the objectification of Black women. They include Sibarita, a Peruvian company that produces spices and herbs sold everywhere from corner stores to supermarket chains. The company mascot is a curvaceous Black woman wearing a very short miniskirt, a form-fitting shirt, and a red-and-white polka-dotted head scarf to cover her hair. The head scarf is reminiscent of attire associated with Black servitude and performance as seen in *peñas* or nightclubs that offer dinner and traditional cultural dancing. Peruvians are frequently exposed to the image of the Sibarita woman, and Afro-Peruvian identity is closely associated with traditional dance that features a similar aesthetic (Feldman 2006).

During a Presencia meeting where we discussed violence among Afro-Peruvian women, the women riffed off each other as we sat around the wooden snack-laden table recounting upsetting experiences. Rene mimed taking her headphones off at the bus stop when a man approached her. "I thought he was asking for directions. Instead, he asked me 'How much?' Right there at the bus stop in the middle of the day." We showed our support by offering up sounds of disgust and empathy at the assumption that Rene was a sex worker because she is Black.

These stereotypes do not only hide the violence that Black women in Peru experience, but they themselves are also innately violent; they degrade and deny humanity, personhood, and the right to individual identity and autonomy (Scheper-Hughes and Bourgois 2004, 1). To move from the current status quo to centering Black women's experiences with IPV is not only to understand the fabricated silence around violence but also to dismantle it.

Accounts of Violence

The act of documenting the accounts of violence as told by the usuarias discredits stereotypes and racist tropes that cause ongoing damage to Black women because of their racial and gender identities. This violence has become more visible thanks to the efforts of Afro-Peruvian feminists and women activists who, like their counterparts in other parts of the Latin American region, have taken issue with Afro-Peruvian thinkers and public figures who do not address gender inequality or consider how women's experiences are different from those of men and people of other genders (Carrillo and Carrillo 2011; Carneiro 2003; Caldwell 2007; Safa 2006). Additionally, their critiques of the feminist movement's reluctance, or at times refusal, to recognize the way racism impacts women of different racial identities mirror those made by Black feminists in the United States. Both camps agree that anti-Blackness along with sexism and poverty makes Black women vulnerable to social, political, and economic exploitation and subjugation (Isis Internacional 1983, 77; Carneiro 2003; MIMP 2014; Crenshaw 1991; Curiel Pichardo 2009; Guy-Sheftall 2013; Perry 2010, 2013; Ritchie 1996; DeCosta-Willis 2003). The following excerpts serve as proof of the multiple kinds of violence suffered by Afro-Peruvian women at the hands of their current and former romantic partners. As such, this is a contribution to the written record of abuse, which holds great political importance for Peruvians of African descent collectively.

Naming Violence

Legibility in the eyes of the state in this case requires compliance with standardized measurements that have previously been set (Scott 1998, 27; Merry 2016). The women I interviewed had been registered in the system and passed through the intake CEM process. Therefore, they spoke about the violence they endured using the categories outlined by the state: physical, sexual, economic, and psychological.[4] In this chapter, I am arguing that the suppression of Afro-Peruvian women's accounts of violence via the use of controlling images and systemic anti-Black racism constitutes psychological violence; therefore, I have not included a subsection specifically dedicated to psychological abuse. For further analysis on racial violence and Afro-Peruvian women's identity, see Lewis 2020)

Physical Violence

The presence of physical violence in numerous cases contradicts the myth that Afro-Peruvian women are never hit. In many cases, acts of physical assault occur for the first time early in the relationship. Vanessa, a woman in her late twenties, lived near the sea with her sister, just across the street from her mother. Her house, like the others in the neighborhood, was made of repurposed wood salvaged from the port, a sign of meager income. Vanessa worked as a waitress in a small, informal restaurant and saved her earnings to move into a small apartment. She had been with her boyfriend, Felix, the father of her five-year-old son, for ten years before ending their relationship and returning to the family home. Thinking about the early days of their relationships, she said, "First came the blows, the slaps. The first time was when we first started going out. I was young, probably about sixteen, seventeen years old. The first time he slapped me it shocked us both. He pulled my hair and slapped me across the face. I looked at him, startled, and then he started to cry. I felt that I had to forgive him because he was going through a difficult time."

The final straw was when he showed up at her mother's house for their son's birthday party some months earlier, yelled at her, and dragged her down the stairs by her hair, after which her family threw him out of their home. He continued calling her in hopes that she would resume the relationship as she had in the past, but he wouldn't come to the house because her mother and four sisters were around.

Claudia's husband of some thirty-odd years began to hit her at the beginning of their marriage: "He was upset about dinner and we were arguing about it. He hit me hard, right across the face. I was stunned. In those days you didn't talk about things that went on in your house, so I just went to my room and shut the door. He beat me for years until he got too sick and weak to do it. Then he continued with verbal abuse." Claudia felt she had to stay with her husband because when she was first married, she had no support. Her mother told her she just had to accept the situation, so she endured the violence.

Most usuarias had been physically abused by their partners. Physical violence manifested itself in slaps, hair pulling, kicks, punches, shoves, and stabbings. While in some cases they remembered the instances as few and far between which made them even more jarring, in other cases the violence escalated consistently, in both frequency and severity. Two usuarias were in the process of filing criminal charges against their partners for attempted murder, or femicide.

Jasenia was in her early twenties and came to the CEM with her two children, one who was still breastfeeding and the other who was three years old. She had long curly hair, dark skin, and a raspy voice. Jasenia stayed home all day with her children. She wanted to look for work. Her father promised her a job as a municipal street cleaner, but she waited until her boyfriend's arrest to accept the position so she wouldn't run into him on the street. She told me about the last time she saw him. He had stormed out of a wedding they both attended and then broke into her house through her bedroom window later that night when she was back at home:

> The last time he broke into the house we were yelling at each other, and he pulled out his gun and aimed it at my head. I told my daughter to run to get her grandparents. I ran to the bedroom, and he ran in behind me, pushed me on the ground and started choking me. "If I can't have you then he definitely won't," he said, even though I'm not seeing anyone! I tried to get him off of me, but I fell unconscious. When my family finally got to the house, he was slamming my head into the floor.

Jasenia's family encouraged her to report her boyfriend since he already had criminal antecedents. She chose to come to the CEM when she knew he would be busy so he wouldn't follow her.

Clara was anxious to move forward with her life. A wide smile lit up her round face whenever she spoke about her new partner, an older man in the navy who was well off and adored her. He wanted to buy a new house in a middle-class district and move her out of her current neighborhood. He promised she wouldn't have to work at the stand in the market anymore, but Clara felt she couldn't move on until her former partner was in prison. Clara's father was a neighborhood boxing champion and taught her how to fight when she was young. She was short but scrappy, and her acquired skills helped her stave off her ex-boyfriend's attempts to hit her earlier on in their relationship, but he became increasingly violent and eventually overpowered her. He stabbed her and stomped on her head on more than one occasion in front of their children. Their screams alerted her parents, who lived next door. They threw her boyfriend out and got her medical attention. Clara listed off her ex-boyfriend's favorite tactics: "He's a violent man. He likes to kick me, hit me in the head with this (she points to her elbow, holding her forearm vertically in front of herself as she swings her arm, jerking the point downward). Once on tv I heard that one good blow to the head can kill you. I think to myself 'If he hits me in the head and kills me, who will my children stay with?'" While deeply entrenched views of Black women as strong continue to influence policy decisions reflecting a belief that Afro-Peruvian women do not require specific attention, usuaria experiences clearly show that violence permeates their intimate lives and that they need support.

Sexual Violence

Sexual violence was seldom mentioned in interviews or discussions with usuarias. As with other types of violence, the lack of mention does not mean that it did not happen, especially considering the added stigma of sexual violence and Blackness, and issues of consent in relationships. However, on a few occasions, women did tell me outright that they had been sexually assaulted.

Rosa, a middle-aged woman with twins, was preparing to move out of Lima and back to her hometown in one of the southern departments when we spoke. She left her job handing out fliers to stay home with her daughter because her husband used drugs and would break into the house to steal her savings and other household items to support his addiction. On one occasion, he broke in at night and sexually assaulted her after an argument. She never told anyone but the CEM staff and me during our interview. Rosa no longer felt safe in her house and was hoping to rent it to someone else while away in hopes of generating some income to support herself and her child.

Ines's husband viciously attacked her when she told him he could no longer live with her and their children in their small home. He held her down and inserted a broken stick into her vagina, causing major internal damage to her vaginal tract and her uterus. The neighbors heard her screaming and called the police. She was rushed to the emergency room for reconstructive surgery.

During a Presencia meeting, Gladys stood up from her chair and put her hands on her hips. We all laughed as we took in the sight of the seasoned activist known for her no-nonsense demeanor, swinging her hips around at an impressive speed like an electrified dashboard hula dancer. She rolled her eyes and mimicked the comments she'd heard time and again about Black women. "'You're so exotic and sexy!' Ha! They talk about us like our waists move as fast as the highest speed on a blender." Gladys's commentary about lightning-fast waistlines made plain the ridiculous assumption that Black women are sexually insatiable. Later, our discussion became more somber as we spoke about how this deeply ingrained stereotype drowns out the realities of abuse and denies them the support to which they are entitled.

Economic Violence

In recent years, the uptick in national and global awareness and action around the problem of GBV has resulted in the creation of more legislative and policy guidelines in Peru, like Law 30364 which was passed in 2015 (*El Peruano* 2015). It is the first law to criminalize economic violence. While the Afro-descendant population shows elevated levels of poverty (CEDET 2005, 2008; MINCUL and GRADE 2015; Luciano 2012), disaggregate data are key to uncovering the impact of economic violence on Black women. The precarious nature of work in the informal economy means that while most usuarias worked or had worked for most of their lives, the jobs available to them were not always long-term or stable. Most women who worked in these environments did not have signed agreements with their employers, nor did they receive benefits. As a result, they often relied on their partners for financial support to help maintain their households. These women often forwent work to ensure their children were supervised and became dependent on their partners' income. Like many others, these women sought help in the CEM because the services are free, which allows poor and lower-class women to access support they could not otherwise afford.

Several usuarias described how their boyfriends and husbands withheld money to punish, disempower, and control them, exploiting the financially dependent nature of their relationship.

When Solsiret, who worked as a seamstress in a small tailoring business, left her job to care for her first daughter after she was born, her boyfriend, the sole earner, began using his finances as leverage. At the beginning of their relationship, her boyfriend said he admired her independence. Her family was from northern Peru, and Solsiret migrated to Lima and created a life for herself before meeting him and having their child. She was very concerned about how vulnerable and dependent she had become because he controlled their finances: "I don't know anything about our financial situation. I don't know how much he makes or how much he has saved. If he leaves, how would I cover basic costs? I don't have a pension and I can't leave my daughter at home to go out to work." She told me she had been more than capable of managing her finances; she had done it for years before meeting her partner, but by the time she started coming to the CEM, she had to ask him for money for anything she wanted or needed.

Claudia recalled many instances where she went hungry when she and her husband fought: "Whenever he got mad, he would go out and not leave me money for lunch or dinner." She felt upset that he had that level of control over her, and she tried to be strategic about when she would argue with him or avoid bringing up problems at all. Like Solsiret, she resented the control her partner held over her life, but she didn't see any way to change her circumstances at the time.

Inés's ex-boyfriend regularly stole from her, leaving her unable to achieve financial independence. She lived hand to mouth, selling hard candies individually on street corners or on buses all day, earning enough to cover meals, buy more candies to sell, and save to pay her rent: "I would work all day selling candy and come home exhausted with fifty soles (roughly $20 USD). He would wait until I was asleep and then find the hole in the mattress where I kept the money and take it. I would wake up to find five soles left. I had to use that to go buy more candy to sell. No money for breakfast, lunch, snacks, nothing. And I had two small children." Inés explained that her ex-partner made planning and saving impossible. Her plans for moving her children to a different part of the city to be farther away from her ex were stalled, since she couldn't count on having the money she needed to leave.

Jasenia had to sell clothing to feed her children when her partner punished her by withholding money. The sustained threat of violence also stopped her from seeking out work. Jasenia's father worked on a municipal clean-up crew, and he offered to help secure a similar position for her, but Jasenia was scared that her boyfriend would find out. He told her he didn't want her to work because he wanted to provide for her, and she agreed to stay home with the children. Later, she noticed he refused to give her money when he was upset with her: "He wouldn't give me money, not twenty soles (roughly $5 USD) for lunch for myself and the kids. So, I packed my bag and I took two pairs of his shoes to sell since I had no money. He doesn't want me to work. He always says he'll give me money. I'm scared that if I take a job and he finds out or sees me at work, he'll come for me. I don't work out of fear." This controlling behavior not only stymied Jasenia's ability to generate the income she needed to feed herself and her children but further barred her from accumulating the financial resources that would allow her to move toward independence and cut ties with her boyfriend.

Conclusion

My research and the voices of the Afro-descendant women who shared their experiences offer a glimpse into the harsh realities of gendered and racial violence in Peru. This violence is indicative of the social and political problems that exist in a nation-state that is only beginning to critically reflect on its identity as a pluricultural nation and the histories that contribute to the systemic injustices its citizens face. Black women face the compound effects of race, gender, and class-based violence, and their experiences cannot be fully understood without considering the role of these three components in their experiences. The stereotypes of natural aggression and hypersexuality largely serve to allow violence against Afro-Peruvian women to go unseen and unnamed by the wider society. Only by centering the stories of Afro-descendant women and considering their knowledge and expertise acquired through lived experiences, research, observation, and critical reflection can we truly understand the problems they face (see White, this volume).

IPV discourse is expanding to encompass forms of abuse that do not cause immediate physical harm given structural inequalities and other kinds of violence that are not solely a result of interpersonal violence. It is worth noting that the stereotypes that obscure violence against Afro-Peruvian women have roots in the colonial period and only correspond directly to physical and sexual violence—more "traditional" forms of abuse—rather than all four categories. Although they are now receiving more social and institutional attention, psychological, economic, and racial violence are not always tangible in the same ways as the former two, which makes them particularly insidious as they continue to covertly foment systemic inequality. There is still much work to be done in order to fully understand the scope and impact of these forms of abuse, and to offer adequate support to those affected by them.

The question of violence against Afro-Peruvian women invites a much deeper discussion that demands that we push past the interpersonal to the structural, from the private to the public, to take stock of how that violence permeates their lives and affects others around them. Just as we see a demand for a broader understanding of what constitutes racism, we should also demand that IPV discourse expand its scope to seriously consider racial violence in meaningful ways that link the interpersonal to larger current and historical trends of inequality. What effect does economic violence have on poverty for Afro-Peruvian women? How does it tie into more expansive patterns of systemic violence against them? These questions can only be answered when interpersonal dynamics are linked to overarching public trends.

There is a compelling argument for officially considering racial violence as a key dimension of IPV. In Peru, a society deeply marred by racism and one that has been historically hostile toward Africans and their descendants, it is imperative to ask how racial inequality plays into interpersonal violence. Without an awareness of the complex, compound effects of race, class, and gender-based violence, Afro-descendant women's experiences will remain unseen regardless of inclusive policies.

While there is a growing body of information that provides a window into Black women's lives under the current circumstances, it is important to develop a vision for what Peruvian society would look like if the needs of Black and Afro-descendant women were met. This provides a goal to work toward and a way to generate a vision of Afro-descendant women as fulfilled agents. This vision includes the following:

- Universal access to quality education, housing, childcare, health care, dignified work and pay, and leisure time
- Strong social support at the local, regional, and national levels
- Enforcement of the cultural, civil, and political rights and respect for the autonomy and legacy of all groups of peoples in Peru
- Support and services for immigrants
- Ample social and political participation of all Peruvians
- Dedicated commitment to gender parity and the safety of people of all genders and sexual orientations

These are merely a few markers that would signal a radical shift toward a society free of violence dedicated to the well-being and prosperity of all peoples, and a truly safe environment for Afro-Peruvian women.

Notes

1 "IPV" specifically refers to acts of violence committed by a current or former intimate partner, including spouses, civil union partners, or less formal relationships including sexual partners (WHO 2016). The National Demographic and Family Health Survey indicated that in 2020, 54.8 percent of the women interviewed said that they had been abused physically, sexually, or psychologically by their partner or husband in the prior twelve months (INEI 2020), making GBV a rampant problem in the nation. The term "Afro-descendant" or "Afro-Peruvian" largely refers to people with physical characteristics commonly associated with African ancestry like dark skin and thick, curly hair textures but also includes people who may not possess these traits but because of family heritage, geographical location, or cultural practices are considered Afro-Peruvian. When I use the word "Black" I am speaking specifically about Afro-Peruvian women whose physical characteristics would cause them to be socially categorized as someone of African descent.
2 These accords include the International Labor Organization's Convention No. 169 for Indigenous and Tribal Peoples (ILO 1989), the Convention of Belém do Pará (OAS 1994), and the final declaration of the 2001 United Nations Durban World Conference against Racism, Racial Discrimination, Xenophobia, and related Intolerance (WHO 2001), which have collectively supported visibility for women of African descent in the realm of gender violence.
3 Scant in-depth work has been done on same and interracial relationships among Afro-Peruvians. Carrillo and Carrillo (2011) have estimated high levels of race mixing among Afro-Peruvians, which they attribute to a desire to whiten.
4 All the names of the usuarias and Presencia members are pseudonyms and personal information has been altered to protect the identity of the women who participated in this research.

References

Alcalde, M. Cristina. 2007. "'Why Would You Marry a Serrana?' Women's Experiences of Identity-Based Violence in the Intimacy of Their Homes in Lima." *Journal of Latin American Anthropology* 12, no. 1: 1–24.
Ames, Patricia. 2011. "Discriminación, Desigualdad y Territorio: Nuevas y Viejas Jerarquías en Definición (Perú)." In *Desarrollo, Desigualdades y Conflictos Sociales: Una Perspectiva desde los Países Andinos*, edited by Marcos Cueto and Adrián Lerner, 15–34. Lima: IEP Instituto de Estudios Peruanos.
Caldwell, Kia Lilly. 2007. *Negras in Brazil: Re-Envisioning Black Women, Citizenship, and the Politics of Identity*. New Brunswick, NJ: Rutgers University Press.
Carneiro, Sueli. 2003. "Enegrecer o feminismo: A situação da mulher negra na América Latina a partir de uma perspectiva de gênero." *Racismos Contemporâneos* 17: 49–58.
Carrillo, Mónica, and Giovanna Carrillo. 2011. *Diagnóstico sobre la Problemática de Género y la Situación de Mujeres Afrodescendientes en el Perú: Análisis y Propuesta de Políticas Públicas*. Lima: MIMDES.
CEDET (El Centro de Desarrollo Étnico). 2005. *El Estado y El Pueblo Afroperuano: Balance y Propuestas del Proceso Afroperuano ante los Acuerdos de la Conferencia Regional de las Américas*. Lima: Bellido Ediciones E.I.R.L.

———. 2008. *La Poblacion Afroperuana y Los Derechos Humanos: Diagnóstico sobre el Plan Nacional de Derechos Humanos en Localidades con Presencia Afroperuana.* Lima: Bellido Ediciones E.I.R.L.
Crenshaw, Kimberle. 1991. "Mapping the Margins: Intersectionality, Identity Politics, and Violence against Women of Color." *Stanford Law Review* 43, no. 6: 1241–1299.
Cuche, Dénis. 1975. *Poder Blanco y Resistencia Negra en el Perú: Un Estudio de la Condición Social del Negro en el Perú después de la Abolición de la Esclavitud.* Lima: Instituto Nacional de Cultura.
Curiel Pichardo, Rosa Ynés Ochy. 2009. "Descolonizado el Feminismo: Una Perspectiva desde Américal Latina y el Caribe." 1–8. https://feministas.org/IMG/pdf/Ochy_Curiel.pdf. Accessed on: March 15, 2022.
Davis, Angela Y. 1981. *Women, Race, and Class.* New York: Vintage Books.
Davis, Dána-Ain. 2006. *Battered Black Women and Welfare Reform: Between a Rock and a Hard Place.* Albany: State University of New York Press.
DeCosta-Willis, Miriam. 2003. *Daughters of the Diaspora: Afra-Hispanic Writers.* Kingston: Ian Randle.
El Peruano. 2015. "Ley para Prevenir, Sancionar y Erradicar la Violencia contral las Mujeres y los Integrantes del Grupo Familiar." http://busquedas.elperuano.com.pe/normaslegales/ley-para-prevenir-sancionar-y-erradicar-la-violencia-contra-ley-n-30364-1314999-1/.
Feldman, Heidi Carolyn. 2006. *Black Rhythms of Peru: Reviving African Musical Heritage in the Black Pacific.* Middletown, CT: Wesleyan University Press.
Guy-Sheftall, Beverly, ed. 2013. *Words of Fire: An Anthology of African-American Feminist Thought.* New York: New Press.
Harris-Perry, Melissa. 2011. *Sister Citizen: Shame, Stereotypes, and Black Women in America.* New Haven, CT: Yale University Press.
Hautzinger, Sarah. 2007. *Violence in the City of Women: Police and Batterers in Bahia, Brazil.* Oakland: University of California Press.
Hill Collins, Patricia. 1990. *Black Feminist Thought: Knowledge, Consciousness and the Politics of Empowerment.* New York: Routledge.
hooks, bell. 1981. Ain't I a Woman: Black Women and Feminism. London: Pluto Press.
ILO (International Labor Organization). 1989. "Convention C169: Indigenous and Tribal Peoples' Convention, 1989 (No. 169)." www.ilo.org/dyn/normlex/en/f?p=NORMLEXPUB:12100:0::NO::P12100_IL O_CODE:C169.
INEI (Instituto Nacional de Estadística e Informática). 2020. *Encuesta Demográfica y de Salud Familiar (ENDES).* Lima. www.inei.gob.pe/media/MenuRecursivo/publicaciones_digitales/Est/Lib1795/.
Isis Internacional. 1983. *II Encuentro Feminista Latinoamericano y del Caribe: Lima, Peru.* Santiago, Chile: Isis Internacional.
Lewis, Eshe. 2020. "*Negras* and *Trigüeñas*: Blackness and Afro-descendants in Women's Emergency Centers in Peru." *Latin American and Caribbean Ethnic Studies* 15, no. 2: 154–169.
Luciano, José. 2012. *Los Afroperuanos: Racismo, Discriminación e Identidad.* Lima: Bellido Ediciones E.I.R.L.
Merry, Sally Engle. 2016. *The Seduction of Quantification: Measuring Human Rights, Gender Violence, and Sex Trafficking.* Chicago: University of Chicago Press.
MINCUL (Ministerio de la Cultura) and GRADE (Grupo de Análisis para el Desarrollo). 2015. *Estudio Especializado sobre Población Afroperuana.* Lima: Proyecto Gráfico S.A.C.

Muñoz Flores, Rocío. 2014. "Representaciones Sociales de las Mujeres Afroperuanas." In *Afroperuanas: Situación y Marco Legal de Protección de sus Derechos*, edited by el Ministerio de la Mujer y Poblaciones Vulnerables. Tomo 5. Lima: Editorial Súper Gráfica E.I.R.L.

OAS (Organization of American States). 1994. "Inter-American Convention on the Prevention, Punishment, and Eradication of Violence against Women (Convention of Belém do Pará)." June 9. www.oas.org/en/mesecvi/docs/BelemDoPara-ENGLISH.pdf.

Perry, Keisha-Khan Y. 2010. "Racialized History and Urban Politics: Black Women's Wisdom in Grassroots Struggles." In *Brazil's New Racial Politics*, edited by Bernd Reiter and Gladys L. Michell, 141–164. Boulder, CO: Lynne Reinner.

———. 2013. *Black Women against the Land Grab: The Fight for Racial Justice in Brazil*. Minneapolis: University of Minnesota.

Portocarrero, Gonzalo. 2009. *Racismo y Mestizaje y Otros Ensayos*. Lima: Fondo Editorial del Congreso del Perú.

Ritchie, Beth E. 1996. *Compelled to Crime: The Gender Entrapment of Battered Black Women*. New York: Routledge.

Safa, Helen I. 2006. "Racial and Gender Inequality in Latin America: Afro-descendant Women Respond." In *Feminist Africa 7: Diaspora Voices*, edited by Rhoda Reddock, 49–66. Cape Town: African Gender Institute.

Scheper-Hughes, Nancy, and Philippe I. Bourgois, eds. 2004. "Introduction." In *Violence in War and Peace: An Anthology*, 1–32. Malden, MA: Blackwell.

Scott, James C. 1998. *Seeing Like a State: How Certain Schemes to Improve the Human Condition Have Failed*. New Haven, CT: Yale University Press.

Solórzano, Daniel, Miguel Ceja, and Tara Yosso. 2000. "Critical Race Theory, Racial Microaggressions, and Campus Racial Climate: The Experience of African American College Students." *Journal of Negro Education* 69, no. 1/2: 60–73.

Sue, Derald Wing. 2010. *Microaggressions in Everyday Life: Race, Gender and Sexual Orientation*. Hoboken, NJ: John Wiley & Sons.

Sue, Derald Wing, Christina M. Capodilupo, Gina C. Torino, Jennifer M. Bucceri, Aisha M. B. Holder, Kevin L. Nadal, and Marta Esquilin. 2007. "Racial Microaggressions in Everyday Life." *American Psychologist* 64, no. 4: 271–286.

Trouillot, Michel-Rolph. 1995. *Silencing the Past: Power and the Production of History*. Boston: Beacon.

van Dijk, Teun A. 2007. *Racismo y Discurso en América Latina*. Barcelona: Gedisa.

Walker, Tamara J. 2017. "Black Skin, White Uniforms: Race, Clothing, and the Visual Vernacular of Luxury in the Andes." *Souls* 19, no. 2: 196–212.

WHO (World Health Organization). 2001. "World Conference against Racism, Racial Discrimination, Xenophobia and Related Intolerance Declaration," September. www.un.org/WCAR/durban.pdf.

———. 2005. WHO Multi-country Study on Women's Health and Domestic Violence against Women. Geneva: WHO.

———. 2016 "Violence against Women: Intimate Partner and Sexual Violence against Women. Fact sheet." www.who.int/mediacentre/factsheets/fs239/en/.

Williams, Erica Lorraine. 2013. *Sex Tourism in Bahia: Ambiguous Entanglements*. Champaign: University of Illinois Press.

Zamudio, Delia. 1995. *Piel de Mujer*. Lima: FOVIDA.

8

A Creole Christmas

Sexual Panic and Reproductive Justice in Bluefields, Nicaragua

ISHAN GORDON-UGARTE

Notions of Black women's sexual deviance are ubiquitous in scholarly and popular considerations of Afro-Atlantic communities including Nicaragua. Social scientists Webster and Ethel (2014) assert that women in Afro-Nicaraguan Creole communities engage in premarital sexuality, often become pregnant as adolescents, and contribute to a communal moral breakdown through their deviant sexuality. Many Creoles in Bluefields, a town on Nicaragua's Caribbean Coast, share this viewpoint and concur that the community must address this issue.[1]

However, personal experience and ethnographic research demonstrate that Western values of respectability regarding women's sexuality are the idealized norm in Creole Bluefields and are also held by young women themselves. These values include married women's foundational reproductive role in the patriarchal nuclear family, the sexual abstinence of unmarried women, and fear of unmarried women's sexuality and reproduction as threats to Creole society's moral fabric (Cooper 2017, 7). This chapter demonstrates that within patriarchal politics of respectability, the stereotype of Black women's hypersexuality has generated complex social processes—a "sexual panic." At the center of this panic is the disciplining of unmarried young women's erotics understood in Creole society to already be illicit or "pornographic" (Lorde 2007, 88). Under the contradictory conditions of sexual panic, young Creole women (YCW) participate in behaviors that both conform to respectable values and contradict them as they struggle to enact empowering "erotic" practices (Lorde 2007, 87–88) and/or succumb to the sexual desires of consuming men.[2] Deprived of reproductive justice by the conditions of "sexual panic," the occasional but regular result of such erotic practices and sexual consumption is premarital pregnancy. Such pregnancy, which brings on intense shame and social marginalization for individual women, is the proof of and fulfillment of the community's and social scientists' expectations of deviance from the sexual norms of respectable society, while the norms themselves remain strongly held by all.

Creole society in Bluefields and its historic and contemporary conditions of existence are unique. However, careful analysis of the ways in which Creole women's erotics and reproductive justice are disciplined as aberrant within the context of sexual panic can be useful for understanding similar processes elsewhere in the hemisphere. Accordingly, this chapter does not concern itself with rates of out-of-wedlock pregnancy that are so prominent in the social science literature. Such questions are underpinned by the hegemonic sanctity of the nuclear family and covert moralism regarding Black women's erotics. Instead, it analyzes the complex and contradictory structural, cultural, and social forces that create sexual panic in Bluefields, which regulates young Black women's erotic power. It starts from the counterintuitive observation that despite strongly held ideal societal values that prohibit sexual behavior outside of marriage for women, premarital pregnancy among YCW regularly occurs.

I explore the factors that compose sexual panic through the analysis of a Christmas play enacted at the Moravian Church in Bluefields' Old Bank neighborhood. Based on my ethnographic research, I explore the panic's consequences for YCW's reproductive and erotic lives. I engaged in ethnographic participant observation in Bluefields throughout the formal fieldwork portion of my research from June 2016 to June 2017. I undertook these activities in family, recreational, and religious institutional settings as well as on the internet. To augment the information and analysis garnered from such participant observation, associates and I conducted semistructured interviews with eighty-five Creole women and fifteen men, aged eighteen years and older. We also interviewed leaders and influential members of local Creole religious institutions. In addition, for the background knowledge that animates the descriptions and analysis, I make ample use of information garnered from reflexive autoethnography. I was born and spent my preschool years and summers in Bluefields, and all my mother's family remains there.

Bluefields, Nicaragua, is the peri-urban administrative capital of the South Caribbean Coast Autonomous Region of Nicaragua. It is a bustling port city of around 50,000 people located at the mouth of the Escondido River. Afro-Caribbean Creoles, who were once the majority, now make up about a third of the population, with the remainder made up of Mestizxs, Miskitu, and other urbanizing Indigenous people. In Nicaragua, Creoles occupy a middle social and economic stratum benefiting from familial remittances and transnational labor (Goett 2017).

Creoles are understood and understand themselves to be *the* Black population of Nicaragua though they are phenotypically highly varied. As such, Creoles are marginal to the nation socially, politically, and economically. They are tainted with foreignness—often referred to as *negros Jamaicans* (Black Jamaicans). They are stereotyped as criminal, hypersexual, athletic, musical, and intellectually inferior in the ways that Black people are stereotyped elsewhere in the world. In the Nicaraguan imagination, the Caribbean Coast in general and Bluefields in particular are racially Black, thus culturally backward and underdeveloped—a threat to national identity (Gordon 1998; Goett 2017).

Creoles emerged as a group with a distinct culture and identity in the early nineteenth century. They were originally a maroon community within the Mosquitia, a Caribbean Central American region under British colonial indirect rule that became an enclave of U.S. capitalism in the early twentieth century (Hale 1994; Goett 2017). British colonial and American neocolonial domination were executed in part "through the sexual objectification and often violent sexual consumption of Black women by occupying Euro-American male agents and by the imposition of capitalist, anti-Black, and patriarchic Protestant values and norms of respectability that positioned blackness as inferior and Black women as hypersexual" (Gordon-Ugarte 2022, 53). Missionary churches, particularly the Moravian Church, played an important role in this colonial and neocolonial domination of the region's people. Creole women in Bluefields were the first to be evangelized, though men soon followed. In response, Creoles developed a "politics of respectability" (Higginbotham 1993).[3]

I argue elsewhere (Gordon-Ugarte 2022) that sexual control of women (a) through the civilizing moral imperative of Protestant Respectability and (b) through the sexual violence and coercion associated with colonialism and slavery were central features of the colonial and neocolonial racial and gender structuration of Mosquitian society. Creole cultural practices, beliefs, and values did not merely mimic European practices. Rather, they were produced through processes specific to them as they created their own unique and complex culture. Creole Respectability, for example, was modeled on the colonial version of "private [nuclear] family values of the old Elizabethan poor-law tradition" (Cooper 2017, 15) in which the disciplining of Black women's erotic power was central. This colonial model included, as a central feature, the often-coercive consumption of Black women's sexuality as men's prerogative.

A Christmas Play

The Moravian Church has the largest number of Creole adherents of any denomination, and Bluefields' main church is the largest in Caribbean Nicaragua. The Moravians also have chapels in Bluefields' principal Creole neighborhoods. The following ethnographic vignette took place in the Old Bank neighborhood chapel on Christmas Eve. It was part of a traditional Christmas celebration featuring school-aged performers that annually attracts Creole Moravians from all over town. This Christmas Eve, the chapel was packed.

Toward the end of the two-hour program, a young Creole boy walks onto the stage where the pulpit usually stands. He announces that the Christmas program will be presenting a drama about why people "should be careful of the internet." Suddenly, a young Creole woman (thirteen years-old) walks through a wooden door placed at the front of the stage. She assumes the role of the character Ms. Joan, wearing a white skirt with red embroidered designs that reaches her ankles. Over the skirt, she wears an apron topped with a red sleeveless blouse (this is the stereotypical attire of a traditional mature and respectable Creole woman). Ms. Joan sits in her rocking chair talking on her cell phone until she hears a knock on the front door. She dashes to the front door to greet family friend Jennifer, a young Creole woman dressed modestly in white jeans and a red blouse with elbow-length sleeves. Both take seats in rocking chairs.

Ms. Joan announces to Jennifer, "I want give my daughta [sixteen-year-old Soan] a nice present this year for her birthday. She want an iPhone."

Immediately Jennifer snaps back, "You crazy gyal? You no have enough money for an iPhone!"

Ms. Joan responds quickly, "I been putting up money for a long time gyal." The scene ends.

A boy (thirteen years old) acting as the bill collector appears at Ms. Joan's front door wearing khaki brown shorts and a blue-colored collared shirt. "Hey, Ms. Joan, I come to tell you that your light bill is due and no matter what I will cut it tomorrow if you no pay!" The boy walks out, closing the door behind him. The audience erupts in laughter. The scene ends.

Jennifer appears on stage and is seen helping Ms. Joan set up her daughter's birthday party. Jennifer has brought a cake, Coca-Cola, and a small gift. Shortly after, Soan's friends arrive to celebrate. Ms. Joan gives her daughter the iPhone and Soan is thrilled. The scene ends with Soan jumping for joy at having received the present.

The next scene opens with Soan at school. There are six chairs aligned in two rows with a student sitting in each. The Creole woman teacher can be heard lecturing: "The internet is a very dangerous place. You must be careful when using it!" Soan sits in the back row taking selfies on her new iPhone. The students begin to turn in their homework while Soan sleeps on her friend's shoulder. Suddenly Soan wakes up: "I no did my schoolwork Professor. I'm sorry Professor. Please do not tell my mom. My mama mean. Please no tell she!" The scene ends.

In the following scene, Soan and her friend Shandi sit in rocking chairs in Soan's living room.

"Gyal I just get one man and him have 25 years!" Soan boasted, "I stay up to three in the mawning chatting with him every day. Now him begging me fa send one picture to him."

"What? Are you crazy? That man could put your picture up online or something!" Shandi gripped back.

"He would never do anything to me."

"Cho! With everyone picture being put up on the internet you neva know!" Shandi states. The scene ends.

Soan's teacher knocks on Ms. Joan's front door. She is dressed formally, wearing black closed-toed shoes with an inch heel, black slacks, and a dark blue–colored blouse with elbow-length sleeves. The teacher walks in and tells Ms. Joan her daughter is sleeping in class and not doing homework. "Nothing is wrong with my daughter. Mind your business! She must have had an off day. She wouldn't just sleep in class like that!" Angry and embarrassed, Ms. Joan throws Soan's teacher out of the house. As the teacher walks out, she screams, "You owe the light bill and everyone knows you can't pay it! You need to watch Soan!" The scene ends.

The next scene opens to Soan's friend Shandi holding her up as they run into Ms. Joan's house. With pleasure, Ms. Joan stands up to greet her daughter. Suddenly the daughter bursts out in tears, weeping, bent over at the waist.

"Something happened! I'm so sorry!" Shandi said concernedly.

"Aye no tell her no tell her!" Soan screams before she blurts out, "The truth is, I meet somebody on the internet, and I get to like him so much and I sent my picture to him."

"And what's wrong with that?" Ms. Joan asks.

"It was a naked picture!" Shandi screams. "And he put it on Facebook and everywhere, sent it to several people and now everyone molesting [bothering] her and making fun of she!"

Soan and Ms. Joan drop to their knees crying and holding one another. Jennifer suddenly appears in the house and suggests they call the police, then screams at Ms. Joan, "I told you not to give that little girl that iPhone! And Shandi, how you could let this happen? You is a bad, bad friend!" Everyone walks off stage as Ms. Joan holds her distraught daughter.

The pulpit is pushed back to its usual place on stage. A Creole woman in her thirties appears standing behind the pulpit and begins talking: "The internet is very dangerous if you do not pay attention to what your children are doing. Parents, you must set boundaries. You need to know what your child is doing. Set a time for internet use. Excessive internet use could affect academic performance, family relationships, and emotional development because when you should be enjoying your family you are on your phone. Young people, don't put pictures of yourself on the internet. The internet is something very public. If you have to hide to put up a picture, it is not good. Nothing stays a secret. What you put on the internet, you need to be able to identify what is good versus what is bad and you need to learn how to behave respectfully online, not just in the streets and school and at home but also on the internet. The internet is a global health crisis that can affect the whole family. Negative consequences in school performance and greater family problems arise—even suicide. Parents, be more engaged with our children and young people to ask the Lord for guidance. God will always lead the way. Do not let anyone depose you from your youth but walk in conduct and prosperity. God loves me and he loves you unconditionally."

The characters from the play gather back on stage in two rows and begin singing in chorus: "Stay safe on the internet. Don't talk to people that you never met," repeating the message just given by the lay pastor.

This vignette highlights the contradictory and fraught circumstances surrounding YCW's erotics. The turbulent relations with family and close friends, church and school officials, and men in the community surrounding their erotics are all aspects of sexual panic. Below, I explore five mutually constituted social processes operating on the structural, cultural, and individual levels that make up sexual panic as exhibited in the play. Their manifestation as themes in this annual ritual is but one demonstration of the centrality of sexual panic to Bluefields' Creole society.

The Colonially Derived Stereotype of Black Women's Hypersexuality

The church through the play constructs Soan's character as a naïve girl who is predisposed to the temptations of sex and sexuality. Although the man who sexually harassed Soan is a main protagonist in the plot, he remains uncritiqued and physically absent. Instead, the play blames Soan and, through her, YCW for their inability to control their sexuality. This is demonstrated by Jennifer, Shandi, and the pastor's criticism of Soan's actions. Soan's shame is extended to her mother and by extension to Creole mothers for not surveilling and disciplining their wayward daughters. The man's actions are completely naturalized, while Soan's actions are demonized. The Christmas drama illustrates the tendency, deeply ingrained in Creole culture, to hold only women responsible for premarital sexuality—unregulated sexuality is blamed on the deviant hypersexuality of YCW.

My ethnographic work in Bluefields reinforces this example of the important role played by the church in the construction of YCW as hypersexual. Through its liturgy, sermons, organizations, and schooling, the church plays a leading role in reproducing the image of young Black women who cannot control their innate pornographic sexual urges and who need the discipline of others to maintain respectability.

Soan is not just Black but young and unmarried. Post-menarche women are considered sexually potent. As they age, they spend more time outside the direct control of their parents at school and in other activities outside the home. This is depicted in the play. At the same time, they and their sexuality are not yet under the control of husbands or limited by the responsibilities of childcare. In this drama, as in young YCW's lives, the stereotype of Black hypersexuality is compounded by that of youthful hypersexuality (Tafari-Ama 2016, 299). My research indicates that men and parents in the Creole community assume that YCW are "hot," better at sex," and always-already available for sexual relations (Martinez and Ethel 2014, 76).

The stereotype of young Black women's hypersexuality is a key aspect of sexual panic. It saturates Bluefields' Creole culture and is encapsulated, both in the Christmas play's choice to blame Soan for the sexual harassment and in the use of a young woman as the prime exemplar of wanton sexuality. As portrayed in the play, because YCW are assumed to be hypersexual, they are viewed as a potential threat to the respectability of Creole societies, families, and themselves. Slavery and colonially derived anti-Black stereotypes of Black women's hypersexuality are contemporarily reproduced in Creole institutions like the church and family. This is an important basis for sexual panic and the prevalent narrative of YCW's propensity to unregulated premarital sexuality.

Creole Respectability: A Hegemonic Value System

The Christmas play annual ritual is an artifact of colonial Victorian culture. My archival work on British colonialism in the Mosquitia demonstrates that Christmas and other key rituals of Protestantism were concerned with reproducing the forms of expression and moral concerns of respectability in Creoles as colonial subjects (Gordon-Ugarte 2022).[4] The Christmas program, and in particular the Christmas play, asserts the importance of conservative Protestant values inherited by Creole Respectability including piety, nuclear families, orderly households, disciplined temperament, conservative dress, frugality, and chastity as a heritage of this past (Offen and Rugeley 2014).

Self-presentation is central to such politics of respectability (Higginbotham 1993), and the congregation/audience's and cast's attire conformed to the norms of Creole Respectability that emerged from this colonial experience. The young woman playing Ms. Joan and the congregation, mostly women, were dressed in modest, dark-colored clothes. The women wore loose midlength or long dresses and skirts with most women's calves, elbows, and forearms visible, while most shoulders were covered. Men wore buttoned-up shirts and slacks.

The hair of each YCW in the congregation and the play was styled fitting the norms of Creole Respectability—maintained in a way considered by the Western conservative mainstream to be well groomed. Most of the YCW under fifteen had their hair brushed and gelled back into midsize braids. The women above sixteen years of age had their hair in three styles: permed straight down their back, in a gelled-back bun, or in thin braids with extensions. No one's hair was visibly frizzy, kinky, or tightly curled. In Bluefields, as elsewhere in the Caribbean, kinky hair violates the precepts of Creole Respectability (Wilson 1974). Long, straight hair is regarded as "good." The kinkier or curlier a young Creole woman's hair is, the greater the chance it will be considered "undone" and in need of control through family intervention. Creole women spend a significant amount of time correcting their hair and that of their younger dependents. They know that if they do not do so, others will criticize them.

In Bluefields, the disciplining of Black women's erotic bodies through clothing, hair texture, and styles is directly related to public assessment of young women's sexuality as pornographic. For example, twenty-three-year-old Natalie describes how people judged her through her hair: "I have dry hair, so from young I did man it [cut hair short]. And people used to say it didn't suit me." This is illustrative of the normative gender identities assigned to kinky hair and short hair ("man head"). Women with either hairstyle disrupt the heteronormative standards of Creole Respectability. The YCW I interviewed stated that kinky hair evoked accusations of "slackness"—unregulated hygiene and hypersexuality.

When the play is over, the pastor states that young women's naked pictures are appearing on the internet because young people (implied YCW) "do not act with respect on the internet." Here, she is referring to the Creole Respectability mandate that young people, particularly YCW, act with modesty and chastity. In addition, the song at the end of the performance contains the ultimate moral lesson to be taken from the play: that "young people need to act responsibly [respectably] on the internet"—exposing the sexualized Black women's body as disreputable and bringing shame to all concerned, except the men involved.

Sexual Consumption of Young Creole Women

At the center of the Christmas play's plot is Soan's disreputable behavior in response to her seduction by the unnamed and unseen man. Similarly, my ethnographic research in Bluefields finds that men play a central role in the creation of sexual panic. They constantly pressure and entice unmarried women to engage in sexual relations. Additionally, they regularly enact sexual abuse and violence on YCW, a fact that is generally hidden and denied but well known in Bluefields (Hodgson Suarez 2022; Gordon-Ugarte 2022; see also White, in this volume).[5] In addition, disciplining and surveilling YCW's presumed hypersexuality elicits libidinal pleasures for the agents of control in the community—family, friends, pastors, and teachers—who engage in it. As demonstrated below, the play illustrates these crucial aspects of sexual panic.

Men's urge to consume (dominate, own, enjoy) YCW's erotic selves and capitalize on Black women's perceived hypersexuality is displayed daily on the streets of Bluefields. What would be considered harassment in the United States is a constant fact of life for young women there, particularly if in a different neighborhood from one's home. Men often stop whatever it is they are doing—talking, working, getting water from the well, picking up the sacks of rice—to whistle, "*cist*" (teeth sucking), call, stare, comment, and even grab one's hand as women walk near them. This is an opportunity for men to reinscribe their masculinity. Such public performances of sexual consumption are public manifestations of a pattern of masculine assumptions of sexual power that permeate Creole culture and that have been continually mentioned in interviews and oral histories done with Creole women (Woods Downs 2005). The normative right of men to consume YCW is so strong that it often descends into abuse and assault (Suarez 2022), as demonstrated by the incident portrayed in the Christmas drama. In the play, the young man, who pretends to be romantically interested in Soan, dupes her by asking for her naked photo that he posts on social media sites. The church is conveying the message that YCW will naturally encounter men who will attempt to consume their sexuality and that it is their responsibility to decline.

According to Chloë Taylor, the family is also a site of libidinal production in relation to young women's sexuality (Taylor 2012). More precisely, she argues, "One of the ways that the family produces 'incestuous' desire is through parental monitoring of children's sexuality" (Taylor 2012, 208). Creole society's preoccupation with consumption and abuse of as well as surveillance and discipline of YCW's erotic and hypersexualized bodies transforms these women into metaphorical and at times literal sexual objects of their parents, pastors, and teachers and "pornographic" sexual objects in general. Thus, one of the rewards of parenting as seen in the Christmas play is the aroused interest and excitement surrounding the libidinal experience of surveilling and disciplining YCW's hypersexualized bodies (Taylor 2012, 210) in the context of sexual panic. The centrality of young women's sexual deviance to the Christmas play and to other spectacular sermonic performances in the Creole Church, as well as the rapt attention and emotional responses of the audience to it, is evidence of the power of young women's sexuality to stimulate abhorrence-attraction in their domination. YCW enmeshed in sexual panic are sexual objects living at the uncomfortable yet titillating nexus of the fear and shame that produces domination by repression and the lust and desire that yield domination by sexual consumption.

Discipline and Surveillance of YCW's Erotic Lives

Ms. Joan, a main character in the Christmas play, is portrayed as a stereotypical Creole mother. The thirteen-year-old young Creole girl who plays Ms. Joan is dressed differently from everyone else in the play, with a long skirt that reaches to her ankles and an apron tied around her waist. These two clothing pieces are representative of the Creole Respectable mother archetype. In Creole society, mothers are seen as the prime agents responsible for surveilling and disciplining their daughters' whereabouts, behaviors, and communications to ensure that their sexuality and reproductivity are controlled. As an example, when Soan confesses that she sent the naked picture to her boyfriend, Jennifer blurts out to Ms. Joan, "I told you to watch your daughter!" The entire Christmas play is directed at showing the negative consequences for Creole families and young women if mothers do not successfully surveil and control the erotics of their premarital daughters.

Ms. Joan does not talk to Soan in positive terms about her daughter's sexuality or reproductive health. The play encapsulates norms of Creole Respectability that dictate that Creole mothers do not talk about sex with their daughters, do not allow their daughters to curse, and teach their daughters to be quiet, modest, and chaste and to seek marriage at a proper age.[6] Fathers are not mentioned at all in this play. In this regard, the play exemplifies my findings and that of scholars working elsewhere in the Afro-Caribbean that many Creole fathers are only peripherally involved in the direct discipline of their daughters' sexuality (Smith 1988; Rowley 2013). In many Creole families adult men, especially those who are the main economic providers for families, are only able to perform this function by working and living most of the year outside Bluefields. Instead, mothers act on behalf of the patriarch to maintain the family's respectability. It is the mother's responsibility to monitor and discipline the young Creole woman.

The play presents a series of negative potential consequences of young women's aberrant behaviors that results from lax familial control of daughters' sexuality. At the play's end the narrating pastor states, "Academic performance, family relationships, and emotional development . . . because when you should be enjoying your family you are stuck to your phone." The play listed numerous negative consequences for YCW who are not appropriately surveilled and disciplined by their mothers on the internet, while giving special attention to the sexual and reproductive consequences for these women. This is visible in the play's climax when the young Creole woman screams in despair to her mother that her naked picture is all over the internet.

The play depicts other mechanisms though which YCW's sexual and reproductive behaviors are surveilled and disciplined. Family friend Jennifer represents the network of Soan's family and friends who also participate in surveilling and disciplining YCW. When Soan and Shandi run to tell Ms. Joan that Soan's naked picture is online, Jennifer randomly pops on stage to reprimand Ms. Joan about her lax mothering and to shame Soan. Jennifer's appearance in the home and interjection of her critical opinion about Soan are symbolic of the way the extended network of Creole family, friends, and acquaintances judges young women and their mothers for undisciplined behaviors. They do this by shaming, gossiping, reprimanding, and telling YCW's parents on them. Key patterns of this interaction are illustrated in the play by people from the neighborhood, family, and close friends coming to the house, stopping by, sitting in the living room, gossiping, and talking together. Jennifer is constantly knocking on Ms. Joan's front door, talking, and chit-chatting with her in her living room about bills, problems, and her daughter. Years of ethnographic work in Bluefields indicate that these behaviors of intimate and constant sociality are typical of the way Creole family and friends interact daily. YCW continuously get reported on by close extended family and friends of their parents for kissing boys, hanging out with friends who are considered bad influences, being places without parental permission, and expressing other forms of erotic fulfillment.

The gossiping about YCW by the extended network of family and friends is also encapsulated in the choir's performance of the moral lesson of the play: "Think about the pictures that you're posting too. Think about the things that people are saying about you." This one line is representative of the way that the church and community use gossip to control YCW's sexuality. It encourages networks of extended family and friends and YCW themselves to surveil and discipline their own and each other's behaviors to avoid shame. The most basic and straightforward message of the play is that mothers and their connected others should surveil and discipline their daughters' sexuality. At the end of the play, the preacher directly asks Creole mothers and extended family and friends to surveil and discipline young Creole daughters: "Be more engaged with your children and young people.... You need to know what your child is doing. Set a time for internet use. Excessive internet could affect academic performance and family cohesion."

One of the main components of sexual panic is the existence of a mother-centered extended network of family and friends who surveil and discipline YCW's lives. This is clearly visible in the Christmas play. It illustrates (a) the primary role of the Respectable Creole mother in this regime as presented in the character Ms. Joan, (b) the way Creole society blames Creole mothers for their daughter's problematic hypersexual behavior, and (c) the role played by extended family and friends in surveilling and disciplining YCW's lives.[7]

However, Creole women's and particularly mothers' disciplinary efforts with young women family members are not simply self-centered righteousness. Mothers and others are also concerned with protecting their daughters. They engage in "strategic" mothering within the context of a sexually and reproductively perilous world in which they have limited options to keep their young daughters safe (Barnes 2016). Creole mothers are protecting their daughter's respectable reputations. Perhaps more importantly, they are trying to protect their daughters from often-coercive forms of male consumption in a context in which neither the society nor the state offers them any protection. As discussed above, YCW are under constant and intense persuasive and coercive pressure of consumption of their sexuality as well as under the continual threat of various forms of sexual violence. The sexual panic surrounding YCW occurs within a context in which YCW have no safety net, few laws, or other effective measures of the society or state to support and protect them from male predation. As such, the mother-centered network of family and friends in the context of generalized sexual panic enacts strategic mothering as their only, albeit restrictive and disciplinary, safety net. This is one of the strongest messages and the moral of the Christmas play and an important component of the disciplinary aspects of sexual panic.

Young Creole Women's Erotic Agency

YCW in Bluefields are agentive. They make decisions within the restraints of racial, gender, and class structures and the Creole cultural repertoire to enact or not enact their erotic desires. Accordingly, at times they resist the restrictive mandates of Creole Respectability. This is evident in the Christmas play in which Soan makes various choices. She asks for an iPhone and enjoys the sociality and other pleasures it enables. She engages in friendships and intimacies, and she decides to send nude pictures to a twenty-five-year-old man she desires.

My extensive interviewing and ethnographic observation show that ideally, YCW follow strict rules: stay within the immediate parameters of the house and yard, do not wander and socialize with friends in the street, do not go to dance halls, dress chastely and modestly, do not interact with men until they are at least eighteen years old, do not have romantic relations, and so forth. My ethnographic research indicates that YCWs are keenly aware of and generally follow these rules but admit to breaking them at times. Most snuck out of the house and/or lied about their whereabouts on occasion to walk around town with friends. Some listened to loud music disturbing the neighbors; some wore prohibited clothing or hung out with friends they were not supposed to or danced sexually and provocatively at ranches and discotheques.

Venturing into the realm of the erotics of interpersonal sexuality, most flirted, some held hands and/or kissed men, some "made out" with boy or girlfriends, and some had clandestine sex with men and/or women. For YCW there is a difference between behavioral ideals and actual behavior. In general, moralistic disciplining of YCW's erotic behavior achieves its repressive goals. However, to greater or lesser degrees, depending on the individual and the circumstances, YCW resist these restraints to enact aspects of their erotic desires.

In Bluefields, when a woman bears her first child, she becomes an adult and gains more freedom from the discipline of her extended network of family and friends. The urge to adulthood and its relative freedoms impels some YCW to pursue romantic relations with the hopes of marriage and/or childbearing. If a YCW is unmarried and becomes pregnant, she first endures a period of extreme social ostracism and isolation during pregnancy. As an unmarried woman with a child gets older and has more children, she is considered more respectable. All women are recognized as adults and are considered respectable after marriage, at which point they are expected to have children unless they are publicly known to be unfaithful to their husbands.[8] Regardless of the original circumstances of childbirth, women, married or not, enforce respectable values upon their children.

This social process is partially represented in the Christmas play. Soan's mother is the pillar and enforcer of respectability in relation to Soan by virtue of being her mother and family authority. A family father figure is never mentioned or implied in the play. The absence of a patriarchic male family authority in the moralistic setting of the church, where nuclear families headed by men are the expectation, must have been a choice of its authors. The implication is that this is a single-parent, woman-headed family and that Ms. Joan may very well have had Soan outside of wedlock. Though Ms. Joan when pregnant would have experienced a period of extreme shame and even now is living in somewhat disreputable circumstances, in the absence of a male authority in the family she now heads, she is the enforcer of patriarchic respectable sexualities. Sexual panic is reproduced from generation to generation, as the potentially disreputable hypersexual YCW with erotic agency transforms, through childbirth, into a respectable asexual adult Black mother who in turn disciplines her daughter's sexuality. YCW's agentive resistance to the exigencies of respectability is motivated by a variety of factors including their own erotic desires and the desire to achieve adulthood—free of the strict surveillance and discipline.

Some YCW, influenced by Western media, enact their agency by sexually objectifying themselves and transforming themselves from prisoners of respectability to the potential status of autonomous participants in the happiness, freedom, comfort, and desirability of Afro-modernity (Curtis 2009). Dressed "sexy" and dancing at the ranch or on Instagram and Facebook, some YCW model their public image after the potent sexuality of the celebrity *mulatta* or "*Rachet* feminism" (refusal of feminine vulnerability) (Tinsley 2018, 70). YCW then often resist the disciplinary elements of sexual panic as they seek to engage with the gendered autonomy of Afro-modernity.

Sexual Panic and Reproductive Justice

Among Creoles in Bluefields, there is a multifaceted sexual panic that, as demonstrated in the Christmas play, exists at a deep cultural level and regulates YCW's everyday lives. At the level of structural power, Creole sexual panic is the product of heteronormative patriarchy, and anti-Blackness and is part of the afterlife of slavery and colonialism in Nicaragua. The historical and contemporary constitutive elements of sexual panic are the following: (a) The colonially derived anti-Black stereotype of YCW's hypersexuality, which both threatens women's respectability and animates men's consumption of Black women's sexuality; (b) The colonially derived ideal values and beliefs of Creole Respectability that form a guiding moral framework that norms YCW's everyday comportment and sexual and reproductive practice; (c) Women's sexual consumption by men who actively sexually pressure, consume, and sometimes abuse YCW; (d) Creole institutions such as the church and particularly extended family networks and peers that internalize values of Creole Respectability and generally accept notions of Black hypersexuality. As part of a politics of respectability, they discipline and surveil YCW's sexuality, while normalizing men's aggressive sexualities. Strategic mothering is an important motivating force in respectability-based disciplining and surveillance of YCW as older women (mothers and grandmothers) attempt to protect young women and their reputations from men; (e) YCW's engagement in their own agentive forms of erotic empowerment in resistance to hypersexualization, consumption, and discipline. This constituted "sexual panic" around YCW's lives is the basis for the Creole community's mobilization to control their sexuality and reproduction, whether that be through surveillance and discipline or sexual consumption.

Sexual panic has negative effects on YCW's access to reproductive justice. As Loretta Ross (2006, 14) states, reproductive justice is not merely a matter of having unequal access to reproductive health care. Rather, it is the repression of women's ability to control their erotic selves and "reproductive destiny." Because of the sexual panic that engulfs them, most YCW have limited freedom to express themselves through hairstyles and clothing, socialize with friends, pick a romantic partner, or engage in sexual satisfaction including those activities that do not carry the risk of pregnancy.

Because of sexual panic, YCW are not educated by their parents and families about sex, sexuality, or reproduction due to a respectability-induced silence in families around sex and sexuality.[9] When interviewed, a twenty-four-year-old Julesi told me, "Well, it's like when you have a dog, when that dog shit inside we beat it but we no teach the dog to go shit outside, same happen with us, we go enjoy as we want, and sometimes maybe not in the proper way, but instead of our women teach us them come row [reprimand] you or call your attention." YCW also report receiving limited sex education in churches and schools that are more focused on abstinence models than free and safe sex (Estrada Halford 2018).

Furthermore, in the grip of sexual panic YCW are disciplined through shame and criticism by their family and often romantic partners for accessing reproductive technology including birth control pills, condoms, and injections otherwise available in Bluefields. Dubie, a twenty-two-year-old I interviewed, stated in this regard, "Them say we is whore, and that we no have shame, we need respect we self, but make if it was a man, them no say that." Almost every young Creole woman interviewed claimed that someone else controlled their access to contraception—their mothers, aunts, grandmothers, or boyfriend and less commonly a sister, brother, father, and/or grandfather. In Bluefields, YCW are refused the benefits of reproductive health. If they are sexually active without access to contraceptives, they sometimes experience the shameful proof of their participation in illicit sexuality: pregnancy out of wedlock. For Creoles, abortions are taboo, and the Nicaraguan government has imposed a total ban on abortion without exceptions.

Conclusion

The situation among unmarried YCW in Bluefields contradicts much of the social science literature (see Bolles 1988; Rowley 2013) and the Bluefields Creole community's understanding of the "problem" of premarital sex and pregnancy. The Christmas play and my ethnographic research demonstrate that contrary to YCW holding deviant values, they are steeped in and have internalized the ideals of Creole Respectability and, for the most part, attempt to conform to its precepts regarding their sexuality.

In this chapter, I argue that hyperawareness and enforcement of the values of respectability contribute to sexual panic through a complex process sometimes resulting in the occurrence of unmarried pregnancy. Such occasional but regular premarital births are the sign of illicit sexuality. This, along with the continuing stereotype of YCW's hypersexuality, creates a situation in which YCW are blamed for sexual deviancy in and outside of Creole society. These intense and contradictory pressures on their erotic selves, from stereotype, consumption, and discipline, place them in circumstances in which their own control of their erotic and reproductive lives is severely limited. In this chapter, I insist on the collective support of healthy erotics for Black women. To this end, the central premise of this chapter is that the sexual panic engulfing YCW's desires and sexuality leads to a disciplinary regime that denies these women the exercise of their erotic power and reproductive justice. This leads to YCW's counterculture of resistant desire that often falls prey to men's consumption and abuse and sometimes to unwanted pregnancy. In this chapter, I seek to untangle the structural and quotidian elements in this complex process in which the strictures of respectability themselves lead to the abhorred results they aim to prevent.

Finally, while Creole women's circumstances are in many ways unique, there are lessons in their case for Black women elsewhere. Our problem is not deviant sexualities or premarital pregnancy. Ubiquitous anti-Black stereotypes of Black women's hypersexuality, the patriarchal values of respectability, and the masculinist consumption of women's sexuality all inhibit Black women's erotic power and deny us reproductive justice. *That* is the problem.

Hortense Spillers (1987, 2003) argues that gender and sexuality are central to racialization processes and that, in dominant discourses, Black women's sexualities are invariably considered deviant. This is the case across the Black Atlantic (e.g., Bolles 1988; Rowley 2013; Cooper 2017). The situation of young Creole women in Bluefields provides insights into the consequences of this central aspect of global anti-Blackness. As in Bluefields, the continual attack on reproductive justice is based on the perceived threat of deviant "women and sex," as exemplified by Black women, to the "traditional" nuclear family and by extension social order. The struggle for young Black women's erotic power and reproductive justice is an essential aspect of the struggle against anti-Blackness.

Notes

1. In the historically and culturally connected regions of the Caribbean Coast of Belize, Nicaragua, and islands of Honduras, the term "Creole" designates Creole-English-speaking, Protestant, mixed-race inhabitants of African descent (Holm 1983, 95).
2. Following Lorde, the erotic is "an assertion of the life force of women; of that creative energy empowered.... The sharing of joy, whether physical, emotional, psychic, or intellectual ... open and fearless underlining of my capacity for joy." "Pornography and eroticism [are] two diametrically opposed uses of the sexual" (Lorde 2007, 89).
3. The "politics of respectability" resists anti-Black racial stereotypes by outperforming the dominant society's norms of moral propriety (Higginbotham 1993, 1–4).
4. This is a major insight of Stoler's (2002) work and has been described in Anglophone Caribbean societies both large (e.g., Abrahams 1983) and small (e.g., Curtis 2009).
5. For a discussion of sexuality and gender-based violence against Black women in Peru, see Lewis, in this volume.

6   This doesn't mean that every Creole woman in the mother role disciplines and surveils YCW to this extent or at all. However, everyone is aware of the respectable ideal expectations for both mother and daughter.
7   A mother, grandmother, or even aunt can take the role of a mother in Bluefields.
8   See Medeiros's (2022) discussion of the relationship between respectability and marriage and Black women's decisions to opt out of remarriage in Northeast Brazil.
9   This statement is supported by Creole intellectual Socorro Woods Downs (2005) and Webster and Ethel (2014).

References

Abrahams, Roger D. 1983. *The Man-of-Words in the West Indies: Performance and the Emergence of Creole Culture.* Baltimore: Johns Hopkins University Press.
Barnes, Riche J. Daniel. 2016. "She Was a Twin: Black Strategic Mothering, Race-Work, and the Politics of Survival." *Transforming Anthropology* 24, no. 1: 49–60.
Bolles, A. Lynn. 1988. "My Mother Who Fathered Me and Others: Gender and Kinship in the Caribbean." *Women and International Development, MSU*, working paper no. 175 (December): 21.
Cooper, Melinda. 2017. *Family Values: Between Neoliberalism and the New Social Conservatism.* Cambridge, MA: MIT Press.
Curtis, Debra. 2009. *Pleasures and Perils: Girls' Sexuality in a Caribbean Consumer Culture.* New Brunswick, NJ: Rutgers University Press.
Estrada Halford, Nazyra. 2018. "Conocimiento que Poseen los Estudiantes de Décimo y Undécimo Año de Secundaria sobre los Factores de Riesgo del Embarazo Precoz, Instituto Nacional Alva Hooker Downs, Municipio Corn Island, II Semestre 2017." PhD diss., Bluefields Indian & Caribbean University.
Goett, Jennifer. 2017. *Black Autonomy: Race, Gender, and Afro-Nicaraguan Activism.* Stanford, CA: Stanford University Press.
Gordon, Edmund Tayloe. 1998. *Disparate Diasporas: Identity and Politics in an African Nicaraguan Community.* Austin: University of Texas Press.
Gordon-Ugarte, Ishan Elizabeth. 2022. *"She Too 'Omanish'": Young Black Women's Sexuality and Reproductive Justice in Bluefields, Nicaragua.* PhD diss., CUNY Graduate Center, New York.
Hale, Charles R. 1994. *Resistance and Contradiction: Miskitu Indians and the Nicaraguan State, 1894–1987.* Stanford, CA: Stanford University Press.
Higginbotham, Evelyn Brooks. 1992. "African-American Women's History and the Metalanguage of Race." *Signs: Journal of Women in Culture and Society* 17, no. 2: 251–274.
———. 1993. *Righteous Discontent: The Women's Movement in the Black Baptist Church, 1880–1920.* Cambridge, MA: Harvard University Press.
Hodgson Suarez, Eva. 2022. "Benevolent Patriarchy & Gender Violence: Unveiling Black Men's Illusion of Mea Innocentia in Bluefields Nicaragua." PhD diss., University of Texas, Austin.
Holm, John. 1983. *Central American English.* Amsterdam: John Benjamins Publishing.
Lorde, Audre. 2007. "The Uses of the Erotic: The Erotic as Power." In *Sexualities and Communication in Everyday Life: A Reader*, edited by Karen E. Lovaas and Mercilee M. Jenkins, 87–91. Thousand Oaks, CA: Sage Publications.
Medeiros, Melanie A. 2022. "Rejecting Remarriage: Respectability & Black Brazilian Women's Decisions to 'Opt Out' of Marriage." In *Opting Out: Women Messing*

with Marriage around the World, edited by Dinah Hannaford and Joanna Davidson, 104–120. New Brunswick, NJ: Rutgers University Press.

Offen, Karl, and Terry Rugeley. 2014. *The Awakening Coast: An Anthology of Moravian Writings from Mosquitia and Eastern Nicaragua, 1849–1899*. Lincoln: University of Nebraska Press.

Ross, Loretta. 2006. Understanding Reproductive Justice: Transforming the Pro-Choice Movement. *Off Our Backs*, 36, no. 4: 14–19.

Rowley, Michelle V. 2013. *Feminist Advocacy and Gender Equity in the Anglophone Caribbean: Envisioning a Politics of Coalition*. New York: Routledge.

Smith, Raymond T. 1988. *Kinship and Class in the West Indies: A Genealogical Study of Jamaica and Guyana*. Cambridge: Cambridge University Press.

Spillers, Hortense J. 1987. "Mama's Baby, Papa's Maybe: An American Grammar Book." *Diacritics* 17, no. 2: 65–81.

———. 2003. *Black, White, and in Color: Essays on American Literature and Culture*. Chicago: University of Chicago Press.

Stoler, Ann Laura. 2002. *Carnal Knowledge and Imperial Power: Race and the Intimate in Colonial Rule*. Berkeley: University of California Press.

Tafari-Ama, Imani. 2016. "Historical Sociology of Beauty Practices: Internalized Racism, Skin Bleaching, and Hair Straightening." *Ideaz* 14 (2016): 1–19.

Taylor, Chloë. 2012. "Foucault and Familial Power." *Hypatia* 27, no. 1: 201–218.

Tinsley, Omise'eke Natasha. 2018. *Beyoncé in Formation Remixing Black Feminism*. Austin: University of Texas Press.

Webster, Martinez, and María Ethel. 2014. "Perspectivas de las Comunidades en Torno al Contexto de Vulnerabilidad en que Vive la Juventud en la RACS." *Wani* 69: 75–80.

Wilson, Peter J. 1974. *Oscar: An Inquiry into the Nature of Sanity*. Vol. 197. New York: Random House.

Woods Downs, Socorro. 2005. *"I've Never Shared This with Anybody": Creole Women's Experience of Racial and Sexual Discrimination and Their Need for Self-Recovery*. Bluefields, Nicaragua: Universidad de las Regiones Autónomas de la Costa Caribe Nicaragüense and Centro de Estudios e Información de la Mujer Multiétnica.

9

Digital Black Feminist Activism in Brazil

••••••••••••••••••••

Toward a Repoliticization of Aesthetics and Romantic Relationships

BRUNA CRISTINA JAQUETTO PEREIRA AND CRISTIANO RODRIGUES

> Indeed, all the great movements for social justice in our society have strongly emphasized a love ethic.
> —bell hooks (2000, 98)

Contemporary Black Brazilian activism is defined by its organizational plurality and diverse strategies for political mobilization. The process of pluralization and diversification of themes, formats, and collective action strategies gained strength from the 1990s onward. In the last decade of the twentieth century, the project of a national and unified Black organization, which took shape with the foundation of the Movimento Negro Unificado (Unified Black Movement; MNU) in 1978, began to lose ground to institutional advocacy and transnational activism networks. This trend toward decentralization evolved into several topics and types of Black activism flourishing from different collectives across the country, particularly those revolving around the intersectionality of race, class, gender, and sexuality (Abdalla, this volume; Rodrigues 2020; Rodrigues and Freitas 2021). Another result of that process was the rise of Black women to prominent roles in the Black social movement. Since the 1990s, they have stood out through creating and leading Black feminist and mixed-gender Black organizations. Black women have also played a key role in lending visibility to the cleavages within the Black population, thus expanding the scope of the discussion about racial inequalities in the country (Rodrigues 2020).

Between the 1990s and the 2010s, Black organizations and activists prioritized three modalities of intervention and political mobilization. In the 1990s, the focus was institutional advocacy strategies and strengthening transnational anti-racism networks. In the 2000s, the election of the Partido dos Trabalhadores (Workers' Party, PT) candidate, President Luiz Inácio Lula da Silva, and the formation of a leftist government resulted in a new change of direction for the Black movement. During PT's administration, activists and organizations of the Black movement advanced strategies of collaboration with the state, mainly through institutionalized participation in state-sanctioned spaces and the occupation of positions within the bureaucracy—in line with other social movements in that same period (Abers, Serafim, and Tatagiba 2014).

From 2010 onward, new expressions of Black activism gained momentum. The rapid diffusion of Black university collectives across the country and the emergence of digital Black activism are the most visible representations of this process. This new wave of activism adopts a set of strategies and practices that focus mainly on individual empowerment and representation, in line with what has been called "progressive neoliberalism."[1] It is thus marked by the avoidance of challenging state institutions and the reliance on strategies of "leaning in" and "cracking the glass ceiling" that do not propose or articulate collective alternative projects of resistance or move beyond our current political-economic system (Fraser 2017; Rodrigues 2020).

The emergence of Black university collectives and digital Black feminist activism in contemporary Brazil is part of this innovative configuration of collective action which has broadened the reach of activism. Although heirs to previous and more traditional social movement organizations (such as MNU and Black Women's nongovernmental organizations [NGOs]), the Black collectives and digital Black feminists analyzed in this chapter are not necessarily social movements. In fact, they do not use the category "social movement" to describe their discourses and political action (Facchini, Carmo, and Lima 2020). They employ what Gomes (2018) defines as "flag-bodies," or political tactics that emphasize identity, experiences, and strategic essentialism. In this context, aesthetics and romantic relationships are turned into objects of political dispute in unprecedented ways.

This chapter discusses how digital Black feminist activism mobilizes aesthetics and romantic relationships to advance its cause. We build on our findings to further understand recent transformations in activism and discuss their implications for broader Black women's activism. With this aim, we analyzed 835 Blogueiras Negras (Black Women Bloggers [BN]) blog posts and conducted observational research to determine how people interact and behave in debates around gender and race in the Facebook group Afrodengo.[2]

In the first section of the chapter, we discuss the role of aesthetics and romantic relationships in the history of the contemporary Brazilian Black movement. Next, we discuss the impacts of the internet on the newest social movements and comment on the emergence of new tools, tactics, spaces, and collective actors in the cybersphere. In the third and fourth sections, we analyze how aesthetics and romantic relationships are mobilized in BN and Afrodengo. Finally, we draw on our research findings to reflect on the implications for Brazilian Black activism and Black women's activism.

Aesthetics and Romantic Relationships in Black Activism

Black social movements have prioritized improving the living conditions of Black people, their insertion into the labor market, and their access to education. However, given widespread negative, racist representations of Black people, Black activists have also sought to promote positive symbolic changes. Black social movements, thus, favor the self-identification of a larger contingent of Brazilians as Black people, the aesthetic appreciation of physical traits linked to Blackness, and the Black romantic couple. As a result, racial identity, self-esteem, and appreciation of Black partners have long been present in the discourse and actions of the Black movement.[3]

In the modern Western imagination, aesthetic evaluation is at the core of the arguments supporting the construction of race as a hierarchical category and fundamental category of difference among human beings. Initially formulated by philosophers and theorists of scientific racism in the nineteenth century, the scales of beauty were conceived based on representations of physical differences between Africans and Europeans. African faces were portrayed like those of monkeys and European features were compared to Greek sculptures (Young 2005). Scientists attempted to prove the "inferior" and "anachronistic" nature of both the African female body and the anatomy of "primitive" peoples. From the modern period, stereotypes about the sexuality of social groups have justified the assignment of places on a scale from animal (or primitive) to fully human. According to nineteenth-century scientific racism's conceptions of racial difference, Black people would have "an attractive but dangerous sexuality, an apparently abundant and unlimited, although threatening, fertility" (Young 2005, 118). Their sexual preeminence would be opposed by the intellectual capacities and physiognomy attributed to white people, whose supposedly more developed minds and harmonic appearance were taken as evidence of racial superiority.

The lasting influences of scientific racism in Brazil are visible in the representations of the Black body as hypersexualized, in the association of Black traits with ugliness and in the national version of the eugenics that took shape at the beginning of the twentieth century.[4] Then, Brazilian intellectuals and politicians reviewed and appropriated selected principles of scientific racism theories to formulate national projects for the "improvement" of the population. Fernando de Azevedo, Edgar Roquette Pinto, Afrânio Peixoto, and other doctors, scientists, and social scientists embraced eugenics thought and implemented state programs to address the "racial inferiority" of the population (Dávila 2006), the most tangible of which was the promotion of European immigration. These intellectuals alleged that widespread miscegenation of Black and Indigenous people with white people was a mechanism to gradually whiten and, thus, modernize the mostly non-white nation. They envisioned mirages of a Brazilian people with a fair and racially homogeneous phenotype over a few generations (Bento 2009; Jarrín 2017; Schwarcz 1993). "Modernizing" was also a project to "beautify" society, getting rid of the "ugliest" elements—that is, of those with a darker complexion (Jarrín 2017).

Race and class are still at the core of aesthetic judgments in contemporary Brazil, often encoded in apparently neutral expressions. A place frequented by "beautiful people" refers to a social space dominated by the middle and upper classes and people of light complexions. At the same time, ugliness is generally attributed to Black people and the poor (Gordon 2013; Jarrín 2017). The white beauty ideal prevails and is widely disseminated by media outlets, the fashion industry, and the cosmetic industry. Blonde women, such as model Gisele Bündchen, are the most celebrated beauty icons. On television, which has a substantial influence on the daily life of Brazilians, Black people are underrepresented and, when present, are often portrayed in a derogatory way: in conditions of subservience and poverty (Hordge-Freeman 2015; Pinho 2009).

Whitening ideology (Andrews 2018; Gonzalez 1988) impacts the self-esteem of Black people and unfolds in the search for proximity with white people and in the distancing from other Black people (Bicudo [1945] 2010; Gonzalez 1982; Moura 1988)—including in contexts of intimacy (Pereira 2020). Thus, white supremacy works as a centripetal force, shaping the flow of affection and appreciation toward white people (Pereira 2020). Both white people and Black people often express a preference for white people as romantic partners as far as "official relationships" (dating and marriage) are concerned.

As romantic partners, Black people—especially Black women—are repeatedly rejected, hidden from friends and the family (either not introduced or frankly concealed). A theory known as "status exchange in interracial marriage" posits that when members of racially subordinated groups date or marry members of racially dominant groups, they compensate for their lower social status by bringing other valued characteristics such as social class, professional status, level of education, or more domestic and care work (Pereira, 2020; Telles, 2004). Racialized stereotypes are also at the roots of the country's comparatively high rates of interracial unions. In white person–Black woman couples, the white partner's interest in an "exacerbated" and "exotic" sexuality often emerges as the main drive of attraction to Black women (Pereira 2020).

The Black movement in Brazil has continuously tackled the symbolic valorization of whiteness at the expense of Black aesthetics. In the late 1970s, as the military dictatorship was cooling down and social movements were gradually reemerging, the politicization of aesthetics and romantic relationships was evident in events and demonstrations staged by *afoxé* groups, Afro-Brazilian religious communities, carnival blocks, and Black social clubs.[5] The aim of strengthening the Black identity, self-esteem, and pride inspired moments and spaces of gathering and celebration. For instance, the "Night of Black Beauty," a women's beauty contest, has been held annually since 1975 at Ilê Aiyê's headquarters in Salvador. In the late 1970s, Movimento Black Rio (Black Rio Movement) and Movimento Black São Paulo (Black São Paulo Movement) weekly promoted the so-called *Bailes Soul* (Soul Balls). On these occasions, Black activists and ordinary Black youth, displaying outfits and hairstyles alluding to Black resistance (such as afros), hit the dance floor and performed elaborate dance steps to the sound of U.S. funk music (Giacomini 2006).

The promotion of an "authentic" and affirmative Black aesthetics includes the realm of romantic relationships. Usually, representations of the Black couple have a twofold objective: they promote a counterhegemonic image of love and affection among Black people and indicate resistance against racism. In this context, representations of Black couples are employed to convey two main messages. First, the heterosexual Black couple presents a "dignified" version of Blackness, one in which Black people can control and regulate their sexuality according to social norms to exemplify and perform traditional gender roles. Here, the problematic aspects of heteropatriarchy remain untouched. Second, the Black couple communicates the ability to overcome white supremacist values and internalized racism that lead to the preference for white partners. Moreover, the bond between a Black woman and a Black man shows up as a strategy to fight racism together. In general, the Black couple conveys a reinterpretation of Brazilianness and Blackness, denouncing racial oppression and displaying resistance and pride (Giacomini 2006).

A 1991 issue of the MNU newspaper depicts one of the meanings assigned to the heterosexual Black couple. The cover page presents the photo of a Black couple kissing with the following caption: Reaja à violência policial: Beije sua preta em praça pública (React to police violence: Kiss your Black woman in public)—a poem by writer and activist Lande Onawale. That the message targeted Black men and encouraged them to acknowledge their Black female partners publicly is notably the result of discussions provoked by Black women within the Black movement. The aim was to challenge the discrimination against considering Black women as romantic partners. At the same time, the scene evokes the heterosexual Black couple as a means to fight police brutality. Black love, when assuming the adequate configuration, seems capable of countering both private and public manifestations of racism.

Even though images of the Black couple have been present in formulations of the contemporary Black movement for decades, only recently have Black women's efforts to "politicize love" (Flauzina 2015) evolved into a broader debate. By the mid-2010s, Black women, within and outside activist circles, began to openly discuss the effects of racism and sexism on the romantic and sexual lives of Black people. Until then, these topics were taboo outside of restricted spaces of Black activism. The most common reference in this conversation is "Black women's loneliness" (Moutinho, Alves, and Mateuzi 2016). This expression has been widely used in Black intellectual and activist circles, mainly by Black women. It generally refers to the abandonment, contempt, demotion, humiliation, and suffering experienced by Black women in romantic relationships.[6] The motto also articulates demands for respect, dignity, and pleasure in the context of dating and relationships.[7] Although also featured in offline public spaces, the topic became popular on the internet, where it has reached wider audiences. In this sense, Black activism is also affected by the recent changes that have reconfigured activism and social movements in general.

Black University Collectives, Newest Social Movements, and Digital Black Feminist Activism

Collectives are a form of organization characterized as fluid, informal, horizontal, and ideologically distant from institutional politics and traditional social movements (Perez and Souza 2017). Collectives of Black university students emerged with the implementation of affirmative action policies for public higher education from the 2000s onward. They are inspired by the Black feminist collectives of the 1970s and 1980s, which worked horizontally in decision-making and had nonhierarchical organizational formats. These collectives are characterized by a break in the gender hierarchy, since many of their leaders are women and LGBTQIA+ people, but also by their ideological differences with traditional social movement organizations (Guimarães, Rios, and

Sotero 2020). The agenda of these groups is marked by the articulation between gender, race, and sexuality (Rios, Perez, and Ricoldi 2018).

Black collectives work intensely in digital platforms, especially on social media—Facebook, Twitter, Instagram, WhatsApp, blogs, and YouTube channels (Guimarães, Rios, and Sotero 2020). In fact, the reach and visibility of these groups are far more significant than the number of people who participate daily in their organizing activities (Guimarães, Rios, and Sotero 2020). Thus, Black collectives distance themselves from the institutional activism format that characterized the Black movement organizations in the 1990s and 2000s and are closer to a set of collective actions that emerged from the late 2000s around the world, such as the Arab Spring, 15-M in Spain, Occupy Wall Street in the United States, and the 2013 protests in Brazil. Some theorists have called these emerging and sometimes anti-capitalist collective actions "newest social movements" (Perez 2019). Although collectives are characterized by their use of new communication technologies for mobilization and sociability, they are not social movements, but they have, according to Gohn (2017), the potential to become movements. The absence of leadership, a continuity project, and opponents are factors that explain how collectives are distinguishable from social movements (Perez 2019).

In the same way, Blogueiras Negras and Afrodengo, which we analyze in detail in this chapter, avoid using the term "social movements" to classify their discourses, actions, and strategies. They are part of a new form of activism termed "digital activism," whose consolidation goes hand in hand with the growing importance of new information, communicative technologies, and social media for sociability and political action. Political action via the internet often replaces or complements traditional forms of collective action, dispenses with or even rejects leadership, and acts from ephemeral digital ties between physically distant activists (Bennett and Segerberg 2013; Carty 2015).

Brazilian digital Black feminist activism, which consolidated in the 2010s, materialized in the wake of Black women and girls' experiences in Black university collectives, the popularization of blogs in the 2000s, and the emergence of a fourth feminist wave in Latin America. This wave was characterized by the mass use of social media and technology (such as so-called hashtag feminism) and was deepened through discussions on identity, body, and feminist issues already widely debated but not yet resolved, such as violence, political representation, sexual rights, and reproductive rights (Rodrigues and Freitas 2021).

Digital Black feminist activism in Brazil began to gain visibility with the creation of Blogueiras Negras in 2013. Digital Black feminist activists aim to change how their audience thinks about and treats Black women by challenging racism and sexism. Through their blogs, the debates on hair transition and Black women's aesthetics and romantic relationships have gained momentum.

BN has reached a much wider audience than previous activists and organizations linked to the Black movement.

In the last decade, disputes on hair texture have emerged as the main battleground around Black aesthetics. According to Google, the searches for "afro hair" (*cabelo afro*) between 2015 and 2017 in Brazil increased by 309 percent, eventually surpassing those on "straight hair" (*cabelo liso*) (BRANDLAB 2017). On Instagram alone, hair transition hashtags have surpassed more than 3 million tags.[8] Influencers and audiences are mostly young, Black people who are going or have gone through this experience of hair modification. They share their experiences, products, and techniques dealing with different hair textures on social media such as YouTube, Facebook, blogs, and websites. Thus, they create a network of solidarity and mutual help, encouragement, and support against racist and misogynistic criticism individuals face when changing their style. Additionally, the hair transition movement has contributed decisively to a transformation in the hygiene and beauty industry, which eventually started to create new brands and include a wider range of products for curly and frizzy hair, targeting this emerging group of consumers. The intersection between Black feminist activism and technoculture has turned the internet into a virtual beauty shop (Steele 2021).

The emergence of an online debate on Black aesthetics has been closely followed by discussions of Black love and "Black women's loneliness." Here, we choose to analyze how aesthetics and romantic relationships are mobilized in Blogueiras Negras and Afrodengo to better understand recent changes in Black women's activism. They are distinct communication platforms: the former (BN) employs strategies and discourses aimed at a broader audience and covers a wider range of topics, while the latter (Afrodengo) targets a smaller audience and is more focused. Despite the differences, both reveal essential dimensions of contemporary Brazilian Black feminist activism and, as such, are a privileged locus for observing the approaches, strategies, and themes that emerge as part of their collective action.

Aesthetics, Sexuality, and Romantic Relationships in Blogueiras Negras (BN)

Blogueiras Negras (BN) was launched in May 2013 by intersectional feminists Larissa Santiago, Charô Nunes, and Maria Rita Casagrande. They met through Blogueiras Feministas (Feminist Bloggers), a feminist collective blog and Google group discussion forum founded in 2010.[9] However, Blogueiras Feministas rarely brought up discussions on race and its intersection with gender: from 2010 to 2012, Blogueiras Feministas published 282 texts, but only three discussed gender and race (Rodrigues and Freitas 2021). Due to this lack of representation, Santiago, Nunes, and Casagrande held Blogagem Coletiva Mulher Negra (Black Woman Collective Blogging) from November 20 to November 25, 2012, an online initiative to intertwine discussions on Brazilian Black Consciousness Day (celebrated on November 20) and the International Day for the Elimination of Violence against Women (celebrated on November 25).[10] BN was created after this initiative and as a manifesto to draw attention to the invisibility of young Black feminists in online feminist discussion platforms. BN is currently coordinated by Charô Nunes, Larissa Santiago, and Viviane Gomes, who, with a team of editors, select the texts, oversee the feed, and maintain the platform. Between 2013 and 2020, approximately 400 Black women freelancers and permanent authors contributed to BN's more than 1,000 blog posts. The BN also has profiles on Facebook and Twitter. In August 2021, they had more than 222,000 followers on Facebook and more than 44,000 on Twitter.

Drawing on the experiences of the Black university collectives, BN's targeted audience is mainly urban, lower-middle-class, young, and well-educated Black women. In 2013, when the blog was created, only 51.04 percent of Brazilians had access to the internet; in 2020, this percentage was 73.19 percent.[11] Marked socioeconomic inequalities in Brazil are strongly gendered and racialized; therefore, we can assume that most Black women did not have access to the internet during the years BN enjoyed its peak. However, the posts and dialogues they engender inform and are informed by pressing issues regarding Black women in Brazil and the world.

BN presents itself as a platform that prioritizes Black and intersectional feminism, as can be seen in the blog introduction:

> We are a very productive community of bloggers willing to turn writing into a tool against the [types of] oppression that affect Black women, such as racism, sexism, lesbophobia, transphobia, homophobia, classism, and fatphobia. We are also a community, an area of reception, energy, rehabilitation, and visibility, as well as a space for Black women's questions, words, and requests. We believe that the exchange of experiences and issues through shared activism is not only desirable but essential. We celebrate who we were, who we are, and who we want to be. Black Bloggers is built by a community of Black women committed to gender and race.[12]

We analyzed the contents and central themes of 835 blog posts published between 2016 and 2020 on the BN website. All posts were listed, cataloged, and analyzed with the following goals in mind: (a) to grasp the audience for these posts and where they expressed solidarity and support or opposition; (b) to describe the central narrative of the posts, the most recurrent topics to understand the formation of collective identities and the discursive interplay of political confrontation; and (c) to identify the posts with the highest impact, that is, the most shared posts and the posts that received the highest number of comments (favorable or unfavorable).

We observed that BN's main themes are Black aesthetics, sexual and romantic relationships, and dimensions of individual representation or empowerment. Between 2016 and 2020, forty-one texts were published covering different aspects of sexuality and romantic relationships, with the prominence of the following topics: romantic and sexual relationships, Black women's loneliness, and lesbian and bisexual Black women. In the posts we analyzed, Black women express solidarity with each other because of *dororidade* (the merger of the words *dor* [pain] and *solidariedade* [solidarity]), referring to suffering as a common trait in their romantic relationships. In most posts, the possibility of escaping loneliness by engaging in romantic relationships is perceived with skepticism. The relationship with men is also viewed with reservation, even with Black men, whose romantic preference for white women is perceived as an internalization of racism. By bringing such issues to the limelight, BN reinforces itself as a debate arena for how racism and sexism are experienced by Black women in their romantic lives. In other spaces of activism, this may be regarded as less relevant, accusatory, or even harmful to Black men or the Black community as a whole.

The posts we analyzed focus mainly on heterosexual relationships, making a few references to white women (to point out Black men's perceived preference for white women), and scarcely mentioning lesbian and bisexual relationships—which are mostly regarded through a heteronormative and monogamous lens. The following passage is a sample of the main narrative of these posts: "We know scientifically that they [Black women] cannot find partners or companions to share the good and bad moments of their walks. They are alone in their pains and their glories. They face delivery rooms, hospitals, prisons, and cemeteries alone. They are alone because they studied too much. They are alone because they have been too sexualized. They are alone because they are too strong. They are alone because they are too beautiful and ugly."[13] Between 2016 and 2020, sixteen BN posts covered beauty and aesthetics. Although these themes are central in the BN, we attribute the low number of blog posts to the time period we covered in our research. Many posts on the subject were published between 2013 and 2015, a period not covered in our analysis.

The main topics covered in posts about beauty and aesthetics (according to the blog's categorization) are body acceptance and self-esteem, Black aesthetics, hair transition and beauty, health and beauty standards, mental health and self-esteem. These findings show that Black women appropriate information and communication technologies to produce, consolidate, and propagate alternative knowledge about identity and political and aesthetic-corporeal knowledge (Gomes 2017). Thus, they try to build a counterhegemonic community capable of breaking with forms of subjection that stereotype and objectify Black people. The quest to reframe Black aesthetics and build meaning outside of stereotypes and white standards of beauty as a strategy to move toward collective emancipation is central in BN's narrative. The following excerpt shows an example: "We can say that Black aesthetics is, without a shadow of a doubt, an instrument of self-acceptance, resistance, empowerment, a way of showing that we do not accept the socially imposed standard, but that Black people are beautiful, diverse, versatile. We are political beings, and our aesthetic choice says a lot about us, our beliefs, our values, affirms our existence, and our resistance against attempts to fit in trends that trivialize our culture, our aesthetics."[14] The salience of topics such as Black aesthetics, hair transition, romantic relationships, and Black women's loneliness reveal that body and experience are leading categories in Brazilian digital Black feminist activism, as suggested by Gomes (2018) with the concept of "flag-bodies." On the other hand, the discussions on these topics are profoundly interlocked with capitalist dynamics, particularly market and consumption. Exacerbated emphasis on individual experiences and simplistic notions of empowerment and resistance converge to what Nancy Fraser (2017) calls "progressive neoliberalism."

Afrodengo: A Territory for Black Love or a Battleground?

Turning to apps and social media aimed exclusively at Black audiences, such as AfriDate, Sanka, Pretinder & Afrocentrados, and Afrodengo, is an alternative available for Black people who want to escape the typical dynamics of rejection and sexual objectification or for those who choose to experience an "Afro-centered love" as a political statement.[15]

Afrodengo is a private group on Facebook created in 2016.[16] We observed this group between September and October 2018 and examined previous posts focusing on the experiences of Black women. In June 2020, more than 53,000 members participated in the group. Entry is subject to approval to guarantee that only Black people over eighteen years old gain access. When accepted, the participant has access to the following description:

> "Who doesn't like a *dengo*?[17] A word that comes from the Kikongo language, of African origin (northern Angola), which means 'affection,' 'pleasure.' So present in the language of the Black population and in the Brazilian vocabulary, it expresses our way of loving, hugging, cuddling, hugging, giving love."

Afrodengo, a startup by self-definition, is a virtual dating group created for Black people that aims to be a space for interaction, flirtation, healthy relationship-building, and casual encounters in order to strengthen Black affection. It is also a space for dialogue about the importance of love for the Black population and all its nuances. Further in the description is the following: "Flirt, love each other, match, kiss, hug, give each other a *dengo*, have sex, practice the *sarrada* and the Black love in its maximum essence, beyond the virtual world.[18] Welcome!"

Currently, Afrodengo's profile image is a drawing of a Black cupid. Photographs representing Afrodengo (posted by the administration and containing Afrodengo's logo) depict straight and LGBTQIA+ couples and polyamorous arrangements, always portraying exclusively Black people. In the forums, there are references to WhatsApp groups corresponding with the location of the participants; there are a lot of polls and flirting games, as well as selfies of people seeking their own "*dengo*." The users' profiles reveal some degree of diversity: the participants come from the middle and lower classes, are straight and queer people, light- and dark-skinned. Mostly, they live in capital cities. There is a seminude gallery with posts and hashtags specifying this type of content. Proud Black couples post their photos, tell their stories, and thus raise the hopes of those looking for a partner.

In Afrodengo, we find a broader universe of representations than other spaces of Black activism (Pereira 2020)—including Blogueiras Negras—as the heterosexual couple is not portrayed as the main symbol of Black resistance. We did not observe, for example, offensive comments on the posts of queer people. Derogatory and prejudiced posts are prohibited and, if posted, are quickly deleted by moderators. The use of gender-inclusive language is another feature of the queerization of Afrodengo.

The group's affirmative proposal emerges in most of the posts and interactions. Darker skin tones and frizzy hair are frequently praised, and affectionate treatments with the term "Black" abound—"What a beautiful Black person!"; "Look at me with my Black woman/man." The seminude gallery is an absolute success considering the number of likes. Images of explicit nudity are not accepted. However, pictures of deep necklines, torsos, and booties (very little covered or not covered), reveal bodies of Black men and women of different sizes, shapes, and skin tones. The interactions tend to be sensual and flirtatious but not overt or aggressive. In this sense, the group allows Black women to experience their agency, subjective affirmation, and pleasure that they hardly experience in other public spaces in their daily lives.[19] In short, Afrodengo, as a space for expressing affection among Black people and valuing Black aesthetics, presents a progressive approach to Black aesthetics and love and affirms the diversity of sexual orientations and gender identities.

However, this small "world of Black people" also has drawbacks.[20] Among flirtations, nudes, and declarations of love, some revealing disagreements emerge. Perhaps the most frequent complaints, by men and women, concern participants' preference for people closer to normative standards of beauty (thin and young, for instance). There are also quite a few complaints from women about the *machismo* (misogyny) of Black men. Above all, they denounce what they call the "scams" —men who deceive women. Women's objections to sexist comments unfold in endless discussions about the proper way of making their case: in general, when women claimed that there was machismo, men would speak out and deny it. In one specific situation, women complained about a pickup line coming from a man they considered *machista* (sexist). Women's reactions to the complaints ranged from a more direct approach, such as publicly exposing the machista person, to a more nuanced and conservative approach such as labeling the author of the comments as "ugly" and "old." This choice of words is fascinating because it reveals the persistence of specific beauty standards even in a space dedicated to challenging (other) aesthetic ideals.

The contradictions don't stop there. Some of the group's members defended the accused man with zeal. They claimed that the comment was just a joke and that Black women should be more patient with and respectful of Black men. The most flared-up participants repeated that if a "standard white man had commented," a "hipster"—that is, someone who seems to be a member of "cool," "alternative" groups, or a "Black NBA Player type," Black women would not be complaining but "licking the screen." From then onward, the discussion became heated. Some women indignantly called the commenters "scrooge males," to which they responded by saying they were "deceived by brankkka ideologies," or, more explicitly, by "white-painted feminism" which "proposes the oppression of men."[21] For some of the men, the opinion of these Black women would result in the disunity of the "Black people." The general tone was "You complain about the loneliness of Black women, but this is why we date white women."

Following the disagreements, we noted that the historical pattern of preference for dating white people is an open wound within the Black community that permeates the interactions between Black people, both at the interpersonal level and in collective debates. Even though the heterosexual Black couple is not the dominant symbol of Black resistance in Afrodengo, the centrality of heteronormativity is established through the ways people debate appropriate behavior. The same way Black women accuse Black men of treating white women better while treating Black women "like garbage" (Burdick 1998; see also Pereira 2020), Black men accuse Black women of tolerating to a greater extent white men's sexist attitudes (Moutinho 2004). Both sides resort to the standards considered adequate to form a heteronormative couple. When women mobilized the language and the ideas associated with the struggle for gender equality, even when not explicitly naming them "feminism," the men of the group rallied around the idea of the "people" to call for unity among Black people. According to these men, women would put themselves at risk by summoning what men classify as an exogenous discourse with an oppressive substrate and, therefore, threatening Black collectivity. Black men, in turn, mobilize their relative advantage in getting white partners as a trump card—or element of blackmail—to try to impose on Black women to accept patriarchal patterns of interaction and relationships.

The dynamics mentioned reveal how Black men can rely on patriarchal and racist ideals in their interactions with Black women and how anti-racist discourse can be mobilized to force Black women into submission. Even through participating in a group that seeks to expand the notion of "Black love," some Black men participants seem to look for some degree of the conservative heterosexual Black couple that performs traditional gender roles.[22] For Black women looking for a partner, Black men's expectations may unfold in feelings of loneliness, injustice, and engagement in yet another battle for humanization and equality. As for Black women's activism more broadly, Black men's attitude toward Black women reveals the need to continue building solidarity among Black women and to further an intersectional approach to anti-racist struggles in both public and private spheres.

In sum, through our analysis of these discussions, we observed that Afrodengo identifies with the agenda of dismantling white aesthetic superiority and the preference for a white romantic partner, thus aligning itself with the ideals of the Black movement. As a unique space for the affirmation of the Black (self)-image, it presents itself as a new empowerment strategy and part of the decolonization of subjectivities. The popularity of the Black collectives we have discussed and their success among Black people in general illustrate a widespread perception of racism as a factor of dehumanization in Brazilian society. Members' active participation in the group reveals that racism is very much present and shapes Black people's most personal interactions and relationships. It also reveals that, as Black women have insisted, love, as recognition of humanity, is central to any Black struggle for self-determination in a racist society.

Simultaneously, we noted that the debates on Black love incorporate arguments related to those fostered by activism. Afrodengo's members enter the group based on some affinity with the activist discourse (or fragments of it) or come into contact with it in this virtual space. A virtual group for erotic-loving encounters, in this sense, brings actors who might never identify with a political program or militant modes of action closer to the Black movement. They do so from a punctual interest, with an aesthetic-subjective nature and in a space and format where the level of engagement depends solely on the individual. After all, there is no requirement for consistent membership and participation.

The heated debates we witnessed also reveal that social media are used as a space for "accountability." In the case we described, Black women demanded a review of traditional gender roles and female submission. On the other hand,

Black men demanded, above all, loyalty to the Black community. Simultaneously, the virtual space provides an ephemeral and fragile engagement with the agendas of the Black movement, facilitates collective mobilizations (insofar as it allows for the dissemination of its discourse or fragments of it), and serves as a place for testing affiliation fidelity—no matter the criteria used to measure it.

Aesthetics and Romantic Relationships in the Digital Black Feminist Activism

Reflections on body, aesthetics, and romantic relationships—secondary topics in the agenda of the Black movement in the 1980s and 1990s—are central to contemporary Brazilian digital Black feminist activism. They have played a key role in grabbing the attention of Black women on the internet, spreading some activist vocabulary and topics of interest, and engaging wider audiences in some of their agendas. In this regard, digital Black feminist activism has contributed to the massification of Black activism in Brazil.

In this chapter, we analyzed how Black women question their rejection and hypersexualization and the pervasive patriarchal and racist logics that intervene in their romantic relationships. Through digital activism, Black women reclaim their right to publicly discuss issues that have been traditionally considered intimate and private. Their political activism through social media is twofold. They work to bring awareness to unfair and discriminatory treatment Black women receive because of racist and patriarchal stereotypes, and they also demand the inclusion of dissident bodies (non-white, outside the heteronormative spectrum, far from sexist aesthetic standards). In this sense, digital Black feminist activists update and reclaim the radical potential of one of the main mottoes of the feminist movement, "The personal is political," but considered above and beyond the sexual division of labor and domestic violence themes to which it was initially related. When reappropriated by Black women in the last decade, this feminist jargon reaches the configuration of feelings, sexuality, and desire, as well as the ways in which they are consciously and unconsciously experienced.

Digital Black feminist activism seeks to dismantle hegemonic symbolic formulations that, through their impacts on subjectivity, contribute to the reproduction of racism and sexism (Fanon 2008; Moore 2008). While these are issues of public interest, it is in engaging actors around the more intimate, private sphere of their lives that there is the potential to influence their subjectivity, making them more prone to activism. The focus on individualism and subjectivity has a great appeal to the Black public not engaged with—or interested in—the agenda of more traditional and institutionalized Black movement organizations. Distancing the debate on subjectivity from a more institutionalized agenda contributes to its massification. At the same time, the decentralized structure of the newest social movements, particularly the digital activism, and the circulation of short texts divided into sections by theme, in blogs, WhatsApp groups, and Facebook pages among others, propagate discourses produced by the Black movement to a public that is uninterested or unfamiliar with this intellectual production. It is not necessary to declaim data on the precarious insertion of the Black population in the labor market, for example, to recognize oneself in reports of offenses in relation to curly or frizzy hair or recurrent affective rejections in the course of one's own personal life trajectory. The structural aspects of racial inequalities and racism are, in this context, less visible, and individual ones more prominent, which allows for prompt self-identification and engagement. Therefore, digital Black feminist activism does align, to some extent, with "progressive neoliberalism" and thus risks losing some of the more radical verve that structured the early Black women's movement in Brazil.

Although our study has explored the Brazilian context exclusively, our findings partially apply to Latin America as a whole. Throughout the region, we observe the emergence of Black women bloggers engaging with the issues of Black aesthetics and romantic relationships. This movement does seem to be stronger in Brazil; however, web pages such as Afrofémina (https://afrofeminas.com), Afrocubanas (https://afrocubanas.com), Ese Pelo Tuyo (https://esepelotuyo.com), Miss Rizos (www.missrizos.com), and Negra Cubana Tenía que Ser (https://negracubanateniaqueser.com), for instance, reveal that the emergence of a digital Black feminist activism is gaining momentum in Latin America. In fact, some of the discussions they promote appear to be heavily influenced by Brazilian Black digital activism.

Our study provides intersectoral contributions and sheds light on a variety of current academic debates. It touches on emergent aspects of contemporary activism, thus adding to the literature on (the newest) social movements. Our discussion of the role of information and communication technologies in reshaping activism contributes to communication and technology studies, particularly those concerning race. Examining transformations (and continuities) in gender relations, the emergence of LGBTQIA+ agendas within Black activism, and the reclamation of the body as a locus of activism, this study also contributes to the field of gender and sexuality studies.

Notes

A version of this work, in Portuguese, was published in *Cadernos Pagu*, no. 67, in 2023.

Part of the empirical data presented in this chapter, especially those contained in sections 2 and 3, were collected under the project "Black Women in Movement(s): Trajectories, Intersections and New Scenarios for Black Feminist Theory and Praxis in Brazil." funded by CNPq (Process 432980/2016-4).

1. According to Nancy Fraser (2017), progressive neoliberalism developed in the United States in the last three decades and refers to "an alliance of mainstream currents of new social movements (feminism, anti-racism, multiculturalism, and LGBTQ rights), on the one side, and high-end 'symbolic' and service-based business sectors (Wall Street, Silicon Valley, and Hollywood), on the other. In this alliance, progressive forces are effectively joined with the forces of cognitive capitalism, especially financialization."
2. One of the definitions of "*dengo*" relates to seduction and sweetness. The word has been employed by Black author Davi Nunes (2016) and in certain niches of activism as an alternative to colonized, racist understandings of love and to promote alternative forms of romantic relationship among Black people.
3. Other works have addressed these subject matters. See, for instance, "A Mulher Negra e o Amor" (Nascimento 1990); "Beleza Mulata e Beleza Negra" (Giacomini 1994); and *Sem Perder a Raiz* (Gomes 2019).
4. See also Lewis on Peru and Gordon-Ugarte on Nicaragua, in this volume.
5. *Afoxé* relates to Afro-Brazilian traditions linked to Candomblé (an Afro-Brazilian religion) and performed during the Carnival.
6. See Medeiros's (2018) discussion of Black Brazilian women's experiences of suffering and distress related to their romantic relationships.
7. See Medeiros (2023) on Black Brazilian women's demand for respect in romantic relationships.
8. "Hair transition" is characterized by the passage of chemically treated hair to its natural texture, especially curly and frizzy hair. Hashtags such as #cacheadas, #crespo, #transiçãocapilar, #cabelonatural, #cabeloafro, and #cabelochadeado, among others, have been widely employed in Brazil since the early 2010s by Black women.
9. Blogueiras Feministas is available at https://blogueirasfeministas.com/sobre-o-blog/. Last accessed January 15, 2022.
10. Blogagem Coletiva Mulher Negra is available at https://blogagemcoletivamulhernegra.wordpress.com. Last accessed January 15, 2022.
11. Information on internet access in Brazil is available at www.statista.com/statistics/209106/number-of-internet-users-per-100-inhabitants-in-brazil-since-2000/. Last accessed January 15, 2022.
12. Available at http://blogueirasnegras.org/quem-somos/. Last accessed December 26, 2021.
13. Available at http://blogueirasnegras.org/das-diferentes-solidoes-da-mulher-negra/. Last accessed August 26, 2021.
14. Available at http://blogueirasnegras.org/estetica-negra-opressao-e-resistencia/. Last accessed December 26, 2021.
15. "Afro-centered love" is an idea that advocates for affective-sexual relations exclusively among Black people (Borges 2014).
16. The Afodengo site is available at www.facebook.com/groups/afrodengo/. Last accessed January 11, 2022.
17. In vernacular Brazilian Portuguese, *dengo* also means a romantic partner or a caress.
18. The *sarrada* is a dance move performed as a hip thrust toward the dance partner.
19. On the use of nudes as a strategy for symbolic affirmation by Black women and the ambiguity of social media as a space for empowerment but also oppression, see "Fat, Black, and Butch: The Use of Internet Nudes to Resist Racism and Practice 'Erotic Therapy'" by Gabriela Loureiro (2017).

20 The expression "world of Black people" alludes to Florestan Fernandes's book *O Negro no Mundo dos Brancos* (1972).
21 The use of "kkk" in words like "brankkko/a" by Black activists comes from the influence of texts such as those by the author Assata Shakur (2005), who uses the term "Amerikkka," for example, in reference to the Ku Klux Klan, using the mention as a metaphor to indicate the structural racism and white supremacy that shape American society—and hereby appropriate to refer to a similar situation in Brazilian society.
22 On the performance of traditional, sexist gender roles as a strategy to counter racism, see, for instance, Giacomini (2006). On sexism in the Black movement, see, for instance, Carneiro (1995) and Cláudia Cardoso (2014).

References

Abers, Rebecca, Lizandra Serafim, and Luciana Tatagiba. 2014. "Repertórios de Interação Estado-Sociedade em um Estado Heterogêneo: A Experiência na Era Lula." *Dados* 57, no. 2: 325–357.

Andrews, George R. 2018. *América Afro-Latina: 1800–2000*. São Carlos, Brazil: EdUFSCar.

Bennett, W. Lance, and Alexandra Segerberg. 2013. *The Logic of Connective Action: Digital Media and the Personalization*. New York: Cambridge University Press.

Bento, Maria Aparecida S. 2009. "Branqueamento e Branquitude no Brasil." In *Psicologia Social do Racismo: Estudos sobre Branquitude e Branqueamento no Brasil*, edited by Iray Carone and Maria Aparecida S. Bento, 25–57. Petrópolis-RJ, Brazil: Vozes.

Bicudo, Virgínia L. 2010 [1945]. *Atitudes Raciais de Pretos e Mulatos em São Paulo*. São Paulo: Editora Sociologia e Política.

Borges, Rosane. 2014. "Amor (Afro)Centrado: É Possível Falar Nesses Termos?" Blogueiras Negras. http://blogueirasnegras.org/2014/06/10/amor-afrocentrado/.

BRANDLAB, Google. 2017. "Dossiê BrandLab: a revolução dos cachos." www.thinkwithgoogle.com/intl/pt-br/advertising-channels/v%C3%ADdeo/revolucao-dos-cachos/.

Burdick, John. 1998. *Blessed Anastacia: Women, Race and Christianity in Brazil*. London: Routledge.

Cardoso, Cláudia Pons. 2014. "Amefricanizando o Feminismo: O Pensamento de Lélia Gonzalez." *Revista Estudos Feministas* 22, no. 3: 965–986.

Carneiro, Sueli. 1995. "Gênero, raça e ascensão social." *Revista Estudos Feministas* 3, no. 2: 544–552.

Carty, Victoria. 2015. *Social Movements and New Technology*. New York: Routledge.

Dávila, Jerry. 2006. *Diploma de Brancura*. São Paulo: Editora UNESP.

Facchini, Regina, Íris Nery do Carmo, and Stephanie Pereira Lima. 2020. "Movimentos Feministas, Negro, LGBTI No Brasil: Sujeitos, Teias e Enquadramentos." *Educação & Sociedade* 41: 1–22.

Fanon, Frantz. 2008. *Pele Negra, Máscaras Brancas*. Salvador, Brazil: EDUFBA.

Fernandes, Florestan. 1972. *O Negro no Mundo dos Brancos*. São Paulo: Difusão Européia do Livro.

Flauzina, Ana Luiza P. 2015. *Utopias de Nós Desenhadas a Sós*. Brasília-DF: Brado Negro.

Fraser, Nancy. 2017. "From Progressive Neoliberalism to Trump—and Beyond." *American Affairs* 1, no. 4: 46–64. https://americanaffairsjournal.org/2017/11/progressive-neoliberalism-trump-beyond/.

Giacomini, Sônia. 1994. "Beleza Mulata e Beleza Negra." *Revista Estudos Feministas*: 217–227.

———. 2006. *A Alma da Festa: Família, Etnicidade e Projetos num Clube Social da Zona Norte do Rio De Janeiro—O Renascença Clube*. Belo Horizonte, Brazil: Editora UFMG.

Gohn, Maria da Glória M. 2017. *Manifestações e Protestos no Brasil*. São Paulo: Cortez.

Gomes, Carla de Castro. 2018. "Corpo, Emoção e Identidade no Campo Feminista Contemporâneo Brasileiro: A Marcha das Vadias do Rio de Janeiro." PhD diss., Universidade Federal do Rio de Janeiro.

Gomes, Nilma Lino. 2017. *O Movimento Negro Educador: Saberes Construídos nas Lutas por Emancipação*. Petrópolis, Brazil: Editora Vozes.

———. 2019. *Sem Perder a Raiz: Corpo e Cabelo como Símbolos da Identidade Negra*. Belo Horizonte, Brazil: Autêntica Editora.

Gonzalez, Lélia. 1982. "A Esperança Branca." *Folha de São Paulo*, 5.

———. 1988. "A Categoria Político-Cultural de Amefricanidade." *Revista Tempo Brasileiro* 92/93: 69–82.

Gordon, Doreen. 2013. "A Beleza Abre Portas: Beauty and the Racialised Body among Black Middle-Class Women in Salvador." *Feminist Theory* 14, no. 2: 203–218.

Guimarães, Antônio Sérgio, Flávia Rios, and Edilza Sotero. 2020. "Coletivos negros e novas identidades raciais." *Novos Estudos CEBRAP* 39, no. 2: 309–327.

hooks, bell. 2000. *All About Love: New Visions*. New York: William Morrow.

Hordge-Freeman, Elizabeth. 2015. *The Color of Love: Racial Features, Stigma and Socialization in Black Brazilian Families*. Austin: University of Texas Press.

Jarrín, Alvaro. 2017. *The Biopolitics of Beauty: Cosmetic Citizenship and Affective Capital in Brazil*. Oakland: University of California Press.

Loureiro, Gabriela. 2017. "Fat, Black, and Butch: The Use of Internet Nudes to Resist Racism and Practice 'Erotic Therapy.'" *Graduate Journal of Social Science* 13, no. 1: 48–68.

Medeiros, Melanie A. 2018. *Marriage, Divorce and Distress in Northeast Brazil: Black Women's Perspectives on Love, Respect and Kinship*. New Brunswick, NJ: Rutgers University Press.

———. n.d. "'A Marriage without Fidelity Is a House without a Foundation': Black Brazilian Women's Demands for Respect in Marriage." *Journal of Latin American and Caribbean Anthropology* 28 (1).

Moore, Henrietta L. 2008. *The Subject of Anthropology: Gender, Symbolism and Psychoanalysis*. Cambridge, UK: Polity.

Moura, Clóvis. 1988. *Sociologia do Negro Brasileiro*. São Paulo: Editora Ática.

Moutinho, Laura. 2004. *Razão, "Cor" e Desejo: Uma Análise Comparativa sobre Relacionamentos Afetivo-Sexuais "Inter-Raciais" no Brasil e na África Do Sul*. São Paulo: UNESP.

Moutinho, Laura, Valéria Alves, and Milena Mateuzi. 2016. "Quanto Mais Você Me Nega, Mais Eu Me Reafirmo." *TOMO* 28: 265–291.

Nascimento, Beatriz. 1990. "A Mulher Negra e O Amor." *Jornal Maioria Falante* 17, 3.

Nunes, Davi. 2016. "A Palavra Não É Amor, É Dengo." *Duque dos Banzos*. https://ungareia.wordpress.com/2016/11/09/a-palavra-nao-e-amor-e-dengo.

Pereira, Bruna Cristina Jaquetto. 2020. *Dengos e Zangas das Mulheres–Moringa: Vivências Afetivo-Sexuais de Mulheres Negras.* Pittsburgh, PA: Latin America Research Commons.
Perez, Olívia C. 2019. "Relações entre Coletivos com As Jornadas de Junho." *Opinião Pública* 25, no. 3: 577–596.
Perez, Olívia C., and Bruno Mello Souza. 2017. "Velhos, Novos ou Novíssimos Movimentos Sociais? As Pautas e Práticas dos Coletivos." *Anais do 41º Encontro Anual da Anpocs.* Caxambu, Brazil: ANPOCS.
Pinho, Patrícia S. 2009. "White but Not Quite: Tones and Overtones of Whiteness in Brazil." *Small Axe* 13, no. 2: 39–56.
Rios, Flávia, Olívia Perez, and Arlene Ricoldi. 2018. "Interseccionalidade nas Mobilizações do Brasil Contemporâneo." *Lutas Sociais* 22, no. 40: 36–51.
Rodrigues, Cristiano. 2020. *Afro-Latinos em Movimento: Protesto Negro e Ativismo Institucional no Brasil e na Colômbia.* Curitiba, Brazil: Appris.
Rodrigues, Cristiano, and Viviane G. Freitas. 2021. "Ativismo Feminista Negro no Brasil: Do Movimento de Mulheres Negras ao Feminismo Interseccional." *Revista Brasileira de Ciência Política* 34 (E238917): 1–54.
Schwarcz, Lilia M. 1993. *O Espetáculo das Raças: Cientistas, Instituições e a Questão Racial no Brasil—1870–1930.* São Paulo: Companhia das Letras.
Shakur, Assata. 2005. "A Message to My Sistas." World History Archives, Hartford Web Publishing. www.hartford-hwp.com/archives/45a/669.html.
Steele, Catherine Knight. 2021. *Digital Black Feminism.* New York: New York University Press.
Telles, Edward E. 2004. *Race in Another America: The Significance of Skin Color in Brazil.* Princeton, NJ: Princeton University Press.
Williams, Erica Lorraine. 2013. *Sex Tourism in Bahia: Ambiguous Entanglements.* Champaign: University of Illinois Press.
Young, Robert C. G. 2005. *Desejo Colonial: Hibridismo em Teoria, Cultura e Raça.* São Paulo: Perspectiva.

Notes on Contributors

JULIA S. ABDALLA has a PhD in sociology from the University of Campinas. In 2021, her dissertation won the honorable mention in the national Brazilian prize of theses and dissertations.

ANGELA CRUMDY is a cultural anthropologist and a Provost Postdoctoral Fellow at the University of Pennsylvania in the Graduate School of Education.

ISHAN GORDON-UGARTE is a cultural anthropologist with a PhD in anthropology from the City University of New York Graduate Center.

CASTRIELA E. HERNÁNDEZ-REYES is an anti-racist feminist and activist-scholar and doctoral candidate in anthropology and instructor at the University of Massachusetts–Amherst. Her work builds on Black/decolonial feminism and critical race theories to examine interlocking systems of power, oppression, and exclusion that operate and intersect within the armed conflict and how they are tied to colonial patterns of racism in Colombia. Castriela is a cofounder and the first president of the Colombian Association of Afro-descendant Researchers—ACIAFRO. As a member of the Black women's movement, she was elected as one of its two representatives and spokeswoman within the Instancia Especial de Género, a political space created to protect women's rights and monitor the implementation of the gender approach within the 2016 Peace Accord in Colombia.

BRUNA CRISTINA JAQUETTO PEREIRA is a Marie Slodowska-Currie (UNA4-CAREER) Postdoctoral Fellow at the Universidad Complutense de Madrid (UCM) and member of the Gender and Politics (GEYPO) research group at the same institution.

Notes on Contributors

ESHE L. LEWIS is a cultural anthropologist and project director for *SAPIENS* magazine.

MELANIE A. MEDEIROS is an associate professor in the Department of Anthropology at the State University of New York–Geneseo. Medeiros's ethnographic research focuses on Black Brazilian women's intimate relationships and mental health, youth political activism in Brazil, and the impact of federal and state-level immigration and labor policies on Latin American immigrant farmworker health in western New York. She is the author of *Marriage, Divorce, and Distress in Northeast Brazil: Black Women's Perspectives on Love, Respect, and Kinship* and coeditor of *Ethnographic Insights on Latin America and the Caribbean*.

KEISHA-KHAN Y. PERRY is the Presidential Penn Compact Associate Professor of Africana Studies at the University of Pennsylvania. She specializes in the critical study of race, gender, and politics in the Americas with a particular focus on Black women's activism, urban geography and questions of citizenship, feminist theories, intellectual history and disciplinary formations, and the interrelationship between scholarship, pedagogy, and political engagement. She has conducted extensive research in Mexico, Jamaica, Belize, Brazil, Argentina, and the United States. Her book *Black Women against the Land Grab: The Fight for Racial Justice in Brazil* is an ethnographic study of Black women's activism in Brazilian cities. She is currently writing *Anthropology for Liberation: Research, Writing, and Teaching for Social Justice*.

CRISTIANO RODRIGUES is an assistant professor in the Department of Political Science at the Federal University of Minas Gerais (UFMG) and professor at the Graduate Program in Political Science at UFMG (PPGCP-UFMG).

CHRISTEN A. SMITH is an associate professor of anthropology and African and African Diaspora Studies and Director of the Center for Women's and Gender Studies at the University of Texas at Austin. She is the author of the book, *Afro-Paradise: Blackness, Violence and Performance in Brazil* (University of Illinois Press, 2016) and co-author of the forthcoming book *The Dialectic is in the Sea: The Black Radical Thought of Beatriz Nascimento* (Princeton University Press, 2023). Her public facing work includes *Cite Black Women*—a transnational initiative that she began in 2017 that draws attention to the race and gender inequalities of citational politics.

EDILZA CORREIA SOTERO is a sociologist and professor of education at the Federal University of Bahia. She writes about Black women's intellectual histories and politics in Brazil and their diasporic linkages to the broader Americas.

MAZIKI THAME is a political scientist and senior lecturer in the Institute for Gender and Development Studies at the University of the West Indies–Mona. She is coeditor of the book *Caribbean Reasonings: Rupert Lewis and the Black Intellectual Tradition*.

MELANIE WHITE is a Provost's Distinguished Faculty Fellow and assistant professor of Afro–Latin American and Caribbean Studies in the Department of African American Studies and the Women's and Gender Studies Program at Georgetown University. Her research and teaching interests include hemispheric Black feminist politics, Black diasporic women's art, and the histories, politics, and visual cultures of Black Latin America and the Caribbean. Her first book project traces a history of sexual and gender-based colonial violence against Black and Afro-Indigenous women and girls from the Mosquito Coast in Caribbean Central America, as well as a genealogy of contemporary art by Black women visual artists in the region that addresses this legacy.

Index

Abdalla, Julia, 7
activism, 166–181
"Activity and Inactivity in the Politics of Afro-Latin America" (Dzidzienyo), 9
Adami, Regina, 83
aesthetics, 155, 168–173, 175–176, 180–181
Afoxé, 182n5
African Diaspora Research Project (ADRP), 33n14
AfriDate, 176
Afrocubanas (website), 181
Afrodengo group (Facebook), 168, 172, 173, 176–180
Afroféminas (website), 181
Afro-Latin Project, 9
Afro-Nicaraguan Creole communities, 148–163
Afro-Peruvian women, 131–144
AfroResistance movement, xii
Agentes de Pastorais Negros (Black Pastoral Agents, APNs), 85
Alberto, Paulina L., 10
Alexander, Simone, 127
alternative space for racial healing, reconciliation, and transformations, 128
Améfrica Ladina, as concept, 25, 33n8
Amefricanidade (Amefricanity), 4, 25
Andrews, George, 21
Anizeti, Cristiane, 85–86
anti-Blackness: misogynoir, as term for, x, xv; through state violence, 2–3, 30.

See also racism; violence against Black women
Antonia, 116, 119–121, 124–125
Arboleda-Quiñonez, Santiago, 117
Articulação de Mulheres Negras Brasileiras (National Black Women's Articulation, Brazil), 78
Atrato River, Colombia, 126
Attitudes of Students from School Groups in Relation to the Color of Their Peers (research project), 21–22
Azevedo, Fernando de, 169

Bailes Soul (Soul Balls), 170
Bairros, Luiza, 8, 9, 25–29, 33nn10–11, 79, 83, 91n5
Baker, Ella, xii
Barros, Bruna, 5
beauty contests, 170. *See also* Black aesthetics
"bell hooks' 'The Oppositional Gaze' in Brazil" (Perry), 5
Benedito, Vera, 9, 33n14
Bentes, Nilma, 82–83
Bicudo, Virgínia, 4, 20–23, 32n2
Bilge, Sirma, 75
Biohó, Benkos, 126
Black aesthetics, 155, 168–173, 175–176, 180–181
"Black and White in Latin America" (Gilliam), 8–9

191

Black Autonomy (Goett), 47
Black Culture, as academic course, 23
Black feminism: digital, 166–181; transnationalism and, x–xv, 2–6. See *names of specific countries*
Black Legend (Alberto), 10
Black Matters Conference (2016), xii
Black Power movement, 58
Black Scholar, The (website), x
Black studies, globalizing and engendering, 6–9
Black Women against the Land Grab (Perry), 7
Black women's digital activism, 166–181
Black Women's Front, 82, 84–90, 91
"Black Women's Intellectual Contributions: Perspectives from the Global South" conference (2020), xiii
Black Women's March (Brazil), 75, 82–84, 87
Black women's studies, as academic discipline, xiii–xiv, 12, 13, 37, 39, 47–52
Blandford, Alta Hooker, 42–43
blog communities. See digital Black activism
Blogueiras Feministas (Feminist Bloggers) collective, 173–174
Blogueiras Negras (Black Women Bloggers [BN]), 168, 172–176
Bluefields, Nicaragua, 38, 42, 44, 49, 50, 148–163, 164n7
Bluefields Indian and Caribbean University (BICU), 42, 44
Bolsonaro, Jair, 75, 80
Boyce Davies, Carole, 58
brava, as term, 133, 134
Brazil: Black women in social sciences of, 18–32; contemporary Black feminism in, 13, 75–91; demographics in, 11–12; digital Black feminist activism in, 166–181; state violence in, 2–3
Brazilian Black Consciousness Day, 174
Brown, Angela, 42
Brown-Davis, Dacia, 68
Butler, Kim, 21

Cáceres, Berta, 4
Caldwell, Kia Lilly, 7, 39
Carmo, Íris do, 81

Carneiro, Sueli, xii–xiii, 80, 115
Carrillo, Sofia, 135
Casagrande, Maria Rita, 173, 174
Castro, Fidel, 100–101, 110n9
CEM (Centro emergencia de la mujer, Women's Emergency Centers), 132–134
Center for Studies and Information of the Multiethnic Woman (CEIMM), 43–52
Central Única dos Trabalhadores (CUT), 85
Chisholm, Shirley, xii
Christmas play annual ritual, 149, 151–153, 154
Cimarrónes, 121, 126, 129n4. See also maroon communities
Circum-Caribbean, as region, xiv
citation, as practice, xi, 2
citational erasure, 8
"Cite Black Women: A Critical Practice (A Statement)" (Smith et al.), xi
Cite Black Women Collective, xi, 2
"Cite Black Women Collective Statement on behalf of the Cite Black Women Collective" (Smith et al.), xi
City of Women, The (Landes), 7
civil war (Nicaragua), 12, 41, 42
Clara, 140
Claudia, 133–134, 142
collectives, 170, 171–173. See also digital Black activism
Colombia, xii, 12, 113–128
colonial/modern racial project of war, 122–123, 125. See also Colombia
Combahee River Collective, xiii
Commission for the Defense of Women, 31
Commission on Human Rights, 30
Committee of Women for Progress (CWP), 56–71, 71n5, 72nn7–8, 72n11, 72n13
communists wearing panties, as phrase, 57, 59–60
Comrade Sister (Lambert), 56
Convention No. 169 (ILO), 145n2
counterrevolutionary ("Contra") war movement, 42
"creating our own references," as concept, 18–19
Creole, as term, 163n1
Creole group (Nicaragua), 40, 41, 43, 148–163

Creole Respectability, 150, 154–155, 157, 159, 161, 162
Crumdy, Angela, 8
Cuba, 11, 95–109, 109nn1–6
Cuban Revolution, 100–101, 108
cuentapropismo, 96–97. *See also* private tutors in Cuba
Cunningham Kain, Myrna, 42
currencies, 99, 103, 104, 105, 109n2, 110n9

dance balls, 170
Danticat, Edwidge, 3
Davis, Angela, 2, 5, 75
Davis, Dána-Ain, 8
dengo, as term, 176–177, 182n2, 182n17
diasporic politics, overview, xii–xiii
digital Black activism, 166–181
domestic violence. *See* IPV (interpersonal violence) in Peru
Doña Luz, 113–114, 116, 118–119, 126
dororidade, 175
double morality, 95–109
Dunham, Katherine, 8, 9
Dzidzienyo, Anani, 9, 24

eco-ethnogenocide, 117
economic violence, 141–143. *See also* violence against Black women
Elena, 95, 102–103, 105–106, 107–108, 109
Encuentro Feminista da América Latina y del Caribe (EFLAC), 79
engendering Black studies, 6–9
epistemic racism. *See* racism
erotic, defined, 163n2
Escola Livre de Sociologia e Política (ELSP), 20, 32n1, 32n3
Escola Normal Caetano de Campos, 20
Escritos de Uma Vida (Carneiro), xii
Ese Pelo Tuyo (website), 181
Estudos sobre Atitudes Raciais de Pretos e Mulatos em São Paulo (Bicudo), 21

Facchini, Regina, 81
Facebook. *See* digital Black activism
Faguagua, María Ileana, 99
favela policing programs (Brazil), 2–3, 30, 33n18
Federal University of Bahia (UFBA), 28

Federal University of Rio de Janeiro (UFRJ), 23
Federal University of Rio Grande do Sul (UFRGS), 27
feminicide, 117–118
feminism. *See* Black feminism
Feva, 5
Figueiredo, Ângela, 79
First National Meeting of Black Women Newsletter, 18
First Young Black Feminists Meeting (I Encontro de Negras Jovens Feministas), 79
flag-bodies, as term, 167–168
"For an Afro-Latin Feminism" (Gonzalez), 4–5
Ford-Smith, Honor, 59
Fórum Afro XXI, 82–83
Fórum de Mulheres Negras (Black Women Forum), 78
Franco, Anielle, 3
Franco, Marielle, ix–x, xii, 2–4, 29–31, 33n15
Fraser, Nancy, 182n1
"Freedom Is a Constant Struggle" event (2019, Brazil), 75
French, Joan, 62, 71n4

Garifuna, 40, 43
gender-based violence. *See* violence against Black women
"Gendered Dimensions of Anti-Black State Violence, The" panel (2016), xii
gender inequality, 11
Gilliam, Angela, 8
Gladys, 98, 101–102, 109, 141
globalizing Black studies, 6–9
Goett, Jennifer, 47
Gomes, Anderson, x, 31, 80
Gomes, Janaína Damasceno, 20, 22
Gomes, Nilma Lino, 91n5
Gomes, Viviane, 174
Gonzales, Lélia, 4–5, 8, 23–26, 91n4
Gordon, Barbara, 66
Gordon, Dereck, 66
Gordon, Edmund T., 7
Gordon, Ishan, 8
Grenada Revolution, 56
Guevara, Che, 100

hair, 49, 155, 172–173, 175, 176, 182n8
hair transition, 172–173, 175, 176, 182n8
Hamer, Fannie Lou, xii
Hamilton, Ruth Simms, 7, 9, 28, 33n14
Harrison, Faye V., 7–8
Hartman, Saidiya, 114, 115, 124
hashtag feminism, 172
Hill Collins, Patricia, 5, 25, 75, 133, 136
Hooker, Juliet, 53n1
hooks, bell, 5, 166
hypersexualization of Black women, 12, 46, 76, 143, 148–163, 169, 180. *See also* respectability politics

Inés, 142
informal curriculum, 7–8
Instituto Cultural Steve Biko, 33n17
Instituto de Pesquisa das Culturas Negras (Research Institute of Black Cultures, IPCN), 23
interculturality, 43–52
International Day for the Elimination of Violence against Women, 174
International Labor Organization (ILO), 145n2
intersectionality, 11
IPV (interpersonal violence) in Peru, 12, 131–144, 145nn1–3. *See also* violence against Black women
"I've Never Shared This with Anybody" (Woods Downs), 47

Jamaica, 11, 13, 56–71
Jamaica Labor Party (JLP), 57–58, 63, 64, 71n2
Jamaica Teachers Association (JTA), 62, 68
Jasenia, 139–140, 143
Jerónimo Kersh, Daliany, 97, 100
Jesus, Carolina Maria de, 20
Joint Committee for Women's Rights (JCWR), 68, 72n12
Jones, Claudia, 24
Juana, 122–123
Julio, Teophilo, 20, 32n2
Junco, Teresa Lara, 98

Kaufman, Michael, 62
"kkk," use of, 183n21
Koch, Adelheid, 21

labor and inequality, 11, 76, 108
Lambert, Laurie, 56
Landes, Ruth, 7
Latin-American and Caribbean Women's Meeting (I Encontro de Mulheres Afro Latino-Americanas e do Caribe), 82–83
Latin American Studies Association, 4
Latinidades Afrolatinas festival, 75–76
"Law, Silence, and Racialized Inequality in the History of Brazil" (Fisher et al.), 10
Law 28 (Nicaragua), 42
"Lembrando (Remembering) Lélia Gonzalez" (Bairros), 4
Lemos, Rosália, 82–84
Leu, Lorraine, xiii
Lewis, Rupert, 61, 67, 69
LGBTQIA+ community: in Brazil, 31, 79, 85, 86, 90, 171, 177; discrimination against, 45, 123. *See also* romantic relationships in Black activism
Lima, Stephanie, 81
Literacy Campaign (Cuba), 98, 100–101, 109n4
loneliness of Black women, 88, 171, 173, 175, 176, 178
love ethic, 166
Lugar de Negro (Gonzalez), 5
Luiza Bairros Award, 28–29
Lula da Silva, Luiz Inácio, 167

Maciel, Regimeire, 79
Magno, M. D., 33n8
Malcher, Maria, 82, 84
Manley, Michael, 56–57, 58, 59, 65, 71
Manley-Duncan, Beverly, 57, 58–59, 60–62, 69
Marco, 135
maroon communities, 78, 81, 84, 91n3, 129n4, 150
Márquez, Francia, xii, 1–2, 3–4
Marriage, Divorce and Distress in Northeast Brazil (Medeiros), 7
Mars, Perry, 60, 62, 63
Maternity Leave Law (Jamaica), 63, 67–70
Matute, Susana, 136–137
Mayangna, 40

Memória Viva (de Olivero), 3
Mendes, Magali, 88
Meridians (publication), 4, 6
"mestizo multiculturalism," 37, 48, 53n1
mestizx politics, 40–41, 47–51
migration, 20
Ministry of Women and Vulnerable Populations (Ministerio de la mujer y poblaciones vulnerables, MIMP), 132
Misión de Observación Electoral, United Nations, xii
Miskitu, 40
misogynoir, x, xv
Miss Rizos (website), 181
modern/colonial racial project of war, as term, 123–124, 125. *See also* Colombia
"monocultural mestizaje," 37
Mora, Mariana, 3
Morais, Mariana, 90
Moravians and Moravian Church, 41, 53, 149–153
Moreira, Núbia, 78
Morris, Courtney, 39, 47
Morrison, K. C., 28
Morrison, Toni, 127
Movimento Black Rio (Black Rio Movement), 170
Movimento Black São Paulo (Black São Paulo Movement), 170
Movimento Negro Unificado (MNU), 26, 27, 166–167
Munroe, Ingrid, 7n5
Munroe, Trevor, 63

Nacional Conference for Promoting Racial Equality (Conferência Nacional de Promoção da Igualdade Racial, Brazil), 83
NACLA: Report on the Americas (publication), 3
Nascimento, Abdias, 20
Natalie, 155
National Association for Graduate Studies and Research in Social Sciences (ANPOCS), 28
National Black Awareness Day (Brazil), 82
National Black Women's Articulation, 83
National Black Women's Meeting, 77–78
National Center for Historical Memory, 123

National Comprehensive Health Policy for the Black Population (Brazil), 79
National Conference of Black Political Scientists (NCOBPS), 28
National Day for Memory and Solidarity with Victims, 113
National Survey of Aging (Cuba), 105
National Union for Democratic Teachers (NUDT), 62
Negra Cubana Tenía que Ser, 181
Negras in Brazil (Caldwell), 7
Nicaragua, 12, 37–53, 148–163
Night of Black Beauty contest, 170
Nunes, Charô, 173, 174

Office for Policies for Women (SPM, Brazil), 79
Oliveira, Jess, 5
Olivero, Leuvis Manuel de, 3
"On the Imperative of Transnational Solidarity" (Caldwell et al.), ix, x
Os Segredos de Virginia (Gomes), 22

Pacifying Police Units (Brazil), 2, 30, 33n18
palenquera, 113, 120, 121–122, 128n1
Partido dos Trabalhadores (Workers' Party, Brazil), 167
"Pecados no 'Paraíso Racial': O Negro na Força de Trabalho da Bahia, 1950–1980" (Bairros), 27
Peixoto, Afrânio, 169
People's National Party (PNP, Jamaica), 56–57
People's National Party (PNP) Women's Movement, 58, 60–62
Peru, 12, 131–144
physical violence, 138–140. *See also* violence against Black women
Pierson, Donald, 32n4
Pirtle, Whitney, xi
police violence, 2–3, 30
political representation, xi–xii
politics of respectability, 154–155, 163n3, 164n6. *See also* Creole Respectability; hypersexualization of Black women
Pontifical Catholic University of Rio de Janeiro (PUC-RJ), 24, 29
Por um Feminismo Afro-Latino-Americano (Rios and Lima), 26

196 • Index

Presencia y Palabra collective, 132, 134
Pretinder & Afrocentrados, 176
Pré-vestibular-Vestibular para Negros e Carentes (PVNC), 33n17
private tutors in Cuba, 95–109, 109n1
PSOL (Socialism and Freedom Party), 31

quilombolas, 91n3. *See also* maroon communities
quilting, 122–123

racial capitalism, 116–117
racial categorization, overview, 9–13
racial violence. *See* violence against Black women
racism: in Colombia, 118–125; ideologies of, 6; in São Paulo, 20–21; terms for, x, xv; through state violence, 2–3, 30, 33n18; in United States, 183n21
"Racism and Sexism in Brazilian Society" (Gonzalez), 5
Rama, 40
Ramos, Alberto Guerreiro, 20
Reagan administration, 42
"Refusing the God Trick" (Harrison), 7–8
Regina, 104–105, 106–108
Regional Autonomous Educational System (SEAR), 43
Reis, Luciana, 5
repasadoras (private tutors), 95–109, 109n1
reproductive justice, 12, 149, 161–163
respectability politics, 154–155, 163n3, 164n6. *See also* Creole Respectability; hypersexualization of Black women
Revolutionary Armed Forces of Colombia (FARC-EP), 116
Ribeiro, Matilde, 91n5
Rios, Flávia, 79
Robinson, Cedric, 30
Rocha, Luciane, 9
romantic relationships in Black activism, 168–171, 180–181. *See also* LGBTQIA+ community
Roquette Pinto, Edgar, 169
Rosa, 141
Rousseff, Dilma, 27, 80

San Basilio de Palenque, Colombia, 119–121
Sandinista National Liberation Front (FSLN), 42
Sanka, 176
Santiago, Larissa, 173, 174
Santos, Sônia Beatriz dos, 9, 78
sarrada, 182n18
scholarly representation, xi, xiii–xiv, 7–8
Seaga, Edward, 63, 69, 71n2
Secretariat for the Promotion of Racial Equality (Brazil), 9
self-employment in Cuba, 96–97. *See also* private tutors in Cuba
Seprod Jamaica, 67
sexual panic, 148–149, 161–162. *See also* hypersexualization of Black women
sexual slavery, 116, 123
sexual violence, 140–141. *See also* violence against Black women
Shakur, Assata, 5, 183n21
silencing, 124–125
Silva, Benedita da, 5
Smith, Christen, 8
Soares, Judith, 64
social media. *See* digital Black activism
social movements, 171–173. *See also* digital Black activism; *names of specific groups*
Social Security Law (Cuba), 109n3
Sociedade de Intercâmbio Brasil África (Brazil Africa Exchange Society, SINBA), 23
Solsiret, 142
Sousa, Neusa Santos, 22
South, as term, xiv
Special Office for Policies for the Promotion of Racial Equality (SEPPIR, Brazil), 79, 91n5
Special Period in Times of Peace (Cuba), 96–97, 108, 110n9
Spillers, Hortense, 163
state violence, 2–3, 30, 33n18
status exchange in interracial marriage, 170
Susana, 98, 100–101, 103–105, 109
systemic racism. *See* racism

Taylor, Chloë, 156
teachers in Cuba, 101, 103, 109n6. *See also* private tutors in Cuba

Tejedoras de Sueños de Mampuján
  (Weavers of Dreams of Mampuján),
  122–123, 124–125
Temer, Michel, 31
Thame, Amy, 65–66
Thame, Maziki, 8
To Defend This Sunrise (Morris), 47
Tornar-se Negro (Becoming Black) (Sousa),
  22–23
transnational Black feminism, x–xv,
  2–6
transnationalism, defined, xv note 2
tutors in Cuba, 95–109, 109n1
Twitter. *See* digital Black activism

Ubuntu, 30
UNDP (United Nations Development
  Program), 33n11
UNESCO (United Nations Educational,
  Scientific and Cultural Organization),
  21–22, 32n5
United Nations Durban World Conference
  against Racism, Racial Discrimination,
  Xenophobia, and related Intolerance,
  145n2
United States: militarism in Nicaragua of,
  42; response to Franco's death in, x–xi;
  structural racism in, 183n21
Unit for the Attention and Integral
  Reparation for the Victims (Unidad para
  la Atención y Reparación Integral para
  las Víctimas), 113–114
University of the Autonomous Regions of
  the Nicaraguan Caribbean Coast
  (URACCAN), 38–39, 41–52
UPPs (Unidades de Polícia Pacificadora,
  Pacifying Police Units), 2, 30, 33n18

Vargas, Virginia, 33n9
Vassell, Linnette, 58–59
violability, xi
violence against Black women, x–xi, xv; in
  Brazil, 2–3, 11–12; in Colombia, 12, 113–128;
  in Nicaragua, 44–46, 51; in Peru, 12,
  131–144, 145nn1–3. *See also* anti-Blackness
Viveros-Vigoya, Mara, 4, 8
Voluntary Price Inspector (VPI), 59, 63,
  66–67

Wadud, Imani, xi
Walter Rodney riots (1968, Jamaica), 58
war, 12, 41, 42, 122–123, 125
Warner-Lewis, Maureen, 67
Weavers of Dreams of Mampuján, 122–123,
  124–125
Werneck, Jurema, 81–82
Williams, Erica, xi
Wirtz, Kristina, 96
Women's Emergency Centers (CEM), 132–134
Woods Downs, Socorro, 39, 41, 47–48, 51
Workers Liberation League (WLL), 56, 59,
  60–62. *See also* Workers Party of Jamaica
  (WPJ)
Workers' Party (Brazil). *See* Partido dos
  Trabalhadores (Workers' Party, Brazil)
Workers Party of Jamaica (WPJ), 56, 57, 59,
  66–67, 70–71. *See also* Workers
  Liberation League (WLL)
workers' rights, 11, 76, 108
World Conference against Racism, Racial
  Discrimination, Xenophobia and
  Related Intolerance, 78

YCW (young Creole women) in Nicaragua,
  148–163